Common Latin Terms in Hong Kong Legal Language
香港法律語言常見拉丁詞彙

U0130465

Common Latin Terms in Hong Kong Legal Language
香港法律語言常見拉丁詞彙

Benjamin K. Tsou 鄒嘉彥
Andy Chin 錢志安

香港城市大學出版社
City University of Hong Kong Press

Acknowledgements

The compilation of this book has resulted from two projects at the then Language Information Sciences Research Centre of the City University of Hong Kong, viz Electronic Legal Documentation System (ELDoS) and the Bilingual Reference System (BRS). Support from the following sources is gratefully acknowledged.

1. Enhancement of Electronic Documentation Retrieval System (2001–02), Applied Research Grant, Hong Kong Judiciary [Enhancement to ELDoS].

2. Bilingual Reference System, (2003–2004), Applied Research Grant, Judiciary, HKSAR.

3. Bilingual Reference System Part II, (2004–2006), Applied Research Grant, Judiciary, HKSAR.

4. Research on Implementation of Legal Bilingualism in Hong Kong and Jurilinguistic Engineering (2000–2006), RGC/CERG Research Grant.

國際統一書號：978-962-937-362-7

出版

香港城市大學出版社
香港九龍達之路
香港城市大學
網址：www.cityu.edu.hk/upress
電郵：upress@cityu.edu.hk

Common Latin Terms in Hong Kong Legal Language
(in traditional Chinese characters)

ISBN: 978-962-937-362-7

Published by
City University of Hong Kong Press
Tat Chee Avenue
Kowloon, Hong Kong
Website: www.cityu.edu.hk/upress
E-mail: upress@cityu.edu.hk

Printed in Hong Kong

Table of Contents
目錄

Foreword

Robert Tang

Non-Permanent Judge of the Court of Final Appeal (2018–)
Permanent Judge of the Court of Final Appeal (2012–2018)

This is a useful book. It provides examples of the actual use of Latin phrases in legislation and the courts in Hong Kong and their Chinese translation.

It is notoriously difficult to express in English the concepts represented by succinct and elegant Latin phrases. May I say, perhaps tongue in cheek, it is so, *a fortiori*, in Chinese. The expression "*a fortiori*" was rightly highlighted in the Introduction. This book provides 6 instances where the expression was used, and suggests 5 different Chinese translations. These translations, in my view, correctly capture the nuances of the Latin expression.

The translated passages in this book are rendered in elegant Chinese which makes them a joy to read. I commend it highly.

序言

鄧國楨

香港終審法院非常任法官 (2018–)

香港終審法院常任法官 (2012–2018)

這是本極富參考價值的書，收集了很多香港法例和法院中所使用的拉丁文用語實例，提供了它們的中文翻譯。

簡練典雅拉丁文所蘊含的概念，極難用英語表達出來，而要用隔了一層的中文來表達，恕我戲言，恐怕是 *a fortiori* 更不用說，難上加難了。本書導言中就恰當地以 *a fortiori* 這個拉丁詞語作說明，列出了它六個不同的使用例子，提出了五個不同的對應翻譯。在我看來，這些翻譯都正確地反映了這個拉丁詞語在不同用法中細微的語意差異。

本書的中文譯文段落，措辭典雅，行文優美，讀來實屬賞心樂事。我極力推薦。

Foreword

Anthony Neoh
Senior Counsel

One may wonder why Latin, a dead language, still commands such a hallowed place in the vocabulary of English Law. For the answer, one must go to the history of England and the English language.

English as we know it today, did not develop until after the Middle Ages. Prior to that, English was an amalgam of Germanic and Nordic dialects. Thus "Olde Englishe" is difficult to decipher. Try reading the 8th Century *Beowulf* epic and one will see its Germanic influences. The English in Chaucer's *Canterbury Tales* (written towards the end of the 14th Century) would be more recognizable but the way the language was pronounced in its day would not be recognizable by us today.

But why did Latin exert so much influence? It is because the Romans ruled England from AD 43 to AD 409, with the result that Latin was the official language. But after the departure of the Romans in AD 409, the Saxons from Germania settled in England and Germanic dialects entered into the English language. The law which then existed after the departure of the Romans was not the Roman Law, but a Germanic Code developed on English soil, the most well known of which was the Code of Æthelberht of Kent. Despite these developments, Latin continued to be used in the Church and it remained the language used in the monasteries of England. The Church was also the main provider of education in England as it was elsewhere in Europe. As the first millennium drew to a close, there was a revival of classical education, with the result that Latin became the language not only of churchmen but also the language of all educated people throughout Europe.

In 1066, England was conquered by the Normans and French dialects began to be used in the King's Court and in official business alongside English. Norman French also became the language of pleadings in the Courts of England. But Latin, being the language of educated men, continued as the language in which all official records were kept. Thus, the law began to be developed where English was used among the common people, French among the nobility and Latin as the language of educated men who inevitably were the people charged with keeping official records. As time went on, this tripartite use of language became intolerable, creating long delays in justice.

The first solution came in 1363, when the Pleadings in English Act (36 Ed. III c.15) was enacted, mandating that pleadings in Court both oral and in writing shall be conducted in English. This came within the first 30 years of the Hundred Years War (1337–1453) between the English and French Monarchies, when nationalistic feelings ran high and thus promoted preference for the use of English in England. But despite the Pleadings in English Act, Latin continued to be used for official records. It was not until 1730 that English became the official language of court records. In 1730, the Proceedings in Courts of Justice Act (4 Geo II, c. 26) was enacted, mandating the use of English alone in all court records and pleadings. But by then the use of Latin in the vocabulary of English Law had become entrenched and Latin terms have remained to this day, part of the vocabulary of the English Law.

One of the reasons why Latin terms have become so entrenched is the difficulty of finding equivalent terms in English, which conveyed exactly the same meaning as was used in a long line of juridical texts and judicial decisions. As can be seen from this book, a term such as *"actus reus"* would need a longish explanation in the English language and if an English term were used, it would have to be coined. Even if that were to be done, it would take a long time for that term to acquire currency. Doing so might be compared to reinventing the wheel and even then it is a wheel, which would take long to acquire recognition against the long usage and common understanding of the Latin term. This is why we have the legacy of Latin terms in the vocabulary of the English law.

This *Common Latin Terms in Hong Kong Legal Language* introduces the reader to the most commonly used Latin terms in English law. It is a useful guide to readers uninitiated in the English law. To those who are interested in looking deeper into the origins and application of these terms, the Latin phrases they find here may be found in countless treatises and juridical sources. That is the beauty of long usage.

序言

梁定邦

資深大律師

　　有人可能會納悶，作為一門已經消亡的語言，拉丁文為何仍然在英國法詞彙中佔據着如此神聖的地位。若要探其究竟，還須從英國以及英文的歷史說起。

　　我們今日所熟知的英文，直到中世紀之後才開始逐漸形成。此前，英文是日爾曼方言和北歐方言融合的產物。是故「古代英語」（Olde Englishe）的解讀頗為費神。只需讀一讀8世紀的《貝奧武夫》史詩，便不難發現其中日爾曼方言的影響力。喬叟的《坎特伯里故事集》（14世紀末著）中的英文就易讀得多，但當時的發音方式較之今日可謂大相徑庭。

　　但為何拉丁文會產生如此巨大的影響？根源是羅馬人。公元43年到公元409年的英國由羅馬人統治，拉丁文順理成章成為其官方語言。公元409年羅馬人撤走後，來自日爾曼尼亞的薩克遜人在英國定居，日爾曼方言隨即進入英文體系。當時的法律是在羅馬人離開後才出現的，所以並非羅馬法，而是萌芽於英文土壤的日爾曼法典，肯特法典（Code of Æthelberht of Kent）就是其中最著名的一部。不過拉丁文依舊為教會所用，於英國的修道院亦然。此外，彼時的英國乃至整個歐洲，教育多由教會提供。臨近公元1000年，一場古典教育復興運動令拉丁文不僅作為神職人員的用語，更是成為了歐洲所有知識分子使用的語言。

　　1066年，諾曼人征服英國，法國方言從此登堂入室，與英文一併成為王室和官方事務用語。此外，諾曼法語還成為英國法庭上訴辯時使用的語言。不過，作為知識分子的語言，拉丁文保持了官方記錄用語的地位。如此一來，法律開始在多語言環境中發展成型，即普通民眾說英文、貴族講法文、以及注定要負責官方記錄的知識分子使用拉丁文。時間一長，這種三語混用的做法動輒造成司法公正事務的長時間拖延，令眾人頭疼不已。

到1363年才總算有了一個解決辦法。《英國訴狀法案》（*Pleadings in English Act*）（36 Ed. III c.15）於該年制定。該法案要求在法庭上不論是口頭還是書面訴辯都必須使用英文。時值英法兩國百年戰爭（1337–1453）的頭三十年，民族情緒高漲，英文隨即在英國大受推崇。可是即便有《英國訴狀法案》的存在，拉丁文仍繼續作為官方記錄用語。直到1730年英文才成為了法庭記錄使用的官方語言。該年《法庭議事錄法》（*Pleadings in English Act*）（4 Geo II, c. 26）出台，要求所有的法庭記錄和訴辯只能使用英文。事到如今，在英國法律詞彙中使用拉丁文的做法已然根深蒂固，拉丁術語遂保留至今，成為英國法律用語的一部分。

拉丁術語之所以能經久不衰，原因之一是在英文中很難找到在語義上能與那些冗長的法律文本和司法裁決中原有的拉丁術語媲美的替代詞。正如在本書中，像"*actus reus*"這樣的簡單術語，用英文解釋起來卻需要長篇大論，非要用英文術語的話，得現造才行。即便是造出來了，這些新詞的流通也非朝夕之事。這就好比重新發明一遍車輪這種費力不討好的做法，要打破對拉丁文經年累月的使用習慣和理解上的共識又豈是咄嗟便辦之事？

《香港法律語言常見拉丁詞彙》為讀者介紹了英國法律中最常用的拉丁術語。對於完全沒接觸過英國法律的讀者，此書不失為一本非常實用的指南型讀物。而想要就這些術語的起源和應用刨根問底的讀者，則會發現本書囊括的拉丁短語在各種專著和法律資料中無所不在。乃謂經年之美。

註解

1. Different translations were provided for the two terms: English law（英國法律）and English Law（英國法）.

2. Code of Æthelberht of Kent is translated to 肯特法典, as the English version of 《埃塞爾伯特法典》 is Laws of Æthelberht.

3. For the two acts mentioned in the text, no established translation was found: *Pleadings in English Act*（《英國訴狀法案》）；*Pleadings in English Act*（《法庭議事錄法》）.

Foreword

Paul Tang
Solicitor

"*Habemus papam*"—We have a pope. It was April 2015, when Vatican announced the election of Pope Benedict XVI. For the first time, I heard Latin being uttered on the television. The momentary disorientation caused by the brief revival of this antique language set me wondering: what place does Latin have in the modern world?

Latin is the source of a significant portion of the English language. Many words and expressions in untranslated Latin have remained in ordinary English language even today—"*vice versa*", "*ad ho*c", "*affidavit*", "*pro rata*", "e.g." (*exempli gratia*) and "etc." (*et cetera*) are just a few of the more familiar examples.

Further, Latin is the language once used by Roman law and English common law, the two legal systems from which the present civil law and common law systems developed. It is therefore no surprise that Latin continues to take a special place in modern legal lexicon. It is not difficult to find Roman maxims in Latin which influence over modern legal systems.

However, a language cannot be kept alive merely by the incidental use of particular terms. Languages with a base of native speakers are constantly evolving as their speakers encounter new experiences. Since the speakers need to talk about such experiences, they draw from familiar existing language resources to coin new terms.

Consider for a moment the legal term "sexual harassment", which was only coined in the 1970s following the case of Carmita Wood, an administrative assistant at the Cornell University Laboratory of Nuclear Studies. She resigned from her job due to repeated unwelcome sexual advances from her superior, prominent nuclear physicist Boyce McDaniel. The term "sexual harassment" was coined by Lin Farley and her team at the Human Affairs Programme at Cornell University who assisted Carmita Wood, and was publicised after Lin Farley used it in testimony given before the Commission on Human Rights of New York City. With the new term coined, we could understand "sexual harassment" as a legal concept and apply it to the relationship between man and woman.

This marks the limitation of Latin from the perspective of our daily life. Hence, a legitimate question: is Latin already so "dead" that it will eventually be ousted from the legal language altogether? I do not think so.

Latin terms and maxims are relics from a society with different values. As a result, exceptions and rules of interpretation have been constructed to ameliorate their effects. In *Chi Kit Company Limited and Another v. Lucky Health International Enterprise Limited* [2000] 2 HKLRD 503, the Court of Final Appeal found that an on-going personal injury claim against the Incorporated Owners of a building, for which judgment of over HK$25.7 million plus interest and costs was eventually given, exposed the purchaser of a property in that building to a liability *"wholly outside the contemplation of a reasonable purchaser"*. In allowing the purchaser to avoid the contract by reason of the vendor's material non-disclosure, the Court held that the maxim *"caveat emptor"*—let the buyer beware—*"should not be applied so that it leaves a purchaser exposed to a serious detriment the risk of which is solely within the knowledge or the means of knowledge of the vendor."*

While the *literal* meaning of Latin legal maxims is fixed, the *legal* meaning may change through judicial interpretation. Armed with modern scientific knowledge, the Court is now able to consider in *BaWang International (Group) Holding Limited and Another v. Next Magazine Publishing Limited* (HCA No.1109 of 2010, 23 May 2016) whether a shampoo containing 27 ppm of 1,4-dioxane poses a more than *"de minimis"*—about minimal things—cancer risk. Like other daily languages, Latin in law continues to evolve, albeit on a much more limited scale.

It is clear that legal practitioners, law students and anyone interested in the legal language will benefit from an understanding of Latin legal terms. This book provides a ready guide at hand. The examples meticulously collected from statutory and judicial sources will allow readers to understand the terms in context, which is the key to proper legal interpretation.

Further, this book fills a niche unique to Hong Kong, where both English and Chinese are official languages, and bilingualism in statutory and judicial texts prevails. With the English and Chinese contents placed alongside each other, this book makes it very easy for readers to look up the most commonly used Chinese translations of a Latin legal term in the statutory and judicial context. Legal practitioners seeking to use an appropriate term in Chinese submissions or letters should find this feature especially helpful.

Latin is a beautiful language. It deserves to continue to glow, as a tradition carefully preserved by faithful users and diligent academia.

序言

鄧賜強

律師

　　"*Habemus papam*"——我們有一位教皇了。那是2015年4月，梵蒂岡宣布選出了教皇本篤十六世，也是我第一次在電視上聽到拉丁文。這古雅語言瞬間再現，令我霎時不知所措，不禁猜想：拉丁文在現代世界究竟有何位置？

　　有相當部分的英語源自拉丁文，即使現在，日常英語中仍保留了許多拉丁文的原有詞彙："*vice versa*"（反之亦然）、"*ad hoc*"（特設）、"*affidavit*"（誓章）、"*pro rata*"（按比例）、"e.g."（"*exempli gratia*"，「例如」的縮寫）及"etc."（"*et cetera*"，「等等」的縮寫）是幾個較為人所熟悉的例子。

　　再者，羅馬法和英國普通法均曾使用拉丁文，而現時的民法及普通法兩個法律系統又是從其中演變而成，故此拉丁文能夠繼續在現代法律詞彙中佔有特殊席位，乃不足為奇，而影響現代法律制度的拉丁文羅馬法格言，也不勝枚舉。

　　然而，僅是偶然使用某一片言隻字，並不足以令一種語言的生命延續下去。語言隨着恆常使用者遇上新體驗而不斷演變發展：因為他們需要談論這些新體驗，便從熟悉的既有語言素材中，創造出新的詞彙。

　　以法律上的「性騷擾」一詞為例，該詞是直至1970年代卡米塔·伍德（Carmita Wood）一案後才被創造出來。卡米塔·伍德原是康奈爾大學（Cornell University）核研究實驗室的行政助理，因為她的上司著名核物理學家博伊斯·麥克丹尼爾（Boyce McDaniel）屢次向她作出帶有性意味的冒犯行為而辭去工作。在協助卡米塔·伍德的過程中，康奈爾大學人事部門的琳·法利（Lin Farley）和她的團隊創造了「性騷擾」一詞。琳·法利向紐約市人權委員會作供時就曾經使用該詞，該詞因而得以廣泛流傳。有了這個新詞，我們現在便能夠將「性騷擾」理解為一種法律概念，以應用於兩性的關係上。

由此可見，從我們的日常生活體驗出發，拉丁文是有其局限性的。隨之而生的問題是：拉丁文是否已經名存實亡，以至終為法律語言所摒棄呢？我的看法並非如此。

拉丁文詞彙和格言是從一個價值觀不同的社會遺留下來的產物。因此，法庭設定了例外的情況及詮釋的規則，令它們能更切合現代社會的需要。在《致傑有限公司及另一人對祥康國際企業有限公司》（[2000] 2 HKLRD 503）一案中，終審法院就判定一宗針對大廈業主立案法團的人身傷亡訴訟（最終法庭就該訴訟頒下了超過港幣二千五百七十萬元另加利息及訟費的裁決）令該大廈一個單位的買家面對「*完全出乎一個合理的買家意料之外的風險*」。在容許該買家因為賣方未披露重要資料而解除合約的同時，法庭亦裁定「caveat emptor」（買方當心）這格言「*不應用於會令買方遭受重大的、而風險只有賣方才會知道或能夠知道的重大損害的情況。*」

雖然拉丁文法律格言有既定的字面意思，但其法律意義仍可透過司法詮釋而轉變。配合現代科學知識，法庭就得以在《*霸王國際（集團）控股有限公司及另一人對壹週刊出版有限公司*》（高等法院民事訴訟2010年第1109號，2016年5月23日）一案中考慮一款含有百萬分之二十七1,4-二噁烷的洗髮水是否構成超出「*de minimis*」（關於微不足道事物）標準的致癌風險。法律中的拉丁文詞彙與日常用語一樣會不斷演變發展——儘管其規模相對有限。

明顯地，法律執業者、學生和其他對法律語言感興趣的人都能從理解拉丁文法律詞彙中獲得裨益。本書為用家提供了一部便利的指南：從案例和法律條文中精心收集的示例令讀者能夠透過上文下理的脈絡理解相關字詞的意義，而這亦是恰當詮釋法律的關鍵。

　　此外，香港以英文和中文同為法定語言，在案例和法律條文中雙語並用的情況十分普遍，而本書正正就迎合了香港的獨特需要。本書中的英文和中文內容並列，令讀者很容易就能查找到拉丁文法律詞彙在案例和法律條文的框架下最常用的中文翻譯。相信這個特點對於需要在中文陳詞或信件中使用適當字眼的法律執業者而言，尤為有用。

　　拉丁文是一門美麗的語言。作為一個傳統，它值得在忠實的使用者和孜孜不倦的學者悉心保存下，繼續流光溢彩。

Preface

This book utilizes a sizable bilingual legal judgement database to provide a useful reference on the use of Latin terms and their Chinese equivalents in Hong Kong, not only for those in the legal profession but also for any others interested in the language situation of Hong Kong.

Words of Latin or Romance language origin constitute a special and important feature of English legal language.[1] In spite of their introduction into the English language mostly in the distant past, they are still commonly used in modern English, especially in the legal domain, and basically with the preservation of their original meanings. Therefore, these terms (with the majority from Latin) stand out as a special lexical layer which for a long time has served to characterize in English the genre of legal writing, as in the case with medicine.

The use of words derived from a different language variety such as the incorporation of Latin in English is not unique to English, or other languages in Europe. There is also a similar tradition of diglossia[2] among languages of East Asia such as Japanese, Korean, Vietnamese, and Modern Chinese. For them the Classical Chinese language has provided such a lexical stratum, following the incorporation of the study of the Chinese Classics in the education of the elite, and the use of the logographic writing system in the development of indigenous literary traditions within what is known as Sinosphere or logographic circle in East Asia.

---

1. For ease of reference, the term "Latin" used here includes also terms derived from Romance languages such as French, e.g. *estop, estoppel.*

2. See the discussion of *diglossia* in *Chinese Language and Society* (漢語與華人社會) by Tsou, Benjamin and You, Rujie (2003), City University of Hong Kong Press.

A useful example may be provided by "appendectomy" in Japanese, Vietnamese and Chinese[3].

(1) Jixing   mangchangyan   kaidao   shoushu   *Chinese*
     急性   盲腸炎   開刀   手術
     "acute"   "blind intestine "cut with   "operation"
                 inflx"   knife"

(2) Kyusei   kaifuku   chusui   setsujo   *Japanese*
     急性   開腹   蟲垂   切除
     "acute"   "laparotomy"   "hanging   "cutting off"
                                 worm"

(3) phẫu thuật viêm   ruột thừa   cấp tính   *Vietnamese*
     剖術   炎   /   急性
     (SinoV.)   (SinoV.)   (Viet.)   (SinoV.)
     "operation" "inflammation" "extra-   "acute"
                                 intestine"

---

3. The Chinese term *mangchang* 盲腸 "blind intestine" refers to the appendage at the end of the digestive track. It first appeared in Japanese as 蟲垂 "hanging worm", a semantic adaptation of the Latin term "vermiform" (worm shape), through the Dutch language, whose speakers along with the Portuguese were the earliest Western visitors to Japan. As in the case of Japanese, the word order could differ from the Chinese, and Sino-Japanese and Sino-Vietnamese terms could be traced to classical Chinese and to some of the more conservative dialects such as Cantonese in pronunciation. This term would not be easily understood by the man on the street in Japan if it was spoken, but reading the Kanji characters would improve his comprehension to realize that there is involvement of "surgical operation in the stomach", "cutting" and "urgency", almost on par with a Chinese person on the street.

Another example is "subdural hematoma", the term referring to "blood clot under the skull",

(4)   Yinnaomo   xia   xuezhong   *Chinese*
硬腦膜   下   血腫
"hard brain membrane"   "under"   "blood swelling"

(5)   Komaku   ka   kesshu   *Japanese*
硬膜   下   血腫
"hard membrane"   "under"   "blood swelling"

(6)   Tụ   máu   dưới   màng cứng   *Vietnamese*
聚? (SinoV.?)   /(Viet.)   /(Viet.)   /(Viet.)
"accumulation"   "blood"   "under"   "membrane-hard"

The English term draws from Latin "sub" and "dura", and from Greek "hematoma", while the Sino-Japanese term refers to "blood swelling under the (hard) skull/brain membrane". There are clearly parallel word constituents in Japanese and Vietnamese based on Chinese[4].

In the case of Latin terms found in English, the meaning and information encoded in the legal terms are very highly compact and succinct, so the terms cannot be rendered into English with just single

---

4. Lexical stratification is common in languages and serves certain useful social-cognitive functions of differentiation within the society. In the case of modern Chinese, the differentiation in lexical layers to correlate with stylistic and discoursal registers is more subtly manifested through the selected use of elements from the Classical Chinese language as shown in the table below:

No.	Class. lang.		Md. lang.		Eng.	No.	Class. lang.		Md. lang.		Eng.
1	*fu*	腹	*du*	肚	stomach	5	*lu*	顱	*tou*	頭	head
2	*fu*	婦	*nü*	女	female	6	*chi*	齒	*ya*	牙	tooth
3	*kou*	口	*zui*	嘴	mouth	7	*zhi*	脂	*you*	油	fat
4	*zu*	足	*jiao*	腳	foot	8	*yi*	疫	*bing*	病	disease

Chinese technical terms often use classical language elements: （1）腹腔 abdominal cavity, （2）婦科gynecology, （3）口腔oral cavity, （4）足浴footbath, （5）顱骨skull, （6）智齒wisdom teeth, （7）脂肪fat, （8）疫情epidemic.

words or appropriate periphrastic expressions. Therefore, what may appear to be jargonistic terms constitute a major vocational challenge which legal professionals have to overcome[5]. Moreover, some items such as *forum, ex-officio, alibi, pro rata, vis-a-vis* have been incorporated into the basic formal English vocabulary[6]. Given the unassailable and dominant status of English in Hong Kong in the past 150 years, many such Latin terms have been in use for a long time in legal documents. Against this background, the present book intends to provide readers with a useful account of the authentic usage of 105 such Latin terms which are commonly used in the Hong Kong legal domain.

It is notable that in one and a half centuries, the courts in Hong Kong operated almost exclusively in English. In the short run-up to the changeover on sovereignty over Hong Kong in 1997, there was an accelerated move to increase the use of Chinese because it was realized that the use of Chinese in the legal context, especially in the Common Law system, could facilitate and enhance China's exercise of sovereignty over Hong Kong through the Chinese Language. By the time the Hong Kong Special Administrative Region (HKSAR) was formally established in 1997, the official status of the Chinese language has been elevated when compared with the continuing use of English in the courts according to Article 9 of the Basic Law of HKSAR which explicitly states that

---

5. Three Japanese legal dictionaries are also selected for comparison in the preparation of this volume. It is interesting to note that when compared with the 2000 edition, the new edition of the dictionary (ロ―ダス21：法律英語辭典, 2002) has incorporated 9 more Latin terms. Another dictionary (英米法辭典, 1991) which contains Japanese glossary for Anglo-American legal terms also covers a significant number of Latin terms. This shows that Latin terms take up a significant position in legal language.

6. "Republic" from Latin *res publica* "matters of the public" is another example of the full incorporation of Latin into English.

in addition to the Chinese language, English may also be used as
an official language by the executive authorities, legislature and
judiciary of the Hong Kong Special Administrative Region.[7]

However, in contrast to the mature use of English in the legal domain, the use of Chinese has been unprecedented in the Common Law tradition, not only in Hong Kong but anywhere in the world. This jurilinguistic development and localization of Common Law in Hong Kong has meant that the all important Chinese terminology for the Common Law system has had to evolve rapidly and had little lead time to be refined and perhaps codified. It is thus not surprising that many legal terms collected in this book have more than one Chinese rendition, and that quite a few have more than four alternate renditions (e.g. *alibi, quantum*) drawing on the classical language as well as Modern Standard Chinese. Such a situation can be quite bewildering for the neophyte legal professional, and no less a challenge for the seasoned jurist who is not familiar with the use of Chinese in the legal domain but may wish to use legally appropriate Chinese terms.

This book therefore is an ideal reference for lawyers, legal professionals, translators, and students of law and anyone else interested in legal language, including anyone with more than passing interest in the English language in Hong Kong. It has collected 105 Latin terms commonly found in the legal domain of Hong Kong with examples drawn mostly

---

7. This provision offers interesting comparison with Article 50 of the 1852 Sino-British Treaty of Tianjin, which established the predominance of the English language over the Chinese language in Hong Kong for one and a half centuries since its founding.

Article 50:

All official communications, addressed by the Diplomat and Consular Agents of Her Majesty the Queen to the Chinese authorities, shall, henceforth, be written in English. They will for the present be accompanied by a Chinese version, but it is understood that, in the event of there being any difference of meaning between the English and Chinese text, the English Government will hold the sense as expressed in the English text to be the correct sense. This provision is to apply to the Treaty now negotiated, the Chinese text of which has been carefully corrected by the English original.

See also the discussion in Tsou and You, *op. cit.*

from actual bilingual court judgments. Besides providing the meaning of the terms in both English and Chinese, this book has made use of a sizable body of bilingual material and has made several unique provisions:

(1) It lists the alternate Chinese terms for each entry found in official legal documentation in Hong Kong and from a wide range of dictionaries. The number of alternate Chinese renditions can exceed 3 in nearly half of the cases, with a handful having 5 or more;

(2) it provides actual examples of the terms found in parallel bilingual texts; and

(3) it indicates the differential distribution of the alternate renditions by percentage whenever available from the body of legal judgments, a feature may be useful to practitioners and

(4) it provides parts-of-speech information on the item as appropriate. Entries having different parts-of-speech are listed separately, such as *bona fide/bona fides* and *mala fide/mala fides*.

The compilation of this book is a follow-up on two research projects the then Language Information Sciences Centre of the City University of Hong Kong, viz *Electronic Legal Documentation System* (ELDoS) and the Bilingual Reference System (BRS). They represented happy collaboration between computational linguists and translators at the City University of Hong Kong and members from the Judiciary. We would like to thank the Judiciary for providing us with the bilingual judgment corpora. We would also like to express our gratitude to Mr. Tony Yen of the Department of Justice for his advice and support, and to Mr. Paul Tang for additional suggestions.

We are fortunate to have forewords provided by three distinguished and respected legal professionals, the Honourable Justice Robert Tang, from the judiciary, who was an advisor of the first-ever MA programme in Language and Law in Hong Kong launched by the Department of Applied Linguistics of the then City Polytechnic of Hong Kong in 1990. Mr Anthony Neoh, Senior Counsel, and Mr Paul Tang, Solicitor. We have also benefited from the advice and help of Professor Serena Jin, and Professor King Kui Sin, and the thoughtful contributions to the translation of the forewords by Professor King Kui Sin [for Mr Justice Robert Tang's foreword], Dr Constance Yan WANG [for Mr A. Neoh's foreword], and Ms Sylvia Hiu Yan Law [for Mr Paul Tang's foreword].

自序

　　本書取材自大型雙語法律判詞數據庫，詳述了判詞裏拉丁文詞語的使用實例，以及這些詞語在香港中文文本的對應用法，不僅能為法律專業人士提供有用典範，也適合其他對香港語言情況感興趣人士參考。

　　源自拉丁文或羅曼語族的詞語是法律英語的一大特徵[1]。儘管此類詞語引入英語的歷史由來已久，但至今仍然是今日英語的常用詞語。在法律領域中使用這些詞語的情況尤其明顯，而且使用時基本上保留了原有詞義。因此，這些主要源自拉丁文的用語在英語中形成了特殊的詞彙層面，長久以來都是法律及醫學用語的普遍情況。

　　使用本民族以外源於不同語言的情況，例如英語中使用拉丁文，並非英語或其他歐洲語言的特有現象。日語、韓語、越南語和現代漢語等亞洲語言傳統上也是有雙層語言[2]並用的情況。這是因為早期東亞地區的漢字文化圈中，漢語文的習得（包括科舉制度）曾是當地一種精英教育的傳統，而且各地在推展當地文字時都曾採用了漢字以義符為主的文字系統，也引發漢語為上述語言增添了漢語辭彙層。

---

1. 為簡化參照，本文所提及的「拉丁文」詞也包括源自法語等羅曼語族語言的詞彙，如 *estop* 和 *estoppel*。
2. 另見《漢語與華人社會》（鄒嘉彥，游汝傑，2003，香港城市大學出版社）。

日語、越南語和漢語[3] 表達「急性盲腸炎開刀手術」
（Appendectomy）的詞語可以說明這種現象。

(1)	Jixing 急性 "acute"	mangchangyan 盲腸炎 "blind intestine inflx"	kaidao 開刀 "cut with knife"	shoushu 手術 "operation"	漢語

(2)	Kyusei 急性 "acute"	kaifuku 開腹 "laparotomy"	chusui 蟲垂 "hanging worm"	setsujo 切除 "cutting off"	日語

(3)	phẫu thuật 剖術 (SinoV.) "operation"	viêm 炎 (SinoV.) "inflammation"	ruột thừa / (Viet.) "extra-intestine"	cấp tính 急性 (SinoV.) "acute"	越南語

另一個例子是 "subdural hematoma"（硬腦膜下血腫）。

(4)	Yinnaomo 硬腦膜 "hard brain membrane"	xia 下 "under"	xuezhong 血腫 "blood swelling"	漢語

(5)	Komaku 硬膜 "hard membrane"	ka 下 "under"	kesshu 血腫 "blood swelling"	日語

---

3. 漢語的「盲腸」指消化道末端的闌尾。在日語中最先以「蟲垂」出現，該詞透過荷蘭語而來，借用了拉丁詞 "vermiform"（蟲形）的語意。原因是荷蘭人和葡萄牙人是最早踏足日本的西方人傳授外科手術知識。日語的詞序和漢語有所不同，而中日和中越所採用的漢語詞彙有些可以追溯到古漢語，發音方面可以與語音比較保守的粵語和其他方言相近。如果在口語用上這些詞語，一般人不一定能輕易聽懂；但只要看到漢字便能提升理解，意識到該詞涉及「腹部的手術」、「切除」和「急性」，幾乎會像中國人望詞即懂一樣。

(6)	Tụ	máu	dưới	màng cứng	越南語
	聚? (SinoV.?)	/(Viet.)	/(Viet.)	/(Viet.)	
	"accumulation"	"blood"	"under"	"membrane-hard"	

英語詞取材自拉丁語的"sub"（下）和"dura"（層），加上希臘語的"hematoma"（血），而漢語則以"硬（腦）膜下血腫"來代表。顯然，日語和越南語的語構成元素都有漢語的基礎成分[4]。

英語中的拉丁法律詞語所蘊含的意義和詞語所提供的規範化信息不但概括性很強，而且非常簡潔，而只單靠幾個英語詞語或句子來表達個中意思則遜色多了。因此，掌握拉丁法律詞語便成為了法律從業員必須克服的一大挑戰[5]。此外，一些拉丁詞語，如*forum*、*ex-officio*、*alibi*、*pro rata*、*vis-à-vis* 等已經成為常見現代英語的基本詞彙[6]。過去150多年，英語在香港有着主導地位，法律文書中也長期大量使用這種拉丁詞語。有見及此，本書挑選了105個此類在香港法律領域中常用的拉丁詞語，並說明它們最新的實際使用情況，務求為讀者提供有用的參考。

---

4. 詞彙分層是各國語言的常見現象，在社會階層識別中發揮着有用的社會認同功能。以現代漢語為例，詞彙分層的差別跟語言風格和話語語域的相互關係，在使用個別早期漢語元素中有跡可尋，如下表所示：

編號	古漢語		現代漢語		英語	編號	古漢語		現代漢語		英語
1	*fu*	腹	*du*	肚	stomach	5	*lu*	顱	*tou*	頭	head
2	*fu*	婦	*nü*	女	female	6	*chi*	齒	*ya*	牙	tooth
3	*kou*	口	*zui*	嘴	mouth	7	*zhi*	脂	*you*	油	fat
4	*zu*	足	*jiao*	腳	foot	8	*yi*	疫	*bing*	病	disease

漢語技術用詞中也經常使用古漢語元素，例如：（1）腹腔、（2）婦科、（3）口腔、（4）足浴、（5）顱骨、（6）智齒、（7）脂肪、（8）疫情。

5. 在編撰本書時，我們同時選擇了三本日文法律詞典進行比較。我們發現2002年版的《ローダス21：法律英語辭典》比2000年版本增加了9個拉丁詞彙。另外一本包括英美法律詞彙日文譯文的詞典——《英米法辭典》(1991)也收集了大量的拉丁詞彙。這都表明拉丁詞彙在法律語言中佔據了很重要的地位。

6. 英語"Republic"（共和國）來自拉丁語的 *res publica*（公共的事務），是另一個拉丁詞語完全融入英語的好例子。

　　還值得注意的是，在過去的一個半世紀，英語基本上是香港法庭的唯一語言。1997年香港主權移交之前，在香港使用中文的機會迅速提升。在行使《普通法》體系的香港法律領域中使用中文，也體現中國對香港恢復行使主權。《基本法》第九條明確指出，至1997年香港特別行政區正式成立時，中文和英文在法庭上具有同等的地位：

　　「香港特別行政區的行政機關、立法機關和司法機關，除使用中文外，還可使用英文，英文也是正式語文。」[7]

　　然而，相對於在法律領域中使用英語的成熟程度，在《普通法》法律體系中使用中文可以說史無前例，在香港如此，在世界任何地方同樣未有過這種做法。香港出現了這種法律語言學發展，加上《普通法》本地化，意味着所有適用於《普通法》制度的重要中文詞彙都需要急速演進，沒有多少時間可供潤飾和制定成文。因此，本書所收錄的很多法律詞語都有超過一個中文對應詞彙，這點便不足為奇。有些詞語，例如*alibi*、*quantum*，甚至多於四種譯法。這種一對多譯的情況經常使新進法律從業員感受到一定的困難，甚至無所適從，而對資深的法律界人士也是一大挑戰，因為他們一方面對法律領域中的中文使用不太熟悉，但另一方面卻希望能夠適當使用中文法律詞彙。

　　因此，本書可以說是一部有實用參考價值的工具書。它的對象包括律師、法律從業員、翻譯人員、法律系學生以及對法律語言感興趣的人，包括對香港語言狀況感興趣的人士。本書選收了105個香港法律領域中常用的拉丁詞語，輔以主要來自雙語法庭

7.　本條文與1852年中英《天津條約》第50款形成了引人注目的對比，後者導致香港開埠後150年來一直重英輕中：

第50款：

嗣後英國文書俱用英字書寫，暫時仍以漢文配送，俟中國選派學生學習英文、英語熟習，即不用配送漢文。自今以後，遇有文詞辯論之處，總以英文作為正義。此次定約，漢、英文書詳細較對無訛，亦照此例。

另見《漢語與華人社會》（鄒嘉彥，游汝傑，2003，香港城市大學出版社）。

判決書的參考例子。除了以中英雙語說明詞義，本書也採用了大量雙語語料，並具有以下幾個特點：

1. 詳列每個拉丁詞語的不同中文翻譯，這些翻譯源自香港的官方法律文本和多部詞典。根據這些語料，我們發現近半詞條都有三個以上的中文對譯，部分甚至有五個以上。

2. 提供從雙語法律文本中篩選出來的實例。

3. 根據雙語判決書，提供每個中文對譯的使用度百分比，本功能可能對於其他需要就此下更多功夫的業者有用。

4. 在適用時提供詞性信息，有些詞彙有不同詞性，將同時列出，如 *bona fide/bona fides* 和 *mala fide/mala fides*。

本書的編撰是香港城市大學語言資訊科學研究中心和香港特別行政區政府司法機構兩個合作項目的延續，這兩個項目分別是 *Electronic Legal Documentation System* (ELDoS) 和 *Bilingual Reference System* (BRS)。在此特別感謝司法機構提供雙語判詞語料，同時也感謝律政署的嚴元浩先生的建議和支持，還有鄧賜強律師的意見。

我們十分榮幸邀請到三位香港傑出知名法律界人士為本書撰寫序言：鄧國楨法官（1990年擔任香港城市理工學院（現為香港城市大學）應用語言學系的語言和法律碩士課程顧問）、梁定邦資深大律師和鄧賜強律師。此外，我們也十分感謝金聖華教授和冼景矩教授的建議和協助，以及冼景矩教授、黃艷博士和羅曉欣小姐分別提供鄧國楨法官、梁定邦資深大律師和鄧賜強律師的序言翻譯。

Introduction

1. Significance of Latin in modern English

Most of the terms presented in this book have their origins in Latin. In fact, Latin terms in English texts represent a hybrid substratum which serves two main purposes: one is stylistic, the other is more substantive in terms of functionality and content. More specifically, Latin terms can: (1) mark the learned status of the user, and (2) serve as succinct conventionalized designations of legal concepts. In many ways they may be compared with acronyms in English or 4-character idiomatic expressions in Chinese.

Consider the words *stratum/strata* and *layer* in the English language. They have different origins: *Stratum* is from Latin while *layer* is from Norman French. Though they have similar meanings, there are considerable differences between the associated or derived words, and usage substitution is problematical. The following two parallel lists contain possible words from the related word families in English. They provide a useful comparison:

Table 1: Word families of *stratum* and *layer*

stratum	layer
sub-stratum	sub-layer
strata	layers
strata title	(*layer title)
stratify	(layerize ?)
stratification	layerization (?)
stratificational	layerlike (?)
stratified	layerlike (?)
	layered
	multi-layer (ed)
de-stratify	(de-layer??)
strato-sphere	?
?	layer cake

Whereas both *layer* and its plural form *layers* could be readily found in English, *strata* usually appears in the singular form: *stratum*. *Strata* can also have a specialized meaning in real estate transactions as in *strata-title*. In addition, *sub-stratum* appears as a preferred alternative to *sub-layer*. However, there are many more possible derivations from *stratum* than *layer*. In the latter case, the derived-terms mostly appear to refer to a static situation. For example, *stratificational* describes a static situation, whereas the participal form stratified implies the results of a dynamic change from an "*un-stratified*" state with considerable semantic content unexpressed.

The situation is the same for a static description represented by *layerlike* while *layered* (or *layerized*) would be uncommon innovations even though they imply dynamic change. However, *layer* or *multi-layer cake* have become conventional terms which would be unusual if rendered as *stratified cake* or *multi-stratified cake*. Similarly *strato-sphere* has a special meaning in referring to a certain *layer* of the atmosphere above the earth, which cannot be replaced by *layer-sphere*.

From the above we can see that the English language has embedded words of different origins which are associated with at least one of the two special functions. In general, Latin or Latin derived words when used properly in English could project an aura of erudition often related to the high register of a stylistically stratified language even when equivalent English words may be found.

It should be stressed that there is more to using Latinate words to display verbal flair in English, especially as in a formal speech. This is because Latinate words also provide a necessary and convenient as well as concise and specialized terminology compared with any parallel periphrastic alternatives. These functions have been associated with such terminological development in the first place. The latter situation finds a ready and more extensive parallel in the medical field such that students embarking on studies in medicine and law had to have studied Latin beforehand in the past.

While the Latin language has many complex grammatical structures, there are primarily two basic and useful linguistic concepts which are highly relevant to the use of Latin terms in English in this book.

1.1 Plural forms

The rudimentary distinction between singular and plural in the word structure of Latin is different from English but accommodated when Latin terms are used in English. This is because the hybridized Latin found in English differs from both Latin, the original donor language, and English, the recipient language. For example, the plural of *onus* should be *onera* in Latin because it belongs to a noun class (declension) which ends in *–us* and takes *-era* as the plural. However, *onuses* is found instead in English because *onus* has been assimilated as an English word and so its plural is formed in analogy to *bus – buses* and *house - houses*. On the other hand, the plural form of *quantum* is still kept as *quanta*, as in Latin. It is also necessary to learn that the plural form for *quorum* is *quorums* rather than *quora*, because it is now also an assimilated word. In addition, *minutiae* is the plural form of *minutia* (a member of the first declension (Noun class) which ends in *–a* and takes *–e* as the plural maker). The above examples indicate that there are at least three common plural forms for nouns in Latin which are obtained by changing the ending of the noun stem:

Table 2: Some common Latin plural endings

Singular		Plural	Example
-a	→	-ae	(*minutia* → *minutiae*)
-um	→	-a	(*quantum* → *quanta*)
-us	→	-era	(*onus* → *onera*)

We note that English grammar retains some agreement between syntactic classes. For example, an appropriate single or plural verb form is required to go with the subject noun and a nominal quantifier such as "this" or "these" has to agree with the singular or plural subject noun. Thus a plural verb form and a plural quantifier are required to go with the common use of the plural form *minutiae* as the subject, for example, "**these** complex *minutiae* of the case *are* baffling……". Therefore, there is still a need to have some basic understanding of the plural forms for Latinate nouns in English for subject-verb agreement.

1.2 Prefixes in Latin

Many expressions involving prepositions in English can be readily encapsulated by prefixes in Latin. It is useful to have a grasp of the basic meaning of the common prefixes. For example, both *inter* and *intra* mean "into among" in English, but in Latin *inter* clearly mean "into or among members across **different** kinds", while *intra* "among members of the **same** kind". Thus, *intra-group* communication refers to communication among the members **within** the same group while *inter-group* communication refers to the one among the members of **different** groups.

Table 3 below lists some common prefixes in Latin and relative English prepositions.[1]

Table 3: Some common prefixes in Latin

Prefix in Latin	Example
ab (from)	*ab initio* (from the beginning)
ad (toward)	*ad litem* (to the lawsuit)
	ad lib (toward pleasure)
de (by, from)	*de-jure* (by law)
	de novo (from the new)
	de facto (by deed)
ex (out of, from)	*ex facie* (from the face)
	ex gratia (from kindness)
in (in)	*in personam* (into a person, directed to a person)
	in situ (in the place)
per (by means of, through, by)	*per capita* (by heads)
	per se (through itself)
pro (for)	*pro-forma* (for form)
	pro rata (for the rate)
sine (without)	*sine die* (without a day)
	sine quo non (without which not)

---

1. Some Latin prepositions have been already fused into assimilated words found in English: *percent* (on each hundred); *promise* (pro-missio).

One example of each of the above Latin prefixes is listed below for illustration.

(1) ab initio

   –   Suing all 10 defendants, the plaintiff primarily seeks a declaration that the assignment between itself and the 1st defendant is void *ab initio*. (HCA 2251/2002)[2]

(2) ad litem

   –   "It shall be the duty of the guardian *ad litem* to investigate as fully as possible all circumstances relevant to the proposed adoption with a view to safeguarding the interests of the infant ...." (HCAD000003/1992)

(3) ad lib

   –   Pickpocking is an *ad lib* act. There will never be a destined place or a target beforehand. (CACC 430/2004)

(4) de jure

   In order to prove that he was, at the material time, a shadow director, the evidence must show firstly, that he was neither a *de jure* nor a de facto director; (HCCW348/96)

(5) de novo

   The Appellant had appeared earlier before another Magistrate on the same two charges and after the conclusion of the prosecution evidence, he ordered a trial *de novo*. (HCMA 268/2004)

(6) de facto

   –   The respondents were *de facto* directors of each of the companies for which petitions were presented and owed fiduciary duties to each company. (HCMP 838/2007)

(7) ex facie

   –   If the case contains anything *ex facie* which is bad law and which bears upon the determination, it is, obviously, erroneous in points of law. (HCIA1/2002)

---

2. The numbers in the brackets refer to the case number of judgment available at the online Legal Reference System of Hong Kong Judiciary.

(8)   ex gratia

- In addition to this incorporation of a hope value into the calculation of *ex gratia* compensation, the working party recommended a set of principles in terms of which the scheme should be administered. (HCAL 2170/2000)

(9)   in personam

- In order to establish in rem jurisdiction requirement within the terms of section 12B(4) of the Supreme Court Ordinance, Cap 4, it must be demonstrated that the target otherwise liable to the plaintiff *in personam* also must be the "beneficial owner" of the vessel in question. (CACV000234/2006)

(10) in situ

- The metal railings had been left *in situ*, on the site, by the site constructor, Maeda when they vacated the site in or about March 1997. (HCPI 1476/2000)

(11) per capita

- These defendants' claimed that 92% of the compensation should be distributed *per capita* and 8% per stirpes. (CACV 137/2007)

(12) per se

- No employer is entitled to make use of a restrictive covenant to protect himself against competition *per se*. A covenant against competition per se is not reasonable and accordingly void. (HCA 4166/2003)

(13) pro forma

- in addition to fully explaining such standard agreement to the ...... tenant, practitioners should check their *pro-forma* provisional agreement against the standard agreement for conflict or discrepancy in order to protect the interest of the ...... tenant. (DCCJ1287/2005)

(14) pro rata

- In mid-1999, by letters dated 28 June 1999 and 5 and 6 July 1999, the defendants gave instructions to the Escrow Agent for the Escrow Shares and Escrow money to be distributed *pro rata* pursuant to clause 6. (CACV 24/2008)

(15) <u>sine die</u>

- What appears from the file note is it is clear that there was an agreement between the parties, and therefore the summons was adjourned *sine die*. (HCA118/91)

(16) <u>sine qua non</u>

- but he does not suggest that these conditions are a *sine qua non* of validity, for which reason I do not intend to address them. (CACV 327/2006)

2. Difference between legal language and common language

We have noted that the legal language constitutes a distinct genre from the common language. In this book, we include references to an additional database LIVAC (A synchronous corpus of Chinese) [https://en.wikipedia.org/wiki/LIVAC_Synchronous_Corpus], which provides some salient information of the Chinese vocabulary from a number of Chinese speech communities such as Hong Kong, Taiwan, Beijing, Shanghai, Macau and Singapore. LIVAC can thus provide additional useful background comparison on the Chinese renditions of the Latin terms used in the judgment corpus.

2.1 Chinese

The situation for legal Chinese is perhaps more complex because its high register is often still represented by elements of the classical language which forms a continuum with written Modern Standard Chinese (現代漢語). It should be of interest to note that the 105 terms in this book are associated with nearly 500 alternative Chinese terms (i.e. on average, each entry has around 5 Chinese alternatives). Of these over 40% are not found in general usage, as represented by the newspaper coverage in Hong Kong, Taiwan and Beijing for 1998 to 2003 involving 70 million characters of the above mentioned LIVAC database. It should be noted that of the 60 items which have appeared 9 times or less in the Chinese newspaper database of **LIVAC**, about 40% did not appear in the Hong Kong and Taiwan sub-databases, but 75% did not appear in the Beijing sub-database. This situation indicates that there is considerable divergence in the rendition of legal terms in the pan-Chinese context.

The general **language usage** indicated by LIVAC provides more information on the relative frequencies among the Chinese alternatives found in legal references. Take the item *a fortiori* as an example, five Chinese renditions are found in the judgments: 尤其(是), 更加, 更何況, 遑論, 更甚的(是) while 何況, 更不用説 and 更不容置疑地 are found in other legal dictionaries. Among them, 更何況 and 遑論 are used the most, as shown in Table 4.

Table 4: Chinese renditions of *a fortiori* in Chinese legal materials

Chinese rendition	Frequency of the Chinese renditions (%)
1. 更何況	28.6
2. 遑論	28.6
3. 尤其(是)	14.3
4. 更加	14.3
5. 更甚的(是)	14.3
6. 何況	0
7. 更不用説	0
8. 更不容置疑地	0

However, when we examine the bilingual judgment corpus, we note a different distribution of these 8 Chinese renditions. Table 5 shows that those two high frequency renditions for *a fortiori* (i.e. 更何況 and 遑論) are not used very much in the Chinese judgments.

Table 5: Distribution of the 8 Chinese renditions (in Table 4)
in the overall Chinese judgment corpus

Words	Frequency in the judgment corpus (%)
1. 更何況	5.7
2. 遑論	6.3
3. 尤其(是)	55.7
4. 更加	24.7
5. 更甚的(是)	0.6
6. 何況	4.6
7. 更不用説	2.3
8. 更不容置疑地	0

At the same time, we also compare the usage of these Chinese words/ phrases in the LIVAC database. The LIVAC data show that 尤其(是) and 更 加 are used much more frequently as a whole (Table 6). This is true of Hong Kong and Taiwan, though the preference in Beijing seems to be reversed for the colloquial 更加, which has been used more often than the pseudo-classical尤其(是) there. On the other hand, one of the high frequency alternatives 遑論 found in legal sources is rarely used in the daily language.

Table 6: Frequency distributions of the Chinese renditions of *a fortiori* in LIVAC

Items / %	LIVAC	Hong Kong	Taiwan	Beijing
1. 更何況	2.2	2.1	4.11	0.6
2. 遑論	1.1	2.1	1.41	0.06
3. 尤其(是)	49.1	53.5	67.2	29
4. 更加	44.2	35.8	23.1	69.6
5. 更甚的(是)	0.1	0.1	0.03	0
6. 何況	3	5.7	3.7	0.6
7. 更不用説	0.3	0.4	0.42	0.2
8. 更不容置疑地	0	0	0	0
TOTAL	100	100	100	100

2.2 English

The 105 terms also provide interesting comparison with existing English language dictionaries. Whereas a specialized dictionary such as the *Dictionary of Law* contains 55 of the entries in full, 45 are not found there, while partial entries for 5 of them are found. When compared with the popular *Oxford Advanced Learner's English-Chinese Dictionary* (*OALD*), 36 entries are found in full and 56 are not found. This indicates that about a third of the Latin and related legal terms in the book are commonly found in written English represented by the *OALD*. Furthermore, when the entries are compared with the deceptively large *New Shorter Oxford English Dictionary*, 76 entries are found in full and only 16 are not found at all. This would suggest that three-quarters of the items in this book are now considered to be essential vocabulary in modern English by the compilers and they might be familiar to someone with a good knowledge of the English language. In short, there is a continuum in the use of Latin or Latinate words from legal language to the language of the educated, whose English already contains many essentially Latin derived abbreviations such as: *A.D., e.g., etc,* sic and could well include other common words such as *dictum, minutiae, quorum, status quo*, etc.

Biliteracy and Trilingualism (兩文三語), involving written Modern Standard Chinese based mostly on spoken Putonghua, and written English; spoken Cantonese, Putonghua and spoken English, has been an important and unique feature of Hong Kong's bilingual milieu. This has been embodied in its legal system after China resumed sovereignty over Hong Kong in 1997. There is yet a fourth language, Latin, which plays a barely noticeable, but nonetheless significant part in its legal system. This book is an early innovative attempt at Digital Humanities studies, by making use of big data and quantitative analysis to examine the use of legal language in Hong Kong which has both practical value as well as serves broader interests. The underlying rationale and methodology for this book have already led to a similar larger project on the specialized terminologies in Chinese and English patents [http://patentlex.chilin.hk/]. We hope this book will serve to draw further interest in the production of similar reference materials for the Hong Kong legal profession and for the study of the evolving language situation in Hong Kong.

導論

1. 現代英語中的拉丁詞語

　　拉丁詞語在英語的歷史十分悠久。使用拉丁詞語有兩種意義：一是體現風格；另外是增強文本的內容性。具體來說，拉丁詞語一方面可以顯示作者的學識，同時作者透過比較簡潔和固定的片語來表達複雜的法律概念。這種情況跟英語簡縮詞和漢語四字格成語相似。

　　以英語 stratum/strata和layer兩個詞語為例，它們有不同的來源：stratum源於拉丁語，layer源於法語。雖然他們的意思相近，但是他們的搭配詞、派生詞以及用法大不相同，兩個詞語衍生出來的詞語不能隨便互相替換。表 1 列出這兩個詞語派生出來的詞彙。

表1：stratum和layer詞族的比較

stratum	layer
sub-stratum	sub-layer
strata	layers
strata title	(*layer title)
stratify	(layerize ?)
stratification	layerization (?)
stratificational	layerlike (?)
stratified	layerlike (?)
	layered
	multi-layer (ed)
de-stratify	(de-layer??)
strato-sphere	?
?	layer cake

Layer的單數 "layer" 和複數 "layers" 形式同時存在，但stratum的複數形式strata經常取代其單數形式。此外，strata 在房地產交易中有特殊意思：strata-title (分層所有權)。Sub-stratum和sub-layer相比，sub-stratum較常用。由stratum派生出來的詞彙比layer多。由layer派生出來的詞彙主要表示靜態情況。例如，stratificational描述的是靜態情況，而其過去分詞stratified則表示由un-stratified的狀態轉化到 stratified的過程，換句話說，stratified隱含較多的語義資訊。

Layerlike一詞跟stratificational 相近，也是描述靜態狀況，雖然layered (或layerized) 也可以表示動態情況，但這種用法比stratified較少見。值得注意的是，layer或multi-layer cake已經成為習慣用語，如果把這兩個詞改為stratified cake或 multi-stratum cake 則會顯得突兀。同樣，表示大氣層中平流層的stratosphere，不能換為layer-sphere。

我們可以看到在有對應英語詞彙的情形下仍然使用拉丁詞語可以反映作者博學多才和有高度的語言造詣，這在正式演說中可見一斑；另一方面，運用在法律語言這個高層語域的拉丁詞語都是簡潔和專業的詞彙，可以避免使用冗長的英語近義詞/句子而使文本顯得冗贅，甚至詞不達意，或者意義有所偏頗，這個在法律專業裏十分重要和嚴謹。因此，我們可以理解為什麼以前的醫科和法律專業的學生，都需要先掌握拉丁語。

相對英語來說，拉丁語有較複雜的語法和詞彙結構，當中有兩項語言特徵在本書收錄的法律詞彙中有所涉及，值得我們探討。

1.1　複數形式

很多拉丁詞語進入英語後，用法跟拉丁語並不完全一樣。因此了解拉丁詞語的詞法和結構十分重要。同時我們也需要了解拉丁詞語進入英語後的調整，融合和發展。其中一項是名詞的複數形式，比如說，onus屬於以-us結尾並以-era作為複數形式的名詞類，它的複數形式因此是onera，但是在英語裏，其複數形式是

onuses，跟bus和house的複數形式buses, houses一樣，另一個例子是quorum（單數）和quorums（複數），quorum在拉丁語裏的複數應該是quora，這些例子說明onus和quorum已經被視為英語詞彙。不過，有些名詞仍然保留拉丁語的複數形式，例如quantum（單數）和quanta（複數），minutia（單數）和minutiae（複數）。以上這些例子表明，拉丁語名詞其中三種複數形式在英語裏都反映出來（見表2）。

表2：部分拉丁名詞的複數形式

單數		複數	例子
-a	→	*-ae*	(*minutia* → *minutiae*)
-um	→	*-a*	(*quantum* → *quanta*)
-us	→	*-era*	(*onus* → *onera*)

英語的語法要求句子中的主語和動詞的單複數形式要保持一致。如果minutiae作為主語，後面的動詞應為複數形式，它的修飾指示代詞也要以複數形式出現，如these或those。例如，"**these complex minutiae** of the case **are** baffling……"。我們因此需要對拉丁詞語的詞法有一定的了解，才能正確掌握它們在英語中的語法規則。

1.2　前綴

英語中很多介詞在拉丁語都是以前綴形式表示（見表3）。部分前綴有細緻的語義差異，以inter- 和 intra- 為例，inter- 指的是"在**不同**種類的個體中"；intra- 指的是"在**相同**種類的個體中"。例如，intra-group communication指的是同一個團隊裏成員之間的溝通，inter-group communication則指不同團隊成員之間的溝通。表3列出一些常見的拉丁語前綴[1]，接下來的是法律文本中的例句。

---

1. 有些拉丁前綴介詞已經成為英語詞彙的一部分，如percent, promise (pro-mission)。

表3：拉丁語前綴

拉丁言前綴	例子
ab (from)	*ab initio* (from the beginning)
ad (toward)	*ad litem* (to the lawsuit)
	ad lib (toward pleasure)
de (by, from)	*de-jure* (by law)
	de novo (from the new)
	de facto (by deed)
ex (out of, from)	*ex facie* (from the face)
	ex gratia (from kindness)
in (in)	*in personam* (into a person, directed to a person)
	in situ (in the place)
per (by means of, through, by)	*per capita* (by heads)
	per se (through itself)
pro (for)	*pro-forma* (for form)
	pro rata (for the rate)
sine (without)	*sine die* (without a day)
	sine quo non (without which not)

具體例子如下：

(1) <u>ab initio</u>

  – Suing all 10 defendants, the plaintiff primarily seeks a declaration that the assignment between itself and the 1st defendant is void *ab initio*. (HCA 2251/2002)[2]

(2) <u>ad litem</u>

  – "It shall be the duty of the guardian *ad litem* to investigate as fully as possible all circumstances relevant to the proposed adoption with a view to safeguarding the interests of the infant ...." (HCAD000003/1992)

---

2. 括號裏的數字是香港司法機構法律參考資料系統中判決書的案件編號。

(3)   ad lib

–   Pickpocking is an *ad lib* act. There will never be a destined place or a target beforehand. (CACC 430/2004)

(4)   de jure

In order to prove that he was, at the material time, a shadow director, the evidence must show firstly, that he was neither a *de jure* nor a de facto director. (HCCW348/96)

(5)   de novo

The Appellant had appeared earlier before another Magistrate on the same two charges and after the conclusion of the prosecution evidence, he ordered a trial *de novo*. (HCMA 268/2004)

(6)   de facto

–   The respondents were *de facto* directors of each of the companies for which petitions were presented and owed fiduciary duties to each company. (HCMP 838/2007)

(7)   ex facie

–   If the case contains anything *ex facie* which is bad law and which bears upon the determination, it is, obviously, erroneous in points of law. (HCIA1/2002)

(8)   ex gratia

–   In addition to this incorporation of a hope value into the calculation of *ex gratia* compensation, the working party recommended a set of principles in terms of which the scheme should be administered. (HCAL 2170/2000)

(9)   in personam

–   In order to establish in rem jurisdiction requirement within the terms of section 12B(4) of the Supreme Court Ordinance, Cap 4, it must be demonstrated that the target otherwise liable to the plaintiff *in personam* also must be the "beneficial owner" of the vessel in question. (CACV000234/2006)

(10)   in situ

–   The metal railings had been left *in situ*, on the site, by the site constructor, Maeda when they vacated the site in or about March 1997. (HCPI 1476/2000)

(11) per capita
- These defendants' claimed that 92% of the compensation should be distributed *per capita* and 8% per stirpes. (CACV 137/2007)

(12) per se
- No employer is entitled to make use of a restrictive covenant to protect himself against competition per se. A covenant against competition *per se* is not reasonable and accordingly void. (HCA 4166/2003)

(13) pro forma
- in addition to fully explaining such standard agreement to the ...... tenant, practitioners should check their *pro-forma* provisional agreement against the standard agreement for conflict or discrepancy in order to protect the interest of the ...... tenant. (DCCJ1287/2005)

(14) pro rata
- In mid-1999, by letters dated 28 June 1999 and 5 and 6 July 1999, the defendants gave instructions to the Escrow Agent for the Escrow Shares and Escrow money to be distributed *pro rata* pursuant to clause 6. (CACV 24/2008)

(15) sine die
- What appears from the file note is it is clear that there was an agreement between the parties, and therefore the summons was adjourned *sine die*. (HCA118/91)

(16) sine qua non
- but he does not suggest that these conditions are a *sine qua non* of validity, for which reason I do not intend to address them. (CACV 327/2006)

2. 法律語言和一般語言之間的差別

法律語言的使用環境和風格跟日常的語言有很大的差別，以下我們比較法律語言跟漢語和英語的一些語言特徵。

2.1 漢語

根據我們的觀察，法律語言在漢語中的情況也許比英語更複雜。現代漢語由古漢語發展出來，在高層語域中偶然也會使用古漢語（如下文提及"遑論"一詞）。此外，在本書收錄的105個拉丁詞語中，有多達500個對應的中文翻譯（即是平均每個詞條有5種中文譯法）。

編撰這本書時，除了法律語料庫，我們也參考《漢語共時語料庫—LIVAC》[https://en.wikipedia.org/wiki/LIVAC_Synchronous_Corpus]。LIVAC語料庫收集了香港、北京、上海、台灣、新加坡等幾個華語地區的詞彙，可以反映漢語日常詞彙的用法和使用度。LIVAC因此可以讓我們比較判決書中拉丁詞語的漢語翻譯跟一般漢語詞彙之間的差異。透過LIVAC，我們檢索和比較這500個拉丁詞語的中文翻譯。檢索範圍包括1998到2003年LIVAC中香港、台灣、北京三地的新聞語料，共計約七千萬漢字。我們發現其中200個並沒有在LIVAC中出現，60個詞彙出現了九次或以下。這60個詞中，40%沒有在香港和台灣出現；75%的沒有在北京出現。由此可見，拉丁詞語在不同華語地區的翻譯有明顯的差別。

我們現在以 *a fortiori* 為例作具體的分析比較。法律語料中共有五種譯法，另有三種見於法律工具書，表4列出這八個中文詞彙在雙語判決書中的分佈率。

表4：*a fortiori* 中文翻譯在雙語判決書中的分佈

a fortiori	各種中文翻譯的分佈
1. 更何況	28.6
2. 遑論	28.6
3. 尤其(是)	14.3
4. 更加	14.3
5. 更甚的(是)	14.3
6. 何況	0
7. 更不用説	0
8. 更不容置疑地	0

表5列出這八個中文詞語在判決書中的使用度分佈。

表5：*a fortiori* 的8個中文翻譯詞語在中文判決書的整體分佈

	在中文判決書的頻率
1. 更何況	5.7
2. 遑論	6.3
3. 尤其(是)	55.7
4. 更加	24.7
5. 更甚的(是)	0.6
6. 何況	4.6
7. 更不用説	2.3
8. 更不容置疑地	0

　　從表4和表5的資料，我們可以看到，在整個判決書語料庫中，雖然*a fortiori*最常用的翻譯是"遑論"（佔28.6%），但是"遑論"在整個判決書語料裏，出現率只有6.3%。由此可見，部分翻譯拉丁詞語的漢語詞語不一定是常用的漢語詞彙。

　　我們進一步比較這八個中文詞彙在不同華語地區的使用度。

表6：*a fortiori* 的8個中文翻譯詞語在LIVAC中的分佈

詞語/%	LIVAC	香港	台灣	北京
1. 更何況	2.2	2.1	4.11	0.6
2. 遑論	1.1	2.1	1.41	0.06
3. 尤其(是)	49.1	53.5	67.2	29
4. 更加	44.2	35.8	23.1	69.6
5. 更甚的(是)	0.1	0.1	0.03	0
6. 何況	3	5.7	3.7	0.6
7. 更不用説	0.3	0.4	0.42	0.2
8. 更不容置疑地	0	0	0	0
總計	100	100	100	100

　　LIVAC顯示"尤其(是)"和"更加"這兩個詞語在香港和台灣用得最多，北京則傾向使用較口語化的"更加"，使用次數比書面語的"尤其(是)"更高。相反，在法律文本中出現的"遑論"在日常漢語中卻很少使用。

2.2　英語

　　我們分析比較一般英語詞典收錄的拉丁詞語。以法律詞典 *Dictionary of Law* 為例，它收錄了本書當中的55個拉丁詞語，沒有收錄的有50個。但是，在 *Oxford Advanced Learner's English-Chinese Dictionary* (1995) 裏，我們只找到36個詞條，69個沒有收錄。這反映大約三分之一的拉丁法律詞彙也在日常英語中使用。此外，*New Shorter Oxford English Dictionary* (1993) 收錄了76個拉丁詞語。這表明本書中四分之三的拉丁詞語已經被視為現代英語的基本詞彙，雖然這些拉丁詞語跟法律有關，但是對熟悉英語的人來說應該並不陌生。其實，受過教育的人士都會使用一些拉丁詞語，比如說一些簡縮詞，如 A.D., *e.g., sic*。

兩文三語（Biliteracy and Trilingualism, 兩文指中文和英文；三語指粵語、普通話和口語英語）[3]是香港特別行政區的語言特色，回歸後充分體現於香港的法律制度。此外，拉丁語在香港法律制度中也有不容忽視的地位。本書屬於數位人文（Digital Humanities）研究的成果，通過大數據和量化資料，以新穎的角度探討香港的法律語言。相關的數位人文研究方法和成果也見於中英專利詞語的研究項目[http://patentlex.chilin.hk/]。最後，我們希望本書能夠拋磚引玉，讓有興趣研究香港法律語言的同行繼續探討有關課題。

---

3. 「兩文三語」也可稱為「三言兩語」，見《社會語言學教程》（游汝傑、鄒嘉彥，2009，復旦大學出版社）。

Features of the Book

1. Sources of the Latin Legal Terms

The Latin terms collected in this book were initially chosen from a 22 million word monolingual English judgment database in Hong Kong which consists of material predating the period when authentic Chinese equivalent judgments were available. This monolingual database allows reasonable estimation of the relative importance and selection of individual terms on the basis of usage frequency. The Chinese renditions of these Latin terms come from two major sources:

1.1 The ELDoS and the BRS corpora

The bilingual **Electronic Legal Documentation System (ELDoS)** and the **Bilingual Reference System (BRS)** corpora developed by the Language Information Sciences Research Centre of the City University of Hong Kong with the support and assistance of the Hong Kong Judiciary in 2000 and 2003 respectively provide us with possible Chinese renditions of these 105 Latin terms commonly used in the Hong Kong legal domain. The two corpora consist of about 5,500,000 Chinese characters and 3,270,000 English words and provide an initial textual database of bilingually aligned judgments.

1.2 The BLIS database

The Department of Justice of the HKSAR Government has produced a glossary from its Bilingual Legal Information System (BLIS) which is an important basic reference for Chinese legal vocabulary in Hong Kong. The glossary provides useful vocabulary lists which cover the official Chinese translation of legal terms in Hong Kong Laws. Although 55 terms can be found in BLIS, many common and crucial legal terms as well as alternate interpretative terms such as *locus standi* found in the broader incubational medium of legal judgments are thus unfortunately not included in BLIS.

In addition, there are only 37 terms which have similar Chinese renditions in the above two corpora. This indicates that there are quite substantial discrepancies among the Chinese renditions for each term.

In the present book, every effort has been made to systematically document the meanings and usage of the Chinese equivalents of the legal terms in the judgments. The ELDoS and BRS legal corpora has provided a rigorous basis together with information on the relative popularity of various Chinese alternatives of the same legal term. This should be very useful for legal writing and translation.

The two legal databases can be seen to have its roots in Hong Kong because it provides the authentic examples of the legal terms. The items chosen for this book were drawn from both civil cases (61%) and criminal cases (39%), and from amongst about 18,000 vocabulary items found in ELDoS or BRS. Among these, primary legal terms accounted for almost 10,000 of the total.

It is relevant to point out that in exceptional cases, relevant examples of certain Latin terms such as *in personam, mens rea*, are drawn from other bilingual judgments when the terms do not exist in the current version of the judgment corpus. At the same time, when selecting examples for illustrations, we also take context into consideration. For example, the term *mens rea* is usually rendered 犯罪意圖 while sometimes, it is simply rendered as 意圖.

2. Information Provided for The Selected Terms

This book features 105 most common terms of primarily Latin origin, which are found in the legal domain of Hong Kong. The ELDoS/BRS corpus provides an objective and scientific basis for the selection of the frequently used terms. The following information is provided for each selected Latin term in the book.

2.1 Definitions

To ensure consistency between Chinese and English definitions, the definition of each entry is first given in English and the Chinese version is subsequently produced, following mediation between the two versions. A number of legal dictionaries and references in both languages have been consulted and they are listed in the bibliography.

2.2 Chinese alternatives

A comprehensive list of Chinese alternatives is presented for each word entry on the basis of the different sources. To indicate the different origins of the Chinese alternatives, the list is divided into three categories: "ELDoS" and "BLIS" indicate that the items are found in the ELDoS/BRS corpus and BLIS respectively while "Others" refers to those alternatives found in other legal dictionaries or references, their bibliographical details are given at the end of this section. As noted above, about half of the Chinese terms are found only in either ELDoS/BRS or BLIS and so are good candidates for a distinct legal vocabulary.

2.3 Actual usage in context

Apart from legal definition, the book provides useful linguistic and usage information on these legal terms. Drawing on language processing technology, we have been able to provide the relative percentage of use of the different Chinese alternatives from the large legal text database. The relative percentage on frequency is computed using the formula:

$$\frac{\text{Token count of a single rendition}}{\text{Token count of ALL alternate renditions of the same term}}$$

For example, we have 5 different Chinese alternatives for a fortiori from the judgment database. The percentages show that a fortiori is more often translated as 更何況 and 遑論 than other forms, as shown in Table 3. This should help the reader or user to decide on an appropriate form to use in a first try.

2.4 Pronunciations

Pronunciations in standard IPA transcriptions of the 100 terms are also provided. The transcriptions are determined mainly on the basis of bibliographical references. The chief source is the *Longman Pronunciation Dictionary* (1990) by J.C. Wells. Other major references include Lu Gusun's (陸谷孫) *The English-Chinese Dictionary* (英漢大詞典) and the *Black's Law Dictionary* (the 6th and 7th editions). Alternate pronunciations are also included for some terms to reflect the variations in actual usage.

The present book has benefited from the collective efforts of a large number of individuals in the Language Information Sciences Research Centre, City University of Hong Kong and in the Judiciary of the HKSAR. The members of the editorial team are the following:

Jurilinguistic Editorial Team:

Chan Kam Pong

Cheung, Lawrence

Chin, Ian

Choi, Toby

Ho, Louis

Kwong, Olivia

Luk, Zita

Sin, King Kui

Tsoi, Wing-fu

Wong Wei Lung

We also wish to thank the support and assistance of Mrs Juliet Cheng, Mr Y M Lee and Mr Tony Yen.

本書的特點

1. 法律拉丁詞語的來源

本書挑選的105個拉丁詞語主要參考一個約兩千兩百萬字的香港單語英文判決書資料庫。這些單語判決書雖然在有對等中文譯本之前已經出現，但是我們可以從它們的使用度來瞭解這些詞語在法律領域中的重要性。這些拉丁法律詞語的中文翻譯有兩個來源：

1.1 電子法律文書系統（ELDoS）和法律文書中英對照系統（BRS）

「電子法律文書系統」（Electronic Legal Documentation System, ELDoS）和「法律文書中英對照系統」（Bilingual Reference System, BRS）是以中英雙語判決書建立的資料庫，由香港城市大學語言資訊科學研究中心和香港司法機構在2000年和2003年共同研發，共有約5,500,000漢字和3,270,000英文詞彙，我們可以建立雙語法律詞彙表，初步瞭解香港英文法律詞彙的中文翻譯情況。

1.2 雙語法律資訊系統（BLIS）

香港特別行政區政府司法機構建立「雙語法律資訊系統」（Bilingual Legal Information System, BLIS），並製造了一個雙語法律術語表。該表也是香港漢語法律詞語的重要參考資料之一。表中收錄了很多有用的法律詞語，並提供官方的中文翻譯。雖然本書收錄的其中55個詞彙可以在BLIS找到，但是很多常用而且重要的法律術語，如*locus standi*等並沒有收錄。此外，105個拉丁詞語中，只有37個在ELDoS和BLIS中有相近的中文翻譯。
這説明拉丁法律詞語的中文譯法仍然存在着一定的差別。

ELDoS和BRS的語料提供拉丁法律詞語的實例。ELDoS語料
庫裏有18,000多個詞語，當中約61%用於民事案件，其餘則用於
刑事案件。在這18,000個詞語中，10,000個屬於法律核心詞語，
其餘的8,000個都是跟法律有關的詞語。

順帶一提的是，有些重要的拉丁詞語並沒有在ELDoS和BRS
出現，如*mens rea, in personam*，由於它們都是重要的法律概念，
我們都收錄在書裏，例子取自其它雙語判決書。另外，我們挑選
例子時，會注意有關中文譯法的合適性，並考慮語境等因素，如
*mens rea*一詞，一般譯為"犯罪意圖"，但有時會根據上下文，
只譯作"意圖"，為了提供更全面的參考資料，本書都包括"意
圖"這種譯法。

本書透過實際語料，詳細闡釋判決書中拉丁詞語的中文譯法
和用法，這些資訊對法律文本寫作和翻譯都很有用。

2. 詞條訊息

本書收錄的105個拉丁法律詞語常用於香港法律領域。
ELDoS和BRS 語料庫為挑選詞條提供了客觀和科學的依據，每
個詞條包含以下的訊息：

2.1 定義

為了確保詞條定義在中文和英文的一致性，本書首先給出每
個詞條的英文定義，並考慮各種法律詞典和中英文參考資料後，
再給出中文定義。

2.2 對應中文詞彙

透過不同的參考數據，本書為每個拉丁詞條提供中文翻譯
的詞彙表。詞彙表分為三部分："ELDoS和BLIS"指在這兩個

語料庫中出現的中文對譯詞語；"Others"指的是在其它法律詞典和參考資料中找到的中文對譯詞語。這些法律詞典和參考資料請見「參考文獻」。上文曾經提到，只有一半的中文對譯詞語在ELDoS或BLIS中的法律語料庫中出現。因此，這些獨有的中文詞語可以說是香港法律中文的特有術語。

2.3　使用度

除了法律定義之外，本書為這些法律術語提供有用的語言學參考訊息。透過ELDoS和BRS，我們提供不同中文翻譯詞語的使用頻率。其計算如下：

$$\frac{\text{該中文翻譯詞語出現的次數}}{\text{該拉丁詞條所有中文翻譯詞語出現的總次數}}$$

例如，*a fortiori*在判決書資料庫中有五個中文對譯詞語（見表4，頁xliv），當中以"更何況"和"遑論"用得最多。這些訊息有助於讀者和法律專業人士挑選合適的中文翻譯詞語。

2.4　發音

本書也提供拉丁詞條的讀音，以國際音標顯示。參考來源主要是J. C.Wells 的 *Longman Pronunciation Dictionary* (1990)。其它包括陸谷孫的《英漢大詞典》和 *Black's Law Dictionary*（第6版和第7版）。有需要時，本書還提供個別詞條的其它讀法，以反映實際讀音。

本書的編纂有賴香港城市大學語言資訊科學研究中心和香港特別行政區司法機構成員的通力合作。編輯小組成員包括：陳淦邦、張欽良、錢卓康、蔡慧君、何奇峰、鄺藹兒、陸心怡、冼景炬、蔡永富、王偉隆。同時，我們也感謝鄭陳邦媛女士、李育明先生和嚴元浩先生的支持和協助。

a fortiori *adv.*

/ˌeɪ fɔːʃiˈɔːraɪ/   /ˌeɪ fɔːtiˈɔːraɪ/

Latin From the more forceful

【中譯】 香港法庭判詞 ELDoS: **1** 更何況；**2** 遑論；**3** 尤其（是）；**4** 更加；**5** 更甚的（是）；香港法例 BLIS: 一；其他 Others: **1** 更不用說；**2** 更不容置疑地；**3** 更有充分理由；**4** 何況

Interpretations 釋義

Even more so; with stronger reason

比原來的事情程度更進一層；具備更充分的理由

Examples 例句

1. 更何況

a. *Airview Park Property Management Limited vs. Sun Wai Chun*
Case Number: CACV000271_1998

This in effect was that the DMC simply prohibited the actual erection of walls, not their toleration or retention by an owner **a fortiori** by a successor-in-title who did not carry out the works herself.

這理由實際上指該公契僅禁止實際豎立牆壁，沒有禁止業主容忍或保留牆壁存在，**更何況**所有權繼承人自己沒有做修築工程。

b. *Airview Park Property Management Limited vs. Sun Wai Chun*
Case Number: CACV000271_1998

Issues, **a fortiori** fundamental issues, cannot be allowed to be slipped in in such an oblique, obscure fashion.

我不能容許一項爭論點，**更何況**是根本爭論點，以這種轉彎抹角而隱晦方式溜入。

使用百分比	ELDoS: 28.57%
	BLIS: 0.00%

2. 遑論

Sky Heart Limited vs. Lee Hysan Estate Company Limited
Case Number: FACV000009_1998

… a proposed appeal which exclusively involves or turns upon an error of fact … will not attract special leave. **A fortiori**, where there are concurrent findings of fact by the primary judge and the intermediate appellate court.

……如擬提出的上訴完全關於或視乎對事實的裁斷是否錯誤……則不能獲得特別許可，**遑論**是原審和中級上訴法庭的一致事實裁斷。

使用百分比	ELDoS: 28.57%
	BLIS: 0.00%

3. 尤其（是）

Bewise Motors Co. Ltd vs. Hoi Kong Container Services Ltd.
Case Number: FACV000004_1997

Likewise "nor" signals the end of part (2), **a fortiori** in conjunction with the immediately preceding comma.

同樣地，「也不」標誌着第（2）部分的完結，**尤其是**在其前面有一個逗號，兩者連用更突顯了這個作用。

使用百分比	ELDoS: 14.29%
	BLIS: 0.00%

4. 更加

Bewise Motors Co. Ltd vs. Hoi Kong Container Services Ltd.
Case Number: FACV000004_1997

I am unable to read this philosophical observation as authority for what may be perceived by the courts to be the reasonable expectations of honest men, to be utilised at large to modify or reject the plain meaning of the words in a contract, particularly a commercial contract, nor **a fortiori** to be utilised as the starting presumption here.

關於法庭如何理解何為誠實人的合理期望，本席認為上述的富哲學味道的論述不可以作為權威意見；也不可以隨意用這種期望來修改或拒納合約（尤其是商業合約裏的字眼本身明顯的意思；**更加**不可以在此用作最先的推定。

使用百分比	ELDoS: 14.29%
	BLIS:　 0.00%

5. 更甚的（是）

Airview Park Property Management Limited vs. Sun Wai Chun
Case Number: CACV000271_1998

The judge, in my view, was right in refusing to allow Mr Woo to raise the matter, **a fortiori** in the face of the objections made by the plaintiff's counsel, Mr Lam.

本席認為原審法官拒絕容許許胡先生提出這事項做法正確，**更甚的是**法庭受到原告人代表大律師林先生提出反對。

使用百分比	ELDoS: 14.29%
	BLIS:　 0.00%

ab initio *adj./adv.*

/ˌæb ɪˈnɪʃiəʊ/

Latin From the beginning

【中譯】 香港法庭判詞 ELDoS: **1** 從一開始；香港法例 BLIS: **1** 從一開始；**2** 一開始；其他 Others: **1** 自始；**2** 由最初開始；**3** 從開始；**4** 自從；**5** 自行為的發端；**6** 發端；**7** 從頭開始

Interpretations 釋義

From the very beginning

從最初開始

Examples 例句

1. 從一開始

a. *Section 54(4), Family Status Discrimination Ordinance (Cap. 527)*

Without limiting the generality of the power conferred by subsection (3), the District Court may – … (g) make an order declaring void in whole or part and either **ab initio** or from such date as may be specified in the order, any contract or agreement made in contravention of this Ordinance.

在不限制第（3）款所賦予的權力的一般性的原則下，區域法院可——⋯⋯（g）作出命令宣告任何違反本條例的合約或協議**從一開始**或從該命令指明的其他日期開始全部或部分無效。

b. *Lee Sai Kwong and another vs. Wong Wing Fai and another*
Case Number: HCA003710_1997

The issue, then, was the recovery of damages, and amongst other things, the House of Lords was concerned to distinguish between rescission **ab initio** and termination of a contract under which accrued rights and obligations continued to subsist.

由此可見，爭論的焦點是追討損害賠償之事。在這方面，上議院在考慮其他問題之餘，也考慮到：**從一開始**即行撤銷合約有別於終止合約而已產生的權利和義務繼續存在，且對兩者之間的分別頗為關注。

c. *Section 3, Disability Discrimination (Proceedings by Equal Opportunities Commission) Regulation (Cap.487C)*

...the Commission may apply for any remedy available to a claimant under section 72(3) of the Ordinance including...an order declaring void in whole or in part either **ab initio** or from such date as may be specified in the order, any contract or agreement made in contravention of the Ordinance.

……委員會可申請申索人根據本條例第72（3）條可獲得的補救，包括……作出命令，宣告任何違反本條例的合約或協議**從一開始**或從該命令指明的其他日期開始全部或部分無效。

使用百分比	ELDoS: 100.00%
	BLIS: 75.00%

2. 一開始

Section 33(d), Magistrates Ordinance (Cap. 227)

… a warrant of distress shall not be deemed void by reason only of any defect therein, if it is therein alleged that a conviction or order has been made, and there is a good and valid conviction or order to sustain the same, and a person acting under a warrant of distress shall not be deemed a trespasser **ab initio** by reason only of any defect in the warrant or of any irregularity in the execution of the warrant; but this enactment shall not prejudice the right of any person to satisfaction for any special damage caused by any defect in or irregularity in execution of a warrant of distress….

……如財物扣押令上指稱裁判官已作出定罪或命令，並有一項妥當而且有效的定罪或命令為依據，則財物扣押令不得只因其上有任何欠妥之處而當作無效，而任何根據財物扣押令行事的人不會只因手令上的欠妥之處或執行手令時不符合規定而一**開始**便被當作是侵犯者；但任何人如因財物扣押令上的欠妥之處或執行時不符合規定而有特別損害，其要求賠償權利不受本成文法則影響……。

使用百分比	ELDoS:	0.00%
	BLIS:	25.00%

actus reus *n. pl. actus reus*

3

/ˈæktəs ˈreɪəs/   /ˈæktəs ˈrɪəs/

Latin guilty act

【中譯】 香港法庭判詞 ELDoS: **1** 犯罪行為；**2** 行為；香港法例 BLIS:
—；其他 Others: **1** 犯罪行為；**2** 構成行為；**3** 具有犯罪意圖
的行為

Interpretations 釋義

One of the elements of a crime (the other being mens rea, the state of mind of the accused person) that the prosecution must prove before a court can convict a criminal defendant. An actus reus is the "physical part" of a crime and refers to the wrongful act of the accused person. It may also take the form of an omission or a state of affairs.

構成罪行的其中一個元素（另一個元素是「犯罪意圖」，即被告人犯罪時的心理狀態）。控方需要證明被告人有「犯罪行為」，法庭才可以把他定罪。「犯罪行為」是構成罪行的「實體部分」，指被告人的不合法行為，也可以是一項不作為或一個事態狀況。

Examples 例句

1. 犯罪行為

a. *Lau Cheong and Lau Wong vs. SAR*
   Case Number: FACC000006_2001

Criminal liability at common law usually requires proof of relevant prohibited conduct causing certain prohibited consequences (the **actus reus**), accompanied by a defined state of mind on the part of the accused in relation to that conduct and its consequences (the mens rea).

根據普通法，刑事法律責任的構成，通常需要證明有關的禁制行為造成某些禁制的後果（**犯罪行為**），連同被告人對有關的行為及其後果所存有的心態（犯罪意圖）。

b. *Lau Cheong and Lau Wong vs. SAR*
Case Number: FACC000006_2001

It is sufficient if he intends to cause grievous bodily harm and death in fact results. It is this apparent lack of symmetry between what constitutes the mens rea of the offence and the consequence of death as part of the **actus reus** that is the subject of criticism.

只要他有意圖引致身體受嚴重傷害，而且事實上導致死亡，這樣已很足夠。現時的批評所針對的是，指控罪的犯罪意圖的構成成分跟作為**犯罪行為**構成部分的死亡結果，兩者之間明顯缺乏對稱。

c. *Wong Yeung Ng vs. The Secretary for Justice*
Case Number: CACV000161A_1998

It was essential for the Crown to prove that the statement made by the appellant was calculated to bring the administration of justice into disrepute. That is the **actus reus** of this offence. The mere fact the words are capable of bringing the administration of justice into disrepute does not suffice. What must be shown is that, by reason of the statement made by the appellant, there was a serious risk that the administration of justice would be interfered with. The risk or prejudice must be serious, real or substantial.

控方必須證明上訴人的論述旨在誣衊司法，那是構成這項罪名的**犯罪行為**；然而，僅僅因為那些說話可構成誣衊司法還未足夠，控方還必須證明，上訴人的言論使司法有被干擾的重大危險，有關的危險必須是重大的、真實的或實質的。

d. *HKSAR vs. Wong Ping Shui Adam, Leung Chung Michael*
Case Number: FAMC000001_2001

Section 24 therefore defines the **actus reus** of the offence as the handling of goods which are "stolen" goods. It goes on to define the mens rea as the dishonest knowledge or belief that the goods are stolen. The quality or status of the goods being stolen is therefore an element in both the **actus reus** and the mens rea.

因此，第24條界定了該罪行的**犯罪行為**是所處理的貨品屬於「被竊」的貨品。這條例進而界定罪行的犯罪意圖是不誠實地知悉或相信該些貨品是被竊貨品。所以，該些貨品作為被竊貨品的特質或狀況，對**犯罪行為**和犯罪意圖來説，都是一項要素。

| 使用百分比 | ELDoS: 92.86% |
| | BLIS: 0.00% |

2. 行為

Stephen Daryl Barnes vs. Hong Kong Special Administrative Region
Case Number: FAMC000015_2000

If the answer to Question 1 is in the affirmative, whether in relation to SPS2286 & SPS2287 the appellant's conduct could in law have amounted to recklessness having regard to the fact that the **actus reus** of the offences under section 46(1) of the Legal Practitioners Ordinance were committed by a person other than the appellant.

倘若第一個問題的答案是肯定的話，那麼，當顧及在事實上干犯《法律執業者條例》第46（1）條的罪行的**行為**並非是由上訴人，而是由其他人所作的，關乎傳票SPS 2286及SPS 2287中上訴人的行為在法律上是否可以構成罔顧後果的行為。

| 使用百分比 | ELDoS: 7.14% |
| | BLIS: 0.00% |

ad litem *adj.*

/æd ˈlaɪtəm/

Latin for the suit

【中譯】 香港法庭判詞 ELDoS: 一；香港法例 BLIS: **1** 訴訟；**2** 辯護；
其他 Others: **1** 為了訴訟的

Interpretations 釋義

For the purposes of the lawsuit.

For example, a guardian ad litem is a person appointed by the
court to represent the interests of an infant in a lawsuit. An
administrator ad litem may be appointed to represent the interests
of the estate of a deceased person in an action when there are no
proper representatives acting for it.

因訴訟而衍生的。

例如：「訴訟監護人」就是在法律訴訟中，由法庭委任代表未
成年者權益的人。而在訴訟中，若沒有合適的人選代表死者
遺產權益時，法庭則會委任「訴訟遺產管理人」履行此職務。

Examples 例句

1. 訴訟

a. *Rule 9(2), Adoption Rules (Cap. 290A)*

The court may at any time, where it considers it to be in the interests
of the infant, appoint the Official Solicitor to be the guardian **ad
litem** of the infant in lieu of the Director.

凡法院認為符合幼年人的利益時，可隨時委任法定代表律師以
代替署長出任幼年人的**訴訟**監護人。

b. Schedule 1 Part 1-1, Official Solicitor Ordinance (Cap. 416)

To act as guardian **ad litem** or next friend to any person under a disability of age or mental capacity, in proceedings before any court.

以因年齡或智能理由而缺乏自行**訴訟**能力的人的訴訟監護人或訴訟保護人身分，在法庭審理的訴訟中行事。

c. Rule 108(2), Matrimonial Causes Rules (Cap. 179A)

The applicant for an order under paragraph (1)(b) shall, on making the application, file a certificate by a solicitor certifying that the person named in the certificate as the proposed guardian **ad litem** has no interest in the proceedings adverse to that of the child and that he is a proper person to be such guardian.

根據第（1）（b）款申請作出命令的申請人，在提出申請時須提交一份由律師發出的證明書，證明其內被指名為建議的**訴訟**監護人的人，在該法律程序中並無任何與該子女的權益相逆的權益，並證明該人是出任訴訟監護人的適當人士。

| 使用百分比 | ELDoS: | 0.00% |
| | BLIS: | 54.48% |

2. 辯護

a. Order 62 rule 29(4), The Rules of the High Court (Cap. 4A)

...the references to the client shall be construed – (a) if the client was at the material time a mentally disordered person within the meaning of the Mental Health Ordinance (Cap 136) and represented by a person acting as guardian **ad litem** or next friend, as references to that person acting, where necessary, with the authority of the Court....

……凡提述當事人之處——（a）如當事人在關鍵時間是《精神健康條例》（第136章）所指的精神紊亂的人，並由一名以**辯護**監護人或起訴監護人身分行事的人代表，須解釋為提述該人，而該人行事（如有此需要）是已獲法庭授權的……。

b. *Order 80 rule 6(2), The Rules of The High Court (Cap.4A)*

Where a party to an action has served on a person under disability who is not already a party to the action a third party notice within the meaning of Order 16 and no acknowledgment of service is given for that person to the notice, an application for the appointment by the Court of a guardian **ad litem** of that person must be made by that party after the time limited (as respects that person) for acknowledging service and before proceeding further with the third party proceedings.

凡一宗訴訟的一方已向並非已是該宗訴訟的一方的無行為能力的人送達第16號命令所指的協力廠商通知書，而並無認收送達為該人而對通知書作出，則該一方必須在作認收送達的時限（就該人而言）後及繼續進行協力廠商法律程序前，申請由法庭為該人委任**辯護**監護人。

c. *Regulation 4(1), Legal Aid Regulations (Cap. 91A)*

An application for legal aid for an infant shall be made by a person of full age and capacity on his behalf in the manner and form determined by the Director, and where the application relates to proceedings which are required by rule of court to be brought or defended by the next friend or guardian **ad litem**, that person shall be the next friend or guardian **ad litem** or, where proceedings have not actually begun, the person intending to act as next friend or guardian **ad litem**.

為幼年人提出的法律援助申請，須由一名具備完全行為能力的成年人以署長決定的方式及表格代為提出；凡申請所關乎的法律程序是法院規則規定由起訴監護人或**辯護**監護人提出或抗辯的法律程序，則申請人須為該名起訴監護人或**辯護**監護人，如該等法律程序實際上尚未開始，則申請人須為擬以起訴監護人或**辯護**監護人身分行事的人。

d. Section 2(1), Legal Aid Ordinance (Cap. 91)

"guardian" (監護人) , in relation to an infant, includes, without prejudice to the generality of the expression, such person as the Director considers might properly be appointed by the court to be the next friend or guardian **ad litem** of the infant.

「監護人」(guardian) 就幼年人而言，在不損害該詞的概括性的原則下，包括署長認為法院可妥善地委任為該幼年人的起訴監護人或**辯護**監護人的人。

使用百分比	ELDoS:	0.00%
	BLIS:	45.52%

alias *n./adj./adv. pl. aliases*

5

/ˈeɪlɪəs/

Latin on other occasions

【中譯】 香港法庭判詞 ELDoS: **1** 又名；**2** 別字；**3** 化名；香港法例
BLIS: **1** 別名；其他 Others: **1** 其他事物或其他人

Interpretations 釋義

Also called; otherwise known as

別名；人或事物除固有名稱外的其他稱呼

Examples 例句

1. 又名

a. *Ultra Eternal Limited vs. Liu Tai Cheong*
Case Number: HCMP001188_1996

We note that in the Will of Chan Charn Ping, he appointed Ho Moon
Yuen and Chan Jook Lam **alias** Chan Sui Sum to be the Executors
and Trustees of his Will.

我們得指出，在 Chan Charn Ping 的遺囑中，他委任 Ho Moon
Yuen 和又名 Chan Sui Sum 的 Chan Jook Lam 為其遺囑的執行人
和受託人。

b. *Ultra Eternal Limited vs. Liu Tai Cheong*
Case Number: HCMP001188_1996

Chan Jook Lam **alias** Chan Sui Sum being the surviving Executor
and Trustee of the said Will has the absolute right to sell the property
without obtaining the consent of the beneficiaries.

作為在生的遺囑執行人和受託人，Chan Jook Lam，**又名**Chan Sui Sum，有絕對權力出售該物業而毋須取得受益人同意。

| 使用百分比 | ELDoS: 77.78% |
| | BLIS: 0.00% |

2. 別字

Guangdong Foodstuffs Import & Export (Group) Corporation and another vs. Tung Fook Chinese Wine (1982) Co. Ltd. and another
Case Number: HCA007759_1995

Bo Man was the **alias** of his father.

「寶文」是其父鍾昌的**別字**。

| 使用百分比 | ELDoS: 11.11% |
| | BLIS: 0.00% |

3. 化名

Secretary For Justice vs. Jerry Lui Kin Hong
Case Number: FACC000003_1999

In essence, the documents were said to confirm that Chen's name had been used as an **alias** by GIL and that the account out of which the payments to Mr Lui had been made was used for the trade in BAT cigarettes and had nothing to do with Pasto's trade in Japanese cigarettes, let alone any such private trade by Chen.

基本上，控方指那些文件證實了瀚國使用陳先生的名字為其**化名**；而付款給呂先生的帳戶是用來處理與英美煙草所進行的香煙交易，與榮華的日本香煙交易無關，與陳先生這方面的私人交易更加無關。

| 使用百分比 | ELDoS: 11.11% |
| | BLIS: 0.00% |

4. 別名

a. Section 158(2), Companies Ordinance (Cap. 32)

Where the company is an unlisted company, the register shall contain the following particulars with respect to each director – (a) in the case of an individual, his present forename and surname and any former forename or surname, any **alias**, his usual residential address and the number of his identity card (if any) or, in the absence of such number, the number and issuing country of any passport held by him ....

如該公司是一間非上市公司，登記冊須就每名董事記載下述詳情——（a）如屬個人，則記載其現時的名字及姓氏以及任何前用名字或姓氏、任何**別名**、通常的住址及身分證號碼（如有的話），如沒有身分證號碼，則所持有的任何護照的號碼及簽發國家……。

b. Section 22(1), Trade Unions Ordinance (Cap. 332)

A notice giving the names (including any **alias**) of all officers and their titles shall be prominently exhibited in the registered office of every registered trade union and in every office of any branch of a registered trade union.

在各已登記職工會的已登記辦事處及其任何分會的每一辦事處的顯眼處，須展示一份載有全部職員姓名（包括**別名**）及職銜的通告。

c. Rule 74, Bankruptcy Rules (Cap. 6A)

Where a bankruptcy order is made against a firm, the Official Receiver may register a memorial thereof in the Land Registry or in any District Land Registry against any property registered in the name of any partner or partners in the debtor firm or in any **alias** of his or theirs or in any t'ong name of his or theirs, or in the name of any t'ong in which he or they has or have any share or interest, or in the name of the spouse of any partner.

凡有破產令針對商號作出，破產管理署署長可將破產令的提
要，在土地註冊處或任何分區土地註冊處，針對任何屬以下情
況的財產而註冊：該等財產即以債務人的商號的任何一名或多
於一名合夥人的姓名或任何**別名**、該名或該等合夥人的任何堂
的名義，該名或該等合夥人擁有分額或權益的任何堂的名義，
或以任何合夥人的配偶的姓名，在土地註冊處或該分區土地註
冊處註冊的財產。

使用百分比	ELDoS:	0.00%
	BLIS:	100.00%

alibi *n./adv. pl. alibis*

6

/ˈæləbaɪ/ /ˈælɪbaɪ/

Latin elsewhere

【中譯】 香港法庭判詞 ELDoS: **1** 不在犯罪現場；**2** 不在凶案現場；
3 不在犯罪現場證據；**4** 不在凶案現場之辯護理由；**5** 不在場
證據；香港法例 BLIS: **1** 不在犯罪現場；其他 Others: **1** 身在
別處；**2** 以不在犯罪現場為理由的申辯；**3** 不在場；**4** 不在同
一處所；**5** 不在現場；**6** 以不在現場為理由的申辯；**7** 託辭；
8 藉口

Interpretations 釋義

A defence to a criminal charge that the defendant was at a
specified place other than the scene of the crime charged at the
time of its commission and therefore could not have committed it.
刑事控罪的一種抗辯。抗辯理由是被告人於案發時，並不在
案發現場，而是在另一個地方，因此罪案不可能是被告人干
犯的。

Examples 例句

1. 不在犯罪現場

a. Section 85A(1), Magistrates Ordinance (Cap. 227)

A magistrate who commits an accused for trial under section 80C(4)
or section 85(2) shall – …(d) say to the accused – "I must warn you
that at your trial you may not be permitted to give evidence of an
alibi or call witnesses in support of an **alibi** unless you have earlier
given particulars of the **alibi** and of the witnesses…"

根據第80C（4）或85（2）條將被控人交付審訊的裁判官，須採取以下行動——⋯⋯（d）向被控人說——「我必須警告你，除非你已在受審前提交有關**不在犯罪現場**及有關證人的詳情，否則你在受審時可能不獲容許提出**不在犯罪現場**的證據，或不獲容許傳召證人以證明**不在犯罪現場**⋯⋯」

b. Section 75A(8), District Court Ordinance (Cap. 336)

"evidence in support of an **alibi**"（證明不在犯罪現場的證據）means evidence tending to show that by reason of the presence of the accused person at a particular place or in a particular area at a particular time he was not, or was unlikely to have been, at the place where the offence is alleged to have been committed at the time of its alleged commission

「證明**不在犯罪現場**的證據」（evidence in support of an alibi）指有助於顯示被控人於某時間在某地點或某地方出現而於指稱的犯罪時間他並不在或相當不可能在指稱的犯罪現場的證據

c. So Yiu Fung vs. HKSAR
Case Number: FACC000005_1999

The appellant's grounds of appeal are helpfully summarised thus in his supplemental printed case: "(1) there were misdirections by the trial judge in Count 2 on **alibi** (including the failure to direct on the cogency of **alibi** evidence, misdirection on the onus of proof and on the correct methodology in approaching the question of timing) ..."

上訴人的上訴理據有建設性地歸納在他用印刷體寫的補充案由裏：「（1）關於第二項罪名，主審法官就**不在犯罪現場**作出錯誤指引（包括沒有就**不在犯罪現場**證據的說服力作出指引，還有在舉證責任方面作出錯誤指引，以及在時間問題上取向的正確方法，也作出錯誤指引）⋯⋯」

d. *So Yiu Fung vs. HKSAR*
Case Number: FACC000005_1999

And there is one aspect (but only one aspect) of the appellant's complaint against the **alibi** directions which gives me some pause.

還有一樣事情——只是一樣事情——關於上訴人投訴**不在犯罪現場**的指引，使到本席有些猶豫。

使用百分比	ELDoS:	50%
	BLIS:	100.00%

2. 不在凶案現場

HKSAR vs. Tang Sau-Leung
Case Number: CACC000620_1996

On the strength of Liem's evidence, it was clear that he was aware of the importance of timings to the Applicant's defence. This was also abundantly plain to everyone in the Applicant's legal team because of the importance of the period between approximately 6.15 p.m. and 7.30 p.m. on 21 July 1995 to the Applicant's defence of **alibi**.

從林膽強的證據看來，足見他清楚知道時間因素對申請人辯護理據至為重要。同樣清楚的是：1995年7月21日大約下午6時15分至下午7時30分的一段時間乃申請人**不在凶案現場**的辯解關鍵所系。

使用百分比	ELDoS:	18.75%
	BLIS:	0.00%

3. 不在犯罪現場證據

a. *So Yiu Fung vs. HKSAR*
Case Number: FACC000005_1999

I need say nothing more about the **alibi** than what I have already said about it.

本席就**不在犯罪現場證據**已作出了評論，無需再多言。

b. *So Yiu Fung vs. HKSAR*
Case Number: FACC000005_1999

The second offence involved finding a young girl on her own who had done something like litter or jaywalk and who could be intimidated or deceived into following a stranger to a lonely spot. The **alibi** left the appellant with very little time to find such a victim.

第二項罪行牽涉發現一名年幼女童單獨一人，她做了一些像拋棄垃圾或不遵守交通規則亂穿馬路的事情及被人恐嚇或受騙跟隨陌生人去到一處人跡稀少的地點。該**不在犯罪現場證據**留下很少的時間予上訴人碰上這樣的受害人。

c. *HKSAR vs. Tang Sau-Leung*
Case Number: CACC000620_1996

...Mr. Tse put his wife up to support the frame-up by destroying the Applicant's **alibi**....

⋯⋯謝先生着其妻作證，毀掉申請人之**不在犯罪現場證據**，以使其誣陷申請人之計得逞。

使用百分比	ELDoS: 18.75%
	BLIS: 0.00%

4. 不在凶案現場之辯護理由

HKSAR vs. Tang Sau-Leung
Case Number: CACC000620_1996

Following one particular line of enquiry, Ricky Tung stated that it was concluded that a "road test" should be performed in relation to the timings (which were so crucial to the **alibi** put forward).

董先生根據某一線索查問，得出結論認為應進行「測試」，以計算時間（這點對於「**不在凶案現場之辯護理由**」至為重要）……。

使用百分比	ELDoS: 6.25%
	BLIS: 0.00%

5. 不在場證據

Chim Hon Man vs. HKSAR
Case Number: FACC000003_1998

Knowledge of the particular act, matter or thing which is the foundation of the charge is important in enabling the accused to ascertain and prove what, if any, defence, for example, an **alibi**, he may have to the offence charged and to subject a complainant's evidence to searching scrutiny by reference to the surrounding circumstances.

令被控人知道某控罪所依據的特定行為、事情或事物是很重要的，因為這樣被控人才能夠對所控告的罪行，確定可以提出什麼證據（如有的話）來抗辯，例如，**不在場證據**；這樣被控人才能夠根據周遭的情況對申訴人所提出的證據，進行細緻詳盡的盤問。

使用百分比	ELDoS: 6.25%
	BLIS: 0.00%

aliunde *adj./adv.*

7

/ˌeɪlɪˈʌndɪ/

Latin from elsewhere

【中譯】 香港法庭判詞 ELDoS: **1** 來自其他方面的；香港法例 BLIS:
—；其他 Others: **1** 出於別處；**2** 出於別處的；**3** 來自外面的；
4 其他

> ## Interpretations 釋義
>
> From outside; from another source, person or place.
> 事情由其他方面引起；事物從其他源頭、人物或地方引入。

Examples 例句

1. 來自其他方面的

Secretary for Justice vs. Jerry Lui Kin Hong
Case Number: FACC000003_1999

The subsection therefore applied only when the document had been
proved by evidence **aliunde** to be admissible.

因此，第22B（2）條只有在文件已由**來自其他方面的**證據證明
為可接納時才適用。

使用百分比	ELDoS: 100.00%
	BLIS: 0.00%

allocatur *n.*

8

/ˌæləˈkeɪtɜː/

Latin it is allowed

【中譯】 香港法庭判詞 ELDoS: 一;香港法例 BLIS: **1** 訟費評定證明書;**2** 評定……費用的證明書;其他 Others: **1** 訴訟費評定證明書;**2** 命令狀

Interpretations 釋義

A term formerly used to denote a court document granting a request. In modern use the term denotes a court order made at the end of an action deciding on the amount of costs to which the successful party is entitled. (see Li et al (eds), *English-Chinese Dictionary of Law* at 17)

本詞原解作法庭批准請求的文件,現專指法庭在訴訟完結後發出的令狀,判定勝訴一方有權獲得的訟費總額。(見李宗鍔等編《英漢法律大詞典》,頁17)

Examples 例句

1. 訟費評定證明書

a. *Rule 148(2), Bankruptcy Rules (Cap. 6A)*

The expense of preparing, making, verifying and lodging any account, list and statement under this rule shall, after being taxed, be allowed out of the estate, upon production of the necessary **allocatur**.

在擬備、作出、核實及遞交本條所指的任何報告、名單及說明書方面的開支,經評定後可從有關產業中撥付,但須出示必要的**訟費評定證明書**。

b. Rule 7(2), District Court (Fixed Costs in Matrimonial Causes) Rules (Cap. 336F)

For the purposes of enforcement of an order for costs fixed or allowed in accordance with these rules, a certificate issued under paragraph (1) shall have the same effect as an **allocatur** issued in respect of taxed costs.

為強制執行按照本規則所作出有關定額訟費或准予訟費的繳付訟費命令，根據第（1）款所發出的證明書具有與就經評定的訟費而作的**訟費評定證明書**相同的效力。

c. Rule 196, Bankruptcy Rules (Cap. 6A)

When property forming part of a bankrupt's estate is sold by the trustee through an auctioneer or other agent, the gross proceeds of the sale shall be paid over by such auctioneer or agent, and the charges and expenses connected with the sale shall afterwards be paid to such auctioneer or agent on the production of the necessary **allocatur** of the taxing officer.

如受託人透過拍賣商或其他代理人出售構成破產人產業部分的財產，則該拍賣商或代理人須交付該項出售的總收益，而與該項出售有關的收費及開支，須於其後在訟費評定官所發的必需的**訟費評定證明書**提交時，支付給該拍賣商或代理人。

d. Rule 33, Bankruptcy Rules (Cap. 6A)

The solicitor in the matter of a bankruptcy petition presented by the debtor against himself shall in his bill of costs give credit for such sum or security (if any) as he may have received from the debtor as a deposit on account of the costs and expenses to be incurred in and about the filing and prosecution of such petition, and the amount of any such deposit shall be noted by the taxing officer upon the **allocatur** issued for such costs.

凡債務人針對其本人提出破產呈請，如該破產呈請事宜中的律師曾獲債務人付款或提供保證金（如有的話），作為就提出及進行該項呈請所會招致和涉及的訟費及開支而繳存的款項，則該律師須在他發出的訟費單中記入該等款項或保證金；訟費評定官就該等訟費發出**訟費評定證明書**時，須記錄任何該等繳存款項的數額。

使用百分比	ELDoS:	0.00%
	BLIS:	90.91%

2. 評定……費用的證明書

Schedule Table A-Item 9, Bankruptcy (Fees and Percentages) Order (Cap. 6C)

Allocatur by the Registrar for any costs, charges or disbursements, for every $100 allowed or part thereof

司法常務官**評定**任何訟費、收費或墊付**費用的證明書**，以獲准支付的每$100或不足$100計。

使用百分比	ELDoS:	0.00%
	BLIS:	9.09%

alter ego *n.*

9

/ˌæltər ˈiːɡəʊ/

Latin second self

【中譯】 香港法庭判詞 ELDoS: **1** 親密夥伴；**2** 極信任的代理人；香港法例 BLIS: 一；其他 Others: **1** 代辦人；**2** 知己；**3** 心腹；**4** 私人交易的工具

Interpretations 釋義

Under the "rule of alter ego", a court may brush aside corporate entity and hold a person individually responsible for acts done in the name of the corporation if he uses it as a sham for conducting his private business.

在「代理人原則」下，如果一個人利用公司作掩飾以經營私人業務，則法庭可將法團的獨立身分置諸不理，並裁定該人須為他以公司名義作出的行為負上個人責任。

Examples 例句

1. 親密夥伴

Secretary for Justice vs. Jerry Lui Kin Hong
Case Number: FACC000003_1999

Finally, conclusion 7 was that Pasto and GIL (and its **alter ego**, CYJ & Co.) had different shareholders and there was no apparent link between the Chen current account in Pasto's ledger and the CYJ & Co. ledger.

最後，第七項結論是榮華與瀚國（及其**親密夥伴**陳盈仁公司）有不同的股東，而陳先生在榮華之分類帳中的往來帳戶與陳盈仁公司的分類帳沒有明顯的關連。

使用百分比	ELDoS: 50.00%
	BLIS: 0.00%

2. 極信任的代理人

Novatel Communications (Far East) Limited vs. Canadian Imperial Bank of Commerce and another
Case Number: HCA008052_1999

I have been able to detect no suggestion in the evidence that Mr. Shenkman [the Plaintiff's **alter ego**] considered that the prospects of future benefits from the Andover steel centre, or the need to buy time, or the need to save himself from bankruptcy, or any other factor, rendered the proposals which are ultimately implemented on 22 January 1969 beneficial from the point of view of the plaintiff (as opposed to Scottish Steel or Mr. Shenkman personally).

本席察覺到證據中並無跡象顯示，Shenkman先生〔原告人**極信任的代理人**〕認為來自Andover鋼鐵中心未來得益的前景、或爭取時間的需要、或挽救自己避免破產的需要、或其他因素，促使最終在1969年1月22日實施建議，從原告人觀點看來是對他有利的（與蘇格蘭鋼鐵或Shenkman先生本人相比較）。

使用百分比	ELDoS: 50.00%
	BLIS: 0.00%

amicus curiae *n. pl. amici curiae*

/əˌmiːkəs ˈkjʊəriiː/

Latin friend of the court

【中譯】　香港法庭判詞 ELDoS：**1** 法庭之友；香港法例 BLIS：**1** 法庭之友；其他 Others：一

> ## Interpretations 釋義
> A lawyer who does not act for a party to an action but who is invited or volunteers to put forward his argument, give advice or make a suggestion to the court to help it solve a difficult legal point or to explain something in public interest which may have been overlooked by the court or may not have been adequately addressed by the parties.
>
> 訴訟中並非代表任何一方的律師，但獲邀或主動向法庭提出論據，給予意見或建議，以協助法庭解決法律難點，或解釋法庭可能忽略了或案中各方未有充分陳述的公眾利益問題。

Examples 例句

1. 法庭之友

a. *Rule 5, Criminal Procedure (Reference of Questions of Law) Rules (Cap. 221E)*

The Secretary for Justice may withdraw or amend the reference at any time before the Court of Appeal begins the hearing, if the court or the Registrar so directs, be served on – ...(b) an **amicus curiae** appointed under section 81D(2)c of the Ordinance.

律政司司長可在上訴法庭開始聆訊前，隨時撤回或修訂轉交，
如法庭或司法常務官有所指示，關於該撤回或修訂的通知須送
達──⋯⋯（b）根據本條例第81D（2）（c）條委任的**法庭之友**。

b. Section 81D(2), Criminal Procedure Ordinance (Cap. 221)

For the purpose of its consideration of a question referred to them
under this section the Court of Appeal shall hear argument – ... (c)
if the Court of Appeal so directs, by counsel appointed as **amicus
curiae** by the Registrar.

為考慮根據本條所轉交的問題，上訴法庭須聆聽──⋯⋯（c）
如上訴法庭有所指示，由獲司法常務官委任為**法庭之友**的大律
師提出的論點。

c. Schedule 1-20, Land Registry Trading Fund (Cap. 430A)

Appearances by the Land Registrar or his representative as witness or
amicus curiae in court proceedings.

土地註冊處處長或其代表在訴訟程序中出庭作為證人或**法庭之
友**。

d. Secretary For Justice and others vs. Chan Wah and others
Case Number: FACV0011_2000 & FACV000013_2000

The Equal Opportunities Commission has helpfully provided the
Court with the assistance of counsel as **amicus curiae**.

平等機會委員會安排了大律師協助本院，作為**法庭之友**，對本
院幫助甚大。

使用百分比	ELDoS: 100.00%
	BLIS: 100.00%

animus possidendi *n.*

/ˌænɪməs ˌpɑːsəˈdendɪ/

Latin intention to possess

【中譯】 香港法庭判詞 ELDoS: **1** 必需的管有意圖；香港法例 BLIS:
一；其他 Others: **1** 佔有的意圖；**2** 擁有的意圖

Interpretations 釋義

The intention of possessing

佔有、控制、使用的意圖

Examples 例句

1. 必需的管有意圖

Wong Tak Yue vs. Kung Kwok Wai David and another
Case Number: FACV000001_1997

The requisite intention to possess has been referred in various
authorities under its latin tag "**animus possidendi**". I shall refer to it
simply as the intention to possess.

必需的管有意圖的拉丁文版本「animus possidendi」經常見於
各類法律典據。以下稱之為**必需的管有意圖**。

使用百分比	ELDoS: 100.00%
	BLIS: 0.00%

11

autrefois acquit

12

/ˌəʊtrəfwɑː əˈkwɪt/

French previously acquitted

【中譯】　香港法庭判詞 ELDoS: **1** 曾就同一罪行獲裁定無罪；香港法
例 BLIS: **1** 曾就同一罪行獲裁定無罪；其他 Others: **1** 前經開
釋；**2** 原已開釋；**3** 事已獲釋；**4** 曾經宣告無罪；**5** 已獲昭雪之
抗辯

Interpretations 釋義

In common law, autrefois acquit is a plea by an accused person
to an indictment that he has once been tried for the same offence
and has already been acquitted. Autrefois acquit is a bar to
another trial on the same offence.

刑事公訴中的一種普通法抗辯。理由是被告人曾經就同一罪
行受審，並已獲釋。這個抗辯可以避免就同一罪行對已獲法
庭宣佈無罪和釋放的人作重複的審訊。

Examples 例句

1. 曾就同一罪行獲裁定無罪

a. Section 31(1), Criminal Procedure Ordinance (Cap. 221)

In criminal proceedings in any court on a plea of autrefois convict
or **autrefois acquit** the accused person may state that he has been
previously convicted or acquitted, as the case may be, of the offence
charged.

在任何法院的刑事法律程序中，被控人作出曾就同一罪行被定
罪或**曾就同一罪行獲裁定無罪**的答辯時，可述明他以往曾就被
控告的罪行被定罪或獲裁定無罪（視屬何情況而定）。

b. *Section 64, Criminal Procedure Ordinance (Cap. 221)*

On the trial of an issue on a plea of autrefois convict or **autrefois acquit**, the depositions transmitted to the Registrar or Secretary for Justice on the former trial, together with the judge's notes, if available, and the depositions transmitted to the Registrar on the subsequent charge, shall be admissible in evidence to prove or disprove the identity of the charges.

對因曾就同一罪行被定罪或**曾就同一罪行獲裁定無罪**的答辯而產生的爭論點作審訊時，傳送至司法常務官或律政司司長的關於上一次審訊的書面供詞，連同法官的紀錄（如有的話），以及傳送至司法常務官的關於其後的控罪的書面供詞，即為證明或反駁控罪相同的可接納證據。

c. *Chim Hon Man vs. HKSAR*
Case Number: FACC000003_1998

Concern was also expressed that the jury may not have been satisfied as to commission of any particular offence (at 276–277, 283, 287–288) and about the later availability to the accused of a plea of autrefois convict or **autrefois acquit** in relation to offences disclosed by the evidence (at 276–277).

同時值得關注的是：陪審團可能並不信納有任何特定罪行的犯罪事實得以確立（參看第276–277、283、287–288頁）。此外，另一點值得關注的是：就該證據所披露的罪行，被控人其後是否可以提出曾就同一罪行被裁定有罪，或**曾就同一罪行獲裁定無罪**，作為答辯（參看第276–277頁）。

d. *Chim Hon Man vs. HKSAR*
Case Number: FACC000003_1998

Another purpose served by the principle is to secure certainty in the conviction or the acquittal, thereby making available a plea of autrefois convict or **autrefois acquit** to a subsequent prosecution for the same offence.

這個原則要達到的另一個目的是確保裁定,不論是罪名成立抑或是無罪釋放,均有個肯定性,使被控人若其後被檢控同一罪行,可以提出曾就同一罪行被定罪,或**曾就同一罪行獲裁定無罪**,作為答辯的依據。

使用百分比	ELDoS: 100.00%
	BLIS: 100.00%

autrefois convict

13

/ˌəʊtrəfwaː ˈkɑːnvɪkt/

French previously convicted

【中譯】 香港法庭判詞 ELDoS: **1** 曾就同一罪行被定罪；**2** 曾就同一
罪行被裁定有罪；香港法例 BLIS: **1** 曾就同一罪行被定罪；
其他 Others: **1** 前經定罪；**2** 原已定罪；**3** 事已獲罪；**4** 已獲判
罪之抗辯

> ## Interpretations 釋義
> In common law, autrefois convict is a plea by an accused person
> to an indictment that he has already been convicted of the same
> offence. Autrefois convict is a bar to another trial on the same
> offence.
>
> 刑事公訴中的一種普通法抗辯，理由是被告人已經就該罪行
> 被裁定有罪。這個抗辯可以避免對已被定罪的人作重複的審
> 訊。

Examples 例句

1. 曾就同一罪行被定罪

a. Section 31(1), criminal procedure ordinance (Cap. 221)

In criminal proceedings in any court on a plea of **autrefois convict**
or autrefois acquit the accused person may state that he has been
previously convicted or acquitted, as the case may be, of the offence
charged.

在任何法院的刑事法律程序中，被控人作出**曾就同一罪行被定
罪**或曾就同一罪行獲裁定無罪的答辯時，可述明他以往曾就被
控告的罪行被定罪或獲裁定無罪（視屬何情況而定）。

b. Section 64, Criminal Procedure Ordinance (Cap. 221)

On the trial of an issue on a plea of **autrefois convict** or autrefois acquit, the depositions transmitted to the Registrar or Secretary for Justice on the former trial, together with the judge's notes, if available, and the depositions transmitted to the Registrar on the subsequent charge, shall be admissible in evidence to prove or disprove the identity of the charges.

對因**曾就同一罪行被定罪**或曾就同一罪行獲裁定無罪的答辯而產生的爭論點作審訊時,傳送至司法常務官或律政司司長的關於上一次審訊的書面供詞,連同法官的紀錄(如有的話),以及傳送至司法常務官的關於其後的控罪的書面供詞,即為證明或反駁控罪相同的可接納證據。

c. Chim Hon Man vs. HKSAR
Case Number: FACC000003_1998

Another purpose served by the principle is to secure certainty in the conviction or the acquittal, thereby making available a plea of **autrefois convict** or autrefois acquit to a subsequent prosecution for the same offence.

這個原則要達到的另一個目的是確保裁定,不論是罪名成立抑或是無罪釋放,均有個肯定性,使被控人若其後被檢控同一罪行,可以提出**曾就同一罪行被定罪**,或曾就同一罪行獲裁定無罪,作為答辯的依據。

| 使用百分比 | ELDoS: 100.00% |
| | BLIS: 50.00% |

2. 曾就同一罪行被裁定有罪

Chim Hon Man vs. HKSAR
Case Number: FACC000003_1998

Concern was also expressed that the jury may not have been satisfied as to commission of any particular offence (at 276–277, 283, 287–288) and about the later availability to the accused of a plea of **autrefois convict** or autrefois acquit in relation to offences disclosed by the evidence (at 276–277).

同時值得關注的是：陪審團可能並不信納有任何特定罪行的犯罪事實得以確立（參看第276–277、283、287–288頁）。此外，另一點值得關注的是：就該證據所披露的罪行，被控人其後是否可以提出**曾就同一罪行被裁定有罪**，或曾就同一罪行獲裁定無罪，作為答辯（參看第276–277頁）。

使用百分比	ELDoS:	0.00%
	BLIS:	50.00%

bona fide[1] *adj./adv.*

/ˌbəʊnə ˈfaɪdi/   /ˌbəʊnə ˈfiːdeɪ/

Latin in good faith

14

【中譯】　香港法庭判詞 ELDoS: **1** 真正的；**2** 真誠；香港法例 BLIS:
1 真正的；**2** 真誠；**3** 真正；**4** 真誠地；**5** 真誠的；**6** 善意；**7**
真正地；其他 Others: **1** 正當地；**2** 善意地

> ## Interpretations 釋義
>
> In or with good faith, honestly, genuine, without fraud, deceit or
> intent to take unfair advantage.
>
> 真誠、誠實、真實地行事，沒有欺詐、欺騙或拿取不正當利
> 益的意圖。

Examples 例句

1. 真正的

a. Section 11(2), Airport Authority Bylaw (Cap. 483A)

No person other than a **bona fide** airline passenger shall, while in the
Restricted Area and without lawful authority or reasonable excuse,
fail to wear a valid permit issued or authorized to be issued by the
Authority or, in the case of an air crew member, a valid military
identification document or an air crew identity card issued by an air
carrier or an aviation authority in such manner as may be acceptable
to the Authority, so that it is reasonably visible at all times.

---

1. Please note that both *bona fide* and *bona fides* have different parts-of-speech.

除**真正的**航空公司乘客外，任何人在限制區內時，不得在無合
法許可權或合理辯解的情況下，沒有以令人相當容易看見有關
許可證、證明文件或身分證的方式佩帶管理局所發出或授權發
出的有效許可證或 (就空勤人員而言) 有效軍事身分證明文件
或航空承運人或航空當局按管理局可接受的方式發出的空勤人
員身分證。

b. *Union Bank of Hong Kong Limited vs. Chapol Limited and others*
Case Number: HCMP002048_1997

A defendant has to satisfy the court that there is a fair and reasonable probability of a real or **bona fide** defence.

被告人必須令法庭信納，案中存在相當而合理的可能性，會確
立一個真實或**真正的**抗辯理由。

c. *Section 14(1), Mining Ordinance (Cap. 285)*

The holder of a prospecting licence shall have the right to enter upon and prospect on any Government land within the area the subject of the licence and, subject to the provisions of subsection (2), on any private land within such area, and may, whilst engaged in **bona fide** prospecting, make bore holes, dig trenches, sink shafts and generally make the necessary excavations, subject to the terms and conditions of the licence.

探礦牌照持有人有權進入在牌照的標的地區內的任何政府土地
並在其上探礦，以及在符合第 (2) 款條文的規定下，進入該地
區內的任何私人土地並在其上探礦；該持有人並可在**真正的**探
礦過程中，開鑽孔、掘地坑、開鑿豎井及一般地作出所需的挖
掘工程，但受該牌照的條款及條件所規限。

d. Section 17(3), Marine Parks and Marine Reserves Regulation (Cap. 476A)

The Authority may, at his discretion, grant a permit for fishing to a **bona fide** fisherman or to a person who ordinarily resides near a marine park to which the permit relates.

總監可酌情向**真正的**漁民，或向通常居於釣魚或捕魚許可證所關乎的海岸公園附近的人，批給該許可證。

使用百分比	ELDoS: 50.00%
	BLIS: 8.06%

2. 真誠

a. Section 3(4), Civil Liability (Contribution) Ordinance (Cap. 377)

A person who has made or agreed to make any payment in **bona fide** settlement or compromise of any claim made against him in respect of any damage (including a payment into court which has been accepted) shall be entitled to recover contribution in accordance with this section without regard to whether or not he himself is or ever was liable in respect of the damage, provided, however, that he would have been liable assuming that the factual basis of the claim against him could be established.

如任何人已支付或同意支付任何款項，作為就任何損害而向他提出的申索的**真誠**和解或妥協（包括繳存於法院並已獲接納的款項），而若向他提出的申索所根據的事實能確立他即會負法律責任，則不論他本人是否或曾否須就該項損害負法律責任，他均有權按照本條而追討分擔。

b. Section 3(2), Land Registration Ordinance (Cap. 128)

All such deeds, conveyances, and other instruments in writing, and judgments, as last aforesaid, which are not registered shall, as against any subsequent **bona fide** purchaser or mortgagee for valuable consideration of the same parcels of ground, tenements, or premises, be absolutely null and void to all intents and purposes ....

凡上述的所有契據、轉易契及其他書面形式的文書和判決沒有作出註冊，對於就同一幅地、物業單位或處所付出有值代價的任何其後**真誠**買方或承按人，在所有用意和目的上均絕對無效……。

C. Hebei Import and Export Corporation vs. Polytek Engineering Company Limited
Case Number: FACV000010_1998

Whether one describes the respondent's conduct as giving rise to an estoppel, a breach of the **bona fide** principle or simply as a breach of the principle that a matter of non-compliance with the governing rules shall be raised promptly in the arbitration is beside the point in this case.

不論將答辯人的行為描述為：引起不容反悔；違反**真誠**原則；或純粹違反有關在仲裁中有不遵守仲裁規則的事情發生得即時提出的原則，這點與本案毫不相關。

d. Section 55, Occupational Retirement Schemes Ordinance (Cap. 426)

Nothing in section 52, 53 and 54 shall invalidate – ...(b) any **bona fide** contract, dealing or transaction made over any asset of the scheme for valuable consideration.

第52、53及54條的條文均不會使以下的事宜變成無效——……（b）以有值代價而就該計劃的資產訂立的**真誠**合約或作出的真誠交易。

使用百分比	ELDoS: 50.00%
	BLIS: 37.91%

3. 真正

a. Section 110, Landlord and Tenant (Consolidation) Ordinance (Cap. 7)

If the property or any part thereof so removed or carried away under section 108 or 109 has been sold **bona fide** and for a sufficient consideration, before or after removal from the premises distrained, to any person not knowing and not having the means of knowing that the same was liable to distraint for rent, or was removed or carried away, or was to be removed or carried away, so as to prevent or hinder the landlord or lessee from distraining, the same, or so much thereof as has been so sold, shall be restored by the bailiff distraining or by the court on application under section 93.

在第108或109條所述情況下遭搬走或帶走的財物或其中任何部分，如在搬離該遭扣押財物的處所之前或之後，已經以足夠的代價，**真正**售出給任何人，而該人並不知道亦無法知道這些財物可由於欠租而被扣押或這些財物曾被搬走或帶走，或將被搬走或帶走，以阻止或阻礙業主或承租人將財物扣押，則該等已售出的財物或已售出的部分，可由負責執行財物扣押的執達主任歸還，或由法院應根據第93條所作的申請予以歸還。

b. Section 5(1), Aviation Security Regulation (Cap. 494A)

Subject to this section, the provisions of section 4 shall not apply to – ...(b) any **bona fide** air passenger awaiting an onward flight in any area reserved for transit or transfer passengers which is within a restricted area.

在符合本條的規定下，第4條的條文不適用於——……（b）任何在禁區內過境或轉機乘客區等候下一航程的**真正**飛機乘客。

c. Section 3(1), Banking Ordinance (Cap. 155)

Part III of this Ordinance shall not apply to the taking of any deposit by – ...(g) an employer where such deposit is taken from a **bona fide** employee ....

本條例第III部不適用於——⋯⋯（g）僱主接受任何存款，而存款是從**真正**僱員處接受的⋯⋯。

| 使用百分比 | ELDoS: 0.00% |
| | BLIS: 32.23% |

4. 真誠地

a. Section 56, Entertainment Special Effects Ordinance (Cap. 560)

No liability shall be incurred by any person in respect of anything done by him **bona fide** in the exercise or purported exercise of any functions conferred or imposed by or under this Ordinance.

任何人均無須就他在行使或看來是行使由本條例授予或施加或根據本條例而授予或施加的任何職能時**真誠地**作出的任何事情，而負上法律責任。

b. Section 22(1), Fire Services Ordinance (Cap. 95)

No member acting **bona fide** under powers conferred by this Ordinance shall be liable to any action for damages for any act done or omitted to be done by him in connexion with his duties on the occasion of a fire or other calamity.

任何根據本條例授予的權力**真誠地**行事的成員，無須為他在火警或其他災難發生時所作出或不作出的任何與他的職責有關連的作為在任何損害賠償的訴訟中承擔法律責任。

c. Section 86, District Councils Ordinance (Cap. 547)

A member of a District Council or a committee shall not be subjected to any liability, action, claim or demand by reason of anything done **bona fide** for the purpose of carrying into effect the provisions of this Ordinance or any other enactment conferring functions on a District Council.

區議會議員或委員會成員如為了施行本條例的條文或任何其他
向區議會賦予職能的成文法則的條文而**真誠地**作出任何事情，
均無須因此而承擔任何法律責任、訴訟、申索或要求。

| 使用百分比 | ELDoS: | 0.00% |
| | BLIS: | 19.91% |

5. 真誠的

a. Regulation 9(3), Essential Services Corps (General) Regulations (Cap. 197A)

...the Commissioner may exempt from liability any volunteer who, in his opinion, quits the Corps for a reasonable and **bona fide** cause.

⋯⋯總監可豁免任何他認為是基於合理及**真誠的**因由而離開服務團的志願團員承擔法律責任。

b. Section 163D(3), Companies Ordinance (Cap. 32)

References in sections 163, 163A and 163B to payments to any director of a company by way of compensation for loss of office, or as consideration for or in connexion with his retirement from office – ...(b) do not include any **bona fide** payment by way of damages for breach of contract or by way of pension in respect of past services; and for the purposes of this paragraph "pension" (退休金) includes any superannuation allowance, superannuation gratuity or similar payment.

在第163、163A及163B條中，凡提述向公司董事作出付款作為失去職位的補償，或作為其退職或與其退職有關的代價——⋯⋯（ｂ）不包括作為違約的損害賠償或作為過去服務的退休金而作出的任何**真誠的**付款；而就本段而言，「退休金」（pension）乃包括任何離職津貼、離職酬金或類似的付款。

| 使用百分比 | ELDoS: | 0.00% |
| | BLIS: | 0.95% |

6. 善意

Article 5(8), Schedule, Fugitive Offenders (Drugs) Order (Cap. 503J)

The provision of this article shall not be construed as prejudicing the rights of **bona fide** third parties.

本條各項規定不得解釋為損害**善意**協力廠商的權利。

使用百分比	ELDoS:	0.00%
	BLIS:	0.47%

7. 真正地

Section 6(2A), Land (Miscellaneous Provisions) Ordinance (Cap. 28)

Notwithstanding subsection (1), where – ...(b) a structure has been erected on unleased land, otherwise than under a licence or a deed or memorandum of appropriation, and the Authority is reasonably satisfied that the structure is not being habitually and **bona fide** used....

不論第（1）款有何規定，凡——……（b）已有構築物並非根據許可證、撥地契據或撥地備忘錄而在未批租土地上建造，而當局合理地信納該構築物並無慣常及**真正地**使用……。

使用百分比	ELDoS:	0.00%
	BLIS:	0.47%

bona fides[1] *n.*

/ˌbəʊnə ˈfaɪdiːz/   /ˈbəʊnə ˈfiːdeɪz/

Latin good faith

15

【中譯】　香港法庭判詞 ELDoS: **1** 誠意；香港法例 BLIS: **1** 真正的；
2 真誠程度；其他 Others: **1** 真誠善意；**2** 善意；**3** 信譽；
4 正當

Interpretations 釋義

Good faith, honesty, sincerity

真誠、誠實、誠

Examples 例句

1. 誠意

Hebei Import and Export Corporation vs. Polytek Engineering Company Limited
Case Number: FACV000010_1998

Failure to raise such a point may amount to an estoppel or a want of **bona fides** such as to a justify the court of enforcement in enforcing an award (see *Chrome Resources S.A. v. Leopold Lazarus* (*Yearbook Comm. Arb'n. XI* (1986) pages 538–542).

沒有提出這樣的論點可能構成一項不容反悔，或被指為缺乏**誠意**，因而執行法院有理由可以強制執行裁決。（見案例*Chrome Resources S.A. v Leopold Lazarus*（*Yearbook Comm. Arb'n XI*（1986）pages 538–542）。

使用百分比	ELDoS: 100.00%
	BLIS:　　0.00%

---

1. Please note that both *bona fide* and *bona fides* have different parts-of-speech.

2. 真正的

Regulation 5(1), Merchant Shipping (Launches and Ferry Vessels) Regulations (Cap. 313E)

If any licence or licence disc issued under this Part is lost, destroyed or defaced, the Director may, if satisfied as to the **bona fides** of such loss, destruction or defacement and upon payment of the prescribed fee, issue a duplicate licence or duplicate licence disc.

如根據本部發出的任何牌照或航行證遺失、損毀或污損，而處長信納上述的遺失、損毀或污損是**真正的**，則他可在訂明費用繳付後，發出牌照複本或航行證複本。

使用百分比	ELDoS: 0.00%
	BLIS: 50.00%

3. 真誠程度

Regulation 4(2), Import and Export (Carriage of Articles) Regulations (Cap. 60I)

For the purposes of subregulation (1), the owner of a prescribed article shall apply for a carriage licence in writing specifying – … (e) such other particulars that the Commissioner may reasonably require to ascertain the **bona fides** of the shipping arrangements and to identify the applicant, the article, the vessel, transportation arrangements, including any land element of the transportation, and any other persons involved in the transportation of the article.

為施行第(1)款，訂明物品的擁有人須以書面申請運載許可證，申請書須指明——……(e)關長可合理規定須予提供的其他詳情，而該等詳情是為確定裝船安排的**真誠程度**和識別申請人、物品、船隻、運輸安排(包括該運輸的任何陸路成分)和任何涉及運輸該物品的其他人者。

使用百分比	ELDoS: 0.00%
	BLIS: 50.00%

bona vacantia *n. pl. bona vacantia*   16

/ˌbəʊnə vəˈkænʃɪə/

Latin vacant goods

【中譯】　香港法庭判詞 ELDoS: **1** 無主物；香港法例 BLIS: **1** 無主財物；其他 Others: **1** 無主財貨；**2** 政府接管物；**3** 無人繼承的財產

Interpretations 釋義

Property with no owner, such as treasure trove, shipwrecks, the property of a dissolved company, or the estate of a person who died leaving no will and no relatives entitled to succeed. Bona vacantia usually belongs to the government, but in some cases it can be claimed by the first finder.

沒有物主的財產，諸如寶藏、遇難船隻、公司解散後的財產或在死者沒有立下遺囑的情況下，又沒有親屬有權承繼的遺產。無主財物一般屬於政府，但亦有可能由第一位發現者索回。

Examples 例句

1. 無主物

To Kan Chi and others vs. Pui Man Yau and others
Case Number: HCMP000562_1992

The 2nd Defendant may, in Part II of the trial concerning the Scheme of Arrangement, invite the Court to declare those properties registered in the name of Chan Chun Ting who died leaving no claims by anyone who could lawfully claim to be entitled to his estate as **bona vacantia** and/or making it part of the properties of Tsing Shan Monastery in light of the clear intention of Chan Chun Ting.

陳春亭死時既沒有將申索權留予任何人第二被告可在審訊的第
二部分，即聆訊安排計劃的部分，請求法庭宣告有權將那些
以陳春亭名義註冊的產業為**無主物**（bona vacantia）及（或）由
於陳春亭轉讓意圖清晰致令那些產業變成青山寺的產業的一部
分。

使用百分比	ELDoS: 100.00%
	BLIS: 0.00%

2. 無主財物

a. Section 290C, Companies Ordinance (Cap. 32)

Where any property other than immovable property vests in the
Government as **bona vacantia** under section 292, the Government's
title to it may be disclaimed by a notice signed by the Registrar.

凡有任何不動產以外的財產根據第292條歸屬政府為**無主財
物**，政府對該等財產的所有權可藉處長所簽署的公告而予以卸
棄。

b. Section 292(1), Companies Ordinance (Cap. 32)

Where a company is dissolved, all property and rights whatsoever
vested in or held on trust for the company immediately before its
dissolution (including leasehold property but not including property
held by the company on trust for any other person) shall be deemed
to be **bona vacantia** and shall accordingly belong to the Government,
and shall vest and may be dealt with in the same manner as other
bona vacantia accruing to the Government.

凡有公司解散，在緊接其解散前歸屬公司或以信託形式代公司
持有的所有財產及權利（包括批租土地財產，但不包括公司以
信託形式代任何其他人持有的財產），須當作是**無主財物**及據
此而屬政府所有，並須按其他歸於政府的**無主財物**的歸屬方式
而歸屬，亦可以相同的處理方式處理。

c. Section 4(9), Intestates' Estates Ordinance (Cap. 73)

In default of any person taking an absolute interest under the foregoing provisions, the residuary estate of the intestate shall, subject to the Inheritance (Provision for Family and Dependants) Ordinance (Cap 481), belong to the Government as **bona vacantia**....

如根據上述條文，無人享有絕對權益，則除《財產繼承（供養遺屬及受養人）條例》（第481章）另有規定外，該無遺囑者的剩餘遺產即成為**無主財物**，屬於政府所有……。

使用百分比	ELDoS:	0.00%
	BLIS:	100.00%

caveat *n.*

/ˈkæviæt/   /ˈkeɪviæt/

Latin let him beware

17

【中譯】　香港法庭判詞 ELDoS: **1** 知會備忘；香港法例 BLIS: **1** 知會備忘；其他 Others: **1** 警告備忘；**2** 當心；（要求停止某些行為的）警告

Interpretations 釋義

A warning.

In law, the term means a formal warning, usually taking the form of an entry in a register, given by a party interested to a court or public office to the effect that no actions of certain kinds may be taken without notice to him.

一項警告。

在法律界，即指正式警告備忘（形式通常是在登記冊內登記），由案中有利益關係的一方向法庭或公共機構發出，表示他在未收到任何知會之前，有關方面不可作出某些行動。

Examples 例句

1. 知會備忘

a. *Rule 44(5), Non-Contentious Probate Rules (Cap. 10A)*

The Registrar shall maintain an index of **caveats** entered in the Registry and on receiving an application for a grant, he shall cause the index to be searched.

司法常務官須就已在承辦處登記的**知會備忘**備存索引，而每當接獲任何授予的申請時，須安排翻查該索引。

b. *Section 45, Probate And Administration Ordinance (Cap. 10)*

A **caveat** against a grant of probate or administration may be entered in the Registry.

針對遺囑認證或遺產管理的授予的**知會備忘**可在承辦處登記。

c. *Order 75, Rule 1(2), The Rules of the High Court (Cap. 4A)*

In this Order – "**caveat** book" (知會備忘登記冊) means the book kept in the Registry in which **caveats** issued under this Order are entered.

在本命令中——「**知會備忘**登記冊」（caveat book）指備存於登記處登錄有根據本命令發出的**知會備忘**的登記冊。

d. *Secretary for Justice and others vs. Chan Wah and others*
Case Number: FACV0011_2000 FACV000013_2000

This is common ground although Mr Dykes SC for Mr Chan and Mr Tse has entered a **caveat** (as to the meaning of indigenous inhabitant in Article 40 of the Basic Law) which is not material for present purposes.

這是雙方爭論中的共同基礎；儘管代表陳先生及謝先生的資深大律師戴啟思先生曾（就《基本法》第四十條中「原居民」一詞的意義）登錄**知會備忘**，但就本案而言這並非關鍵問題。

e. *Rule 25(4), Non-Contentious Probate Rules (Cap. 10A)*

Upon the issue of a summons under paragraph (2) of this rule the person issuing such summons shall enter a **caveat**.

在根據本條第（2）款發出傳票時，發出該傳票的人須將**知會備忘**登記。

使用百分比	ELDoS: 100.00%
	BLIS:　　100.00%

certiorari *n.*

18

/ˌsɜːʃiəˈreəraɪ/

Latin to be informed

【中譯】 香港法庭判詞 ELDoS: **1** 移審令；香港法例 BLIS: **1** 移審令；
其他 Others: **1** 移解高院令；**2** 移送令；**3** 調卷令；**4** 覆審令；
5 調審令；**6** 移送案件命令

Interpretations 釋義

An order of certiorari can be obtained by an application for judicial review. Such an order brings a decision from a lower court or tribunal, or an administrative body before the Court of First Instance which, if satisfied that the decision was made ultra vires or is contrary to natural justice, has jurisdiction to quash the decision and, additionally, remit it to the lower court or tribunal, or the administrative body.

透過申請司法覆核可取得的移審令。該移審令將下級法院、審裁處或行政機關的判決帶到原訟法庭席前供其審核。如果原訟法庭信納判決有超越許可權的情況，或違反自然公義原則，則原訟法庭有權推翻判決，甚至可以將案件發還下級法院、審裁處或行政團體重新審理或考慮。

Examples 例句

1. 移審令

a. *Order 53, Rule 9(2), The Rules of the High Court (Cap. 4A)*

Where the relief sought is or includes an order of **certiorari** to remove any proceedings for the purpose of quashing them, the applicant may not question the validity of any order, warrant, commitment, conviction, inquisition or record unless before the hearing of the motion or summons he has lodged with the Registrar a copy thereof verified by affidavit or accounts for his failure to do so to the satisfaction of the Court hearing the motion or summons.

凡所尋求的濟助是或包括用以移走任何法律程序以將之撤銷的**移審令**，申請人不得質疑任何命令、手令、交付羈押、定罪判決、調查或紀錄的有效性，但如在動議或傳票進行聆訊前，該人已向司法常務官遞交一份該命令、手令、交付羈押、定罪判決、調查或紀錄的經由誓章核實文本，或已就其沒有如此行事而向聆訊動議或傳票的法庭作出令法庭信納的交代，則屬例外。

b. Section 21K(5), High Court Ordinance (Cap. 4)

If, on an application for judicial review seeking an order of **certiorari**, the Court of First Instance quashes the decision to which the application relates, the Court of First Instance may remit the matter to the court, tribunal or authority concerned, with a direction to reconsider it and reach a decision in accordance with the findings of the Court of First Instance.

如在接獲尋求**移審令**的申請司法覆核後，原訟法庭撤銷該項申請所關乎的決定，則原訟法庭可將有關事宜發回有關的法院、審裁處或主管當局，並指示須按照原訟法庭的裁斷而重新考慮有關事宜和達成決定。

c. Section 28, Protection of Children and Juveniles Ordinance (Cap. 213)

No summary conviction under this Ordinance shall be quashed for want of form or be removed by **certiorari**, and no warrant of commitment shall be held void by reason of any defect therein, provided it is therein alleged that the party has been convicted and there is a good and valid conviction to sustain the same.

任何根據本條例循簡易程序審訊而作出的判罪，不得因形式欠妥而宣告無效，亦不得藉**移審令**將案件移交；此外，拘押令內

如指稱當事人已被判罪名成立，並有適當而有效的判罪來確認
該令，則不得因該令本身有欠妥善之處而宣告無效。

d. Section 104(9), Magistrates Ordinance (Cap. 227)

No application for a review shall be granted and no exercise by a
magistrate shall be made of the power conferred on him by subsection
(5) subsequent to the commencement of proceedings by either party
with a view to questioning the decision of the magistrate by way of
appeal, mandamus or **certiorari**, unless such proceedings shall have
been abandoned.

任何一方如為質疑裁判官的決定而以上訴、履行責任令或**移審
令**的形式開始法律程序後，覆核的申請即不會獲得批准，而裁
判官亦不得行使第(5)款授予的權力，但如該等法律程序已被
放棄，則屬例外。

e. Xie Xiaoyi vs. The Director of Immigration
Case Number: HCAL000013_1998

In the case of Tam Nga Yin, I make an order of **certiorari** to quash
the removal order made against her on 23rd August 1997.

就譚雅賢其案而言，本席頒下**移審令**撤銷在1997年8月23日針
對其所發出遣送離境令。

f. Oriental Daily Publisher Limited vs. Commissioner for
Television and Entertainment Licensing Authority
Case Number: FACC000001_1998

Mr Dykes for the appellant and Mr Bruce for the respondent agree
that if the Tribunal is found to have failed in its duty to give reasons,
then the proper relief is **certiorari**.

代表上訴人的戴啟思先生和代表答辯人的布思義先生同意，倘
若本庭裁定審裁處未有提出理由以履行其職責，那麼本庭所作
的適當濟助便會是作出**移審令**。

g. *Oriental Daily Publisher Limited vs. Commissioner for Television and Entertainment Licensing Authority*
Case Number: FACC000001_1998

I would also uphold this appeal for the reasons given by the Chief Justice and I would grant an order of **certiorari** quashing the determination of the Tribunal on the basis that they have given no adequate reasons for it.

本席同樣會以終審法院首席法官提出的原因判決上訴得直。本席亦會基於審裁處沒有提出充分理由解釋裁決這個原因，發出**移審令**，撤銷審裁處的裁決。

h. *Section 64(3), Interpretation and General Clauses Ordinance (Cap. 1)*

The conferring by any Ordinance of a right of appeal or objection to the Chief Executive in Council shall not prevent any person from applying to the High Court for an order of mandamus, **certiorari,** prohibition, injunction or any other order, instead of appealing or making an objection to the Chief Executive in Council, where an application for such an order would lie....

任何條例授予向行政長官會同行政會議提出上訴或反對的權利，並不因此而阻止任何人向高等法院提出依法有權利提出的履行義務令、**移審令**、禁止令、強制令或其他命令的申請，以代替向行政長官會同行政會議提出上訴或反對……。

使用百分比	ELDoS: 100.00%
	BLIS: 100.00%

contra proferentem rule

n. pl. contra proferentem rules

/ˌkɒntrə ˌprefəˈrentəm ruːl/

Latin contra proferentem = against the offeror

also: contra proferentes rule

【中譯】　香港法庭判詞 ELDoS: **1** 不利提出者法則；香港法例 BLIS: 一；
其他 Others: **1** 不利出者法則；**2** 不利解釋原則；**3** 不利於文
章草擬人和提出人的解釋原則

Interpretations 釋義

This rule dictates that, in interpretation of documents, an
ambiguous term should be construed strictly against the party
who drafted the document or who relies on it.

此法則指在解釋文件時，遇有意義含糊、模稜兩可的字詞，
應嚴選不利於草擬該文件或援引該字詞一方的解釋。

Examples 例句

1. 不利提出者法則

a. *Bevise Motors Co. Ltd. vs. Hoi Kong Container Services Ltd.*
Case Number: FACV000004_1997

Quite apart from "rules of construction" which require courts
to construe standard exemption clauses against the party putting
them forward (the **contra proferentem rule**), there is this further
consideration to bear in mind: The court in its task of interpretation
should look at the exemption clause broadly as a whole, in the same
way as any business person would in assessing the allocation of risk.

法庭除了要按照「釋義法則」對提出標準免責條款的一方作出不利的解釋外（**不利提出者法則**），還要謹記着這一點：法庭應從整體上來看免責條款及對其作出寬鬆的解釋，就像任何生意人在評估風險分配時所做的一樣。

b. *Bevise Motors Co. Ltd. vs. Hoi Kong Container Services Ltd.*
Case Number: FACV000004_1997

In concluding, it must be acknowledged that the wording of clause 4(a) is neither elegant nor ideal. But its meaning from a careful reading is so clear and compelling as to leave no room for ambiguity and obscurity. In the absence of these, there is neither need nor warrant to resort to secondary rules of construction, including the **contra proferentem rule**.

總括來說，必須承認第4（a）條款的措詞用字既不典雅，也不理想。然而，只要仔細的看，便會發覺其意思是很清晰和有力的，完全沒有含糊或費解之處，因此，並無需要或足夠理由去採用釋義的輔助法則，包括了**不利提出者法則**。

使用百分比	ELDoS:	100.00%
	BLIS:	0.00%

de bene esse *adj./adv.*

/ˌdeɪ ˈbiːniː ˈesiː/   /ˌdiː ˈbiːniː ˈesiː/

Latin of well-being

【中譯】 香港法庭判詞 ELDoS: **1** 暫先；**2** 暫行；香港法例 BLIS:
1 暫行；其他 Others: **1** 臨時；**2** 暫先處理的

Interpretations 釋義

Provisionally; valid in the present circumstances but subject to future challenge, examination or exception

暫時的；某事物按現今的情況仍然有效，但仍須依據日後的反對、查證或例外情況而有所改動。

Examples 例句

1. 暫先

Francis Cheung and another vs. Insider Dealing Tribunal
Case Number: CACV000157_1999

The approach adopted by the Judge, whether this was done **de bene esse** or as an integral part of the proceedings, was to consider in particular what was said by Mr. Siu and Mr. Cheung and then see how Mr. Wu responded to the allegations made.

原審法官所採取的處理方式是，無論是**暫先**處理或是作為程序的固有部分，他已特別考慮了蕭先生及張先生所言，然後觀察胡先生對指稱作何反應。

使用百分比	
ELDoS:	50.00%
BLIS:	0.00%

2. 暫行

a. *Francis Cheung and another vs. Insider Dealing Tribunal*
Case Number: CACV000157_1999

The Judge below admitted the evidence **de bene esse** and after taking them into account, in the end rejected the claim for relief by the appellants.

下級法庭法官**暫行**接納了該等證據，並在考慮證據後，最終拒絕了上訴人尋求濟助的申索。

b. *Schedule 1 Taking Evidence, etc. -3, High Court Fees Rules (Cap. 4D)*

For every witness examined **de bene esse** by a judge or the Registrar, per day or part thereof

由大法官或司法常務官**暫行**訊問的每一名證人，每天或不足一天

c. *Schedule Taking Evidence, etc. -3, District Court Civil Procedure (Fees) Rules (Cap. 336C)*

For every witness examined **de bene esse** by a judge or the Registrar, per day or part thereof

由法官或司法常務官**暫行**訊問的每一名證人，每天或不足一天

使用百分比	ELDoS:	50.00%
	BLIS:	100.00%

de bonis non adv.

/ˌdiː ˈbəʊnəs ˈnɒn/

Latin of the goods not (administered)

【中譯】　香港法庭判詞 ELDoS: 一；香港法例 BLIS: **1** 未作管理的遺產；其他 Others: **1** 已故遺產管理人之後繼人；**2** 未作管理遺產的遺產管理書

Interpretations 釋義

A shortened form of "de bonis non administratis". For example, an administrator de bonis non is appointed by court to take over the administration of a deceased person's estate when a previous administrator has died before completing the administration.

「de bonis non administratis」的縮寫，即沒有人管理的遺產。例如，當一名遺產管理人在未完成遺產管理責任前已去世，受法庭委託接任遺產管理工作的人便稱為「已故遺產管理人的後繼人」。

Examples 例句

1. 未作管理的遺產

Schedule 2-3, High Court Fees Rules (Cap. 4D)

Double or cessate probates, or cessate letters of administration or letters of administration **de bonis non**, or duplicate probates or letters of administration

雙重遺囑認證或終止遺囑認證，或終止遺產管理書或**未作管理的遺產**的遺產管理書，或遺囑認證或遺產管理書的複本

使用百分比	ELDoS:	0.00%
	BLIS:	100.00%

de facto *adj./adv.*

/ˌdeɪ ˈfæktəʊ/   /ˌdi ˈfæktəʊ/

Latin in fact

【中譯】 香港法庭判詞 ELDoS: **1** 事實上；**2** 實際；**3** 實際上；
香港法例 BLIS: **1** 事實上；其他 Others: 一

Interpretations 釋義

In fact; actually; as a matter of fact, even though there may be doubts as to the legitimacy

事實；真實情況；不涉及是否正當的考慮，單就現實情況而言

Examples 例句

1. 事實上

a. *Schedule 5, Article 14(1), Arbitration Ordinance (Cap. 341)*

If an arbitrator becomes de jure or **de facto** unable to perform his functions or for other reasons fails to act without undue delay, his mandate terminates if he withdraws from his office or if the parties agree on the termination.

如果仲裁員在法律上或**事實上**不能履行他的職責或由於其他原因未能不過分遲延地行事，他的任命即告終止，如果他辭職或當事各方就終止他的任命達成協議的話。

b. *Novatel Communications (Far East) Limited vs. Canadian Imperial Bank Of Commerce and another*
Case Number: HCA008052_1999

Summary judgment ~ money had and received ~ whether borrowing company bound by agreement for loan to discharge liability of another company to lender ~ whether transaction for legitimate corporate purposes of the Plaintiff ~ whether actual authority from **de facto** unanimous approval of the shareholders.

簡易判決──已有及已收取的金錢──借款公司是否受貸款協議約束而為另一公司解除其對放債人所負法律責任──進行交易是否為了原告人合法的法團目的──是否股東**事實**上一致同意授予實際許可權。

使用百分比	ELDoS:	50.00%
	BLIS:	100.00%

2. 實際

Chen Li Hung alias Chan Chen Li Hung and another vs. Ting Lei Miao and another
Case Number: FACV000002_1999

Lying at the heart of this question (and of the general question of the correct attitude in law to be taken to the orders of courts exercising **de facto** power without de jure authority) is the passage in Lord Wilberforce's speech in *Carl Zeiss Stiftung v. Rayner & Keeler Ltd* (No. 2) [1967] AC 853 at p. 954 C–E where he famously said.

觸及這個問題（以及關於在法律上，對由無法理上許可權而行使**實際**權力的法庭所作之命令應採取之正確態度的一般問題）之核心是Lord Wilberforce在*Carl Zeiss Stiftung v. Rayner & Keeler Ltd*（No. 2）[1967] AC 853第954頁C–E行中一段著名的陳述。

使用百分比	ELDoS:	25.00%
	BLIS:	0.00%

3. 實際上

a. *Chen Li Hung alias Chan Chen Li Hung and another vs. Ting Lei Miao and another*
Case Number: FACV000002_1999

To what extent is effect to be given by our courts to orders made by courts sitting in Taiwan which is part of and under the de jure sovereignty of the People's Republic of China but is presently under the **de facto** albeit unlawful control of a usurper government?

雖然在法理上，中華人民共和國擁有國家的主權，而台灣只是中華人民共和國的一部分，但是**實際**上台灣現正接受一個篡權政府的非法統治。因此，對於由台灣的法庭所作出的命令，香港的法庭應在何種程度上予以執行？

b. *Chen Li Hung alias Chan Chen Li Hung and another vs. Ting Lei Miao and another*
Case Number: FACV000002_1999

All the enactments of the **de facto** Legislatures in the insurrectionary States during the war, which were not hostile to the Union, nor to the authority of the General Government, and which were not in conflict with the Constitution of the United States or of the States, have the same validity as if they had been enactments of legitimate Legislatures.

由戰爭期間叛亂的州內**實際**上的立法機構所制定的法律可以和由合法之立法機構所制定的法律同樣有效，只要它們不反對聯邦或聯邦政府的權威，以及沒有抵觸合眾國或美國的憲法。

使用百分比	ELDoS: 25.00%
	BLIS: 0.00%

de jure *adj./adv.*

23

/ˌdeɪ ˈdʒʊəri/   /ˌdi ˈdʒʊəri/

Latin from the law

【中譯】 香港法庭判詞 ELDoS：**1** 合法；**2** 法理上；香港法例 BLIS：
1 法律上；其他 Others：**1** 按照法律

Interpretations 釋義

Of right; legitimate; as a matter of law

擁有法律權利；合法的；在法律層面上分析事情

Examples 例句

1. 合法

a. *Chen Li Hung alias Chan Chen Li Hung and another vs. Ting Lei Miao and another*
Case Number: FACV000002_1999

In the following year he undoubtedly went further in *Hesperides Hotels Ltd v. Aegean Turkish Holidays Ltd* [1978] 1 Q.B. 205, a case relating to the seizure of hotels in North Cyprus by the government of the so-called Turkish Federated State of Cyprus. No such government or state was recognised **de jure** or de facto by the United Kingdom government.

在翌年的*Hesperides Hotels Ltd v. Aegean Turkish Holidays Ltd*（［1978］1 Q.B. 205）一案中，Lord Denning分明把其論據作進一步的引伸。該案是關於一個所謂土耳其賽普勒斯聯合國的政府佔領了一些位於北賽普勒斯的酒店，而這個組織從未被聯合王國的政府承認為**合法**或實際上的政府或國家。

b. *Chen Li Hung alias Chan Chen Li Hung and another vs. Ting Lei Miao and another*
Case Number: FACV000002_1999

If it were necessary to make a choice between these two conflicting doctrines, I would unhesitatingly hold that the courts of this country can recognise the laws or acts of a body which is in effective control of a territory even though it has not been recognised by Her Majesty's Government **de jure** or de facto: at any rate, in regard to the laws which regulate the day to day affairs of the people, such as their marriages, their divorces, their leases, their occupations, and so forth.

只要一個組織實際上已控制了一個地區，則即使它未獲女皇陛下的政府承認為**合法**或實際上的政府，但是本國的法庭仍可承認其法律或作為，本席所指的是那些控制人們日常事務的法律，例如結婚、離婚、租約和職業等等。

使用百分比	ELDoS: 50.00%
	BLIS: 0.00%

2. 法理上

a. *Chen Li Hung alias Chan Chen Li Hung and another vs. Ting Lei Miao and another*
Case Number: FACV000002_1999

To what extent is effect to be given by our courts to orders made by courts sitting in Taiwan which is part of and under the **de jure** sovereignty of the People's Republic of China but is presently under the de facto albeit unlawful control of a usurper government?

雖然在**法理上**，中華人民共和國擁有國家的主權，而台灣只是中華人民共和國的一部分，但是實際上台灣現正接受一個篡權政府的非法統治。因此，對於由台灣的法庭所作出的命令，香港的法庭應在何種程度上予以執行？

b. *Chen Li Hung alias Chan Chen Li Hung and another vs. Ting Lei Miao and another*
Case Number: FACV000002_1999

What he contemplated was recognition of particular acts of governments recognised neither **de jure** nor de facto "where private rights, or acts of everyday occurrence, or perfunctory acts of administration are concerned".

Lord Wilberforce的觀點是：「如涉及的是私人權利、或每天發生的作為，或例行的行政作為」，則可承認一些特定的政府作為，即使該政府在**法理**上和實際上都不被承認。

c. *Chen Li Hung alias Chan Chen Li Hung and another vs. Ting Lei Miao and another*
Case Number: FACV000002_1999

Lying at the heart of this question (and of the general question of the correct attitude in law to be taken to the orders of courts exercising de facto power without **de jure** authority) is the passage in Lord Wilberforce's speech in *Carl Zeiss Stiftung v. Rayner & Keeler Ltd* (No. 2) [1967] AC 853 at p. 954 C–E where he famously said.

觸及這個問題（以及關於在法律上，對由無**法理**上許可權而行使實際權力的法庭所作之命令應採取之正確態度的一般問題）之核心的，是Lord Wilberforce在*Carl Zeiss Stiftung v. Rayner & Keeler Ltd*（No.2）[1967] AC 853第954頁C–E行中一段著名的陳述。

使用百分比	ELDoS:	50.00%
	BLIS:	0.00%

3. 法律上

Schedule 5, Article 14(1), Arbitration Ordinance (Cap. 341)

If an arbitrator becomes **de jure** or de facto unable to perform his functions or for other reasons fails to act without undue delay, his mandate terminates if he withdraws from his office or if the parties agree on the termination.

如果仲裁員在**法律上**或事實上不能履行他的職責或由於其他原因未能不過分遲延地行事，他的任命即告終止，如果他辭職或當事各方就終止他的任命達成協議的話。

| 使用百分比 | ELDoS: | 0.00% |
| | BLIS: | 100.00% |

de minimis *adj.*

24

/ˌdeɪ ˈmɪnɪmɪs/

Latin insignificant

【中譯】 香港法庭判詞 ELDoS: **1** 瑣碎小事；香港法例 BLIS: 一；
其他 Others: 一

Interpretations 釋義

Small; unimportant. The phrase is a shortened form of the legal maxim "de minimis non curat lex" (the law takes no notice of trifles).

瑣碎的、不重要的。此詞為法諺「de minimis non curat lex」的縮寫，意指法律不計較瑣碎事情。

Examples 例句

1. 瑣碎小事

a. ***Kwan Siu Man Joshua vs. Yaacov Ozer***
Case Number: FACV000019_1998

As to the averments in the statement of claim, the Court of Appeal said they were not "wholly consistent with the open contract found to have been made by the judge" but the matter was **de minimis** and capable of correction by amendment.

至於原告人的申索陳述書，上訴法庭雖説陳述書內容「與法官裁斷的『簡略合約』，不盡相符」，但稱之為**瑣碎小事**，作出修訂即可糾正。

b. *Kwan Siu Man Joshua vs. Yaacov Ozer*
Case Number: FACV000019_1998

The Court of Appeal's conclusion that the variance was **de minimis** cannot be supported.

上訴法庭結論是：雖然原審法官的裁斷有異於原告人所訴，但這只屬**瑣碎小事**。此點，本席不予支援。

使用百分比	ELDoS: 100.00%
	BLIS:　　0.00%

de novo *adj./adv.*

25

/ˌdiː ˈnəʊvəʊ/

Latin anew

【中譯】 香港法庭判詞 ELDoS: **1** 重；香港法例 BLIS: **1** 重；其他
Others: **1** 重新開始；**2** 重新；**3** 更始；**4** 重新審理；**5** 第二次

Interpretations 釋義

Anew; afresh; starting again from scratch
更新；重新開始；由零開始

Examples 例句

1. 重

a. Section 119(1)(d), Magistrates Ordinance (Cap. 227)

the judge may by his order confirm, reverse or vary the magistrate's decision or may direct that the case shall be heard **de novo** by a magistrate or may remit the matter with his opinion thereon to a magistrate, or may make such other order in the matter as he thinks just, and by such order exercise any power which the magistrate might have exercised; and any decision or order made by the judge shall have the like effect and may be enforced in the like manner as if it had been made by the magistrate;

法官可憑其所作的命令維持、推翻或更改裁判官的決定，或指示案件由一名裁判官**重審**，或將有關事項連同其意見發回一名裁判官處理，或就有關事項作出他認為公正的任何其他命令，及憑此命令列使裁判官原可行使的權力；法官所作的決定或命令，猶如裁判官作出的一樣，具相同效力，並可按同樣方式強制執行；

b. *Order 78 rule 2(7), The Rules of the District Court (Cap. 336H)*

Where any such application as is mentioned in paragraph (6) has been part-heard in the Court of First Instance, the Court may either – ...(b) require the application to be heard **de novo**.

凡第（6）款所述的任何申請已在原訟法庭進行部分聆訊，則區域法院可——……（b）規定該申請須予**重審**。

C. *Section 118(1)(F), Magistrates Ordinance (Cap. 227)*

...if any step in or in connection with any appeal or intended appeal is rendered impossible by the death, absence or incapacity of a magistrate, a judge upon motion shall have power for good cause to order that the case be heard **de novo** by a magistrate and the case shall be so heard accordingly.

……如任何上訴或擬進行的上訴中有任何步驟，或有與此等上訴或擬進行的上訴有關的步驟，因裁判官的死亡、缺席或無行為能力而無法進行，則法官根據動議，有權基於好的因由而命令案件由一名裁判官**重審**，而案件則須據此而重審。

d. *To Kan Chi and others vs. Pui Man Yau and others*
Case Number: HCMP000562_1992

The second Trial **de novo** before me commenced on 9 March 1998.3 The hearing ended on 9 September 1998 for 67 hearing days with a number of adjournments in between.

第二次的聆訊屬於**重審**，開審日期為1998年3月10日3，聆訊於1998年9月9日審結，共審訊67天，其間又有延期審理數次之多。

使用百分比	ELDoS:	100.00%
	BLIS:	100.00%

dictum   *n. pl. dicta*

/ˈdɪktəm/

Latin a remark

26

【中譯】 香港法庭判詞 ELDoS: **1** 意見；**2** 附帶意見；**3** 名言；**4** 案例
的決定；香港法例 BLIS: 一；其他 Others: **1** 法官附帶意見；
2 法官的意見；**3** 法官判決的附帶意見

Interpretations 釋義

A shortened form of obiter dictum ("a thing said in passing").
An opinion expressed by a judge in the judgment that is
unnecessary for the decision. It does not form part of the ratio
decidendi and therefore does not set an authoritative precedent.
「obiter dictum」的縮寫，意即順帶提出的意見。法官在判詞
中提出不影響判決的意見。該意見不會作為判決理由的一部
分，因此也不會成為權威性判例。

Examples 例句

1. 意見

***Guangdong Foodstuffs Import & Export (Group) Corporation
and another vs. Tung Fook Chinese Wine (1982) Co. Ltd. and
another***
Case Number: HCA007759_1995

There are **dicta** from which it might be inferred that an action will
lie for any words, whether they are defamatory or not, which are
followed by special damage.

從一些法官在判案時陳述的**意見**可以推論，任何言詞，無論是否帶誹謗性的，只要造成了特殊損害，就符合提起訴訟的條件。

使用百分比	ELDoS: 42.86%
	BLIS:　　0.00%

2. 附帶意見

a. Chen Li Hung alias Chan Chen Li Hung and another vs. Ting Lei Miao and another
Case Number: FACV000002_1999

All of these statements, including Lord Wilberforce's, are admittedly obiter, but they constitute **dicta** of the most carefully considered kind, and I find them wholly persuasive.

誠然，這所有的陳述（包括Lord Wilberforce所作的）都只是**附帶意見**，但它們都是經過最仔細考慮的附帶意見，本席認為它們有十足的説服力。

b. Chen Li Hung alias Chan Chen Li Hung and another vs. Ting Lei Miao and another
Case Number: FACV000002_1999

These ideas began to take shape on the termination of the Civil War (see *U.S. v. Insurance Companies 89 US 99* (1875)), and have been developed and reformulated, admittedly as no more than **dicta**, but **dicta** by judges of high authority, in later cases.

這些想法在南北戰爭時已開始形成（見*U.S. v. Insurance Companies 89 US 99*（1875）），並在以後的案件中被法官加以闡發和再次系統地闡述。誠然，它們只是作為法官的**附帶意見**，但卻是位高權重之法官的**附帶意見**。

使用百分比	ELDoS: 28.57%
	BLIS:　　0.00%

3. 名言

Kwan Siu Man Joshua vs. Yaacov Ozer
Case Number: FACV000019_1998

It is as well to recall, once again, the **dictum** of Lord Bridge in The Chikuma [1981] 1 WLR 314 at 321G – cited in *World Ford Development Ltd v. Ip Ming-wai* [1994] 2 HKLR 1 at 8–9 and 11

且讓我們重溫Lord Bridge在The Chikuma〔1981〕1 WLR 314 at 321G案的**名言**（另在*World Ford Development Ltd v. Ip Ming-wai*〔1994〕2 HKLR 1 at 8–9 and 11亦有引述）

使用百分比	ELDoS: 14.29%
	BLIS: 0.00%

4. 案例的決定

HKSAR vs. Lau Tai Heung
Case Number: CACC000054_1999

We have no hesitation in rejecting that submission. It is contrary to the foregoing **dicta** and would here eliminate the incentive given for the considerable benefits that the courts recognise flow from pleas of guilty.

我們毫不猶疑就拒絕了這番陳詞，因其違反了前述**案例的決定**，並否定了法庭對因被告認罪而給予被告相當大的好處的鼓勵。

使用百分比	ELDoS: 14.29%
	BLIS: 0.00%

estop *v.*

/ɪ ˈstɒp/　/e ˈstɒp/

French to stop up

【中譯】 香港法庭判詞 ELDoS：**1** 不得；**2** 禁絕；**3** 禁止；**4** 不容反悔；香港法例 BLIS：**1** 禁止；其他 Others：**1** 阻止；**2** 防止

Interpretations 釋義

To prevent or bar somebody from doing something; to obstruct by estoppel

阻止或禁止某人做某事；根據「不容反悔法則」阻止某人做某事

Examples 例句

1. 不得

a. *Walton Wai-Tati Li vs. Evelyn Man-York Li*
Case Number: CACV000271_1998

…thirdly, in the circumstances, the Plaintiff ought to have waived or been **estopped** from claiming against the Defendant by the present action.

……第三，既然如此，就本訴訟而言原告人應已放棄權利或**不得**向被告人申索。

b. *Zhou Cui Hao vs. Ting Fung Yee*
Case Number: HCA007558Y_1996

The Deceased (and his successors in title and all persons claiming title through him including the Plaintiff) is **estopped** from reneging from his aforesaid promise and representation by claiming against the Defendant for possession of the premises.

死者（及其業權繼承人和包括原告人在內的所有憑死者的關係
而表示擁有業權的人士）**不得**否認他曾經作出上述承諾及陳述
而向被告人收回該物業的管有權。

| 使用百分比 | ELDoS: 33.33% |
| | BLIS: 0.00% |

2. 禁絕

a. *Gimex Development Limited vs. Cua Wai Tai*
Case Number: CACV000174_1999

If the latter be the case, the appellant might be able to argue that the respondents were **estopped** from asserting their rights.

如果情況屬於後者，那麼上訴人可能可以爭論説答辯人等已遭
禁絕，不可堅稱他們的權利。

b. *Gimex Development Limited vs. Cua Wai Tai*
Case Number: CACV000174_1999

Since the buyer had acted on that representation to his detriment, the defendant was **estopped** from asserting that the agreement was entered into without his authority.

由於買家以該表現為行事基礎而招致損害，故此被告人遭**禁
絕**，不得堅稱協議是未得到他的授權而訂立的。

| 使用百分比 | ELDoS: 33.33% |
| | BLIS: 0.00% |

3. 禁止

a. *Direk Mahadumrongkul vs. Lau Chun Keung and others*
Case Number: CACV000133_1998

In defence, the 1st, 4th and 5th defendants raise the following points: (4) that the plaintiff has waived his right to the parking spaces or is **estopped** from asserting such right.

第一、第四和第五被告人提出以下各點抗辯理由：⋯⋯（4）原告人已經放棄本身對該等泊車位的權利、同時亦受**禁止**宣示這等權利。

b. *Gimex Development Limited vs. Cua Wai Tai*
Case Number: CACV000174_1999

The silence and inaction of the two respondents after being served with the appellant's proceedings would **estop** the two respondents from asserting that they still have an interest in the property.

兩位答辯人獲送達了上訴人的法律程序文件後的沉默和不採取行動，將**禁止**該兩位答辯人堅稱他們仍然擁有該物業的權益。

c. *Section 64(8), Patents Ordinance (Cap. 514)*

An application may be made under this section in respect of a patent notwithstanding that the applicant is already the holder of a licence under the patent; and no person shall be **estopped** from relying on any of the matters specified in subsection.

即使申請人已是在某一專利下的特許的持有人，他仍可就該專利而根據本條提出申請；任何人不得因作出任何承認（不論是否在該項特許中或在其他方面或由於他已接受該項特許）而被**禁止**依賴第（2）款所指明的任何事宜。

| 使用百分比 | ELDoS: 22.22% |
| | BLIS: 0.00% |

4. 不容反悔

Roe Investment Limited vs. Prince Good Limited and others
Case Number: FACV000013_1999

He had in fact earlier in his judgment concluded that the "interpleader summons" was properly constituted – as to which he was plainly wrong – but went on to hold that Prince Good was in any case "**estopped**" from denying the validity of those proceedings, having in effect used them as the vehicle by which the issue as to who lawfully controlled Unionix could be resolved.

事實上，在較早前他已在判案書中作出結論：「互爭權利傳票」乃恰當地組成——這點他明顯是錯了——但是仍然裁定無論如何Prince Good都「**不容反悔**」，否認該等法律程序的有效性，而實際上已把它們用作能夠解決是誰合法控制Unionix這個爭論點的工具。

使用百分比	ELDoS: 11.11%
	BLIS: 0.00%

estoppel *n.*

/ɪ ˈstɒpəl/　/e ˈstɒpəl/

French　to stop up

【中譯】　香港法庭判詞 ELDoS: **1** 不容反悔；**2** 不容反悔法；**3** 禁制；
香港法例 BLIS: **1** 不容反悔法；其他 Others: **1** 不得自駁；
2 不得反言；**3** 不許否認；**4** 禁止改口；**5** 禁止翻供

Interpretations 釋義

A rule of evidence (or a rule of law) that prevents a party from
gaining advantage by denying the truth of a statement he has
asserted previously or the existence of facts that he has alleged
to exist. In order to invoke this rule, the person who, by the
above party's words or conduct, has been led to believe in such
a statement or the existence of such facts and acted accordingly
must show that he would otherwise not have so acted and that his
position has been altered as a result. There are three varieties of
estoppel, viz estoppel of record, estoppel by deed and estoppel
by conduct. The first two are legal estoppel and the last one is
equitable estoppel.

這是證據法規則（或法律規則）裏的其中一個原則。這原則規
定甲方不能從以下行為獲益：（一）否定以前曾對乙方作出陳
述的真實性；（二）否定以前曾對乙方聲稱某事實確實存在。
若乙方要引用此規則，他必先因甲方的言語或行為而相信該
陳述或事實確實存在，並作出相應行動。在此情況下，乙方
必須證明若非甲方這些言行，他根本不會如此行動，使他的
處境與原來的不同。

Examples 例句

1. 不容反悔

a. *Hebei Import and Export Corporation vs. Polytek Engineering Company Limited*
Case Number: FACV000010_1998

Whether one describes the respondent's conduct as giving rise to an **estoppel**, a breach of the bona fide principle or simply as a breach of the principle that a matter of non-compliance with the governing rules shall be raised promptly in the arbitration is beside the point in this case.

不論將答辯人的行為描述為：引起**不容反悔**；違反真誠原則；或純粹違反有關在仲裁中有不遵守仲裁規則的事情發生得即時提出的原則，這點與本案毫不相關。

b. *Gimex Development Limited vs. Cua Wai Tai*
Case Number: CACV000174_1999

Where a person, having a title, right, or claim to property of any kind, perceives that another person is innocently, and in ignorance, conducting himself with reference to the property in a manner inconsistent with such title, right, or claim, it is the duty of the former to undeceive the other party forthwith; if he omits to do so, and if all the other conditions of a valid **estoppel** are satisfied, he is precluded from exercising or asserting his right or title or claim as against such other party on any subsequent occasion.

遇有一個人，他對任何一種物業有業權、權利或申索，而他察覺到另一個人天真無邪地和無知地，就該物業，以一種與這業權、權利或申索並不一致的方式表現他自己，那麼前者就有義務立即使另一方醒悟過來；若他漏了這樣做，和若果所有其他有效的**不容反悔**的條件都滿足了的話，那麼他就不能在日後任何場合向這另一方行使或堅稱其權利或業權或申索。

c. *Gimex Development Limited vs. Cua Wai Tai*
Case Number: CACV000174_1999

The evidence, without more, is insufficient to show a representation by the 2nd respondent that Mr. Choi had her authority to dispose of the property so as to give rise to an **estoppel** by representation or by conduct.

在沒有進一步的證據下，該等證據不足以顯示由第二答辯人作出的表現（即蔡先生有她的授權處置該物業），以惹起因表現或行為而構成**不容反悔**。

使用百分比	ELDoS: 62.96%
	BLIS:　　0.00%

2. 不容反悔法

a. *Hebei Import and Export Corporation vs. Polytek Engineering Company Limited*
Case Number: FACV000010_1998

Estoppel, a term developed in the English law of equity, does not lie comfortably in the context of enforcing a Convention award. It is not a legal concept of universal currency among the contracting states to the New York Convention. If what is suggested by **estoppel** is no more than this, that a party invoking s.44(3) [of the Arbitration Ordinance] must act in good faith; that he must not string the claimant along by taking procedural points in contesting the award, and then, when all else has failed, attempts to resist enforcement by taking a public policy point for the first time, then this is no more than expressing another facet of public policy, as expressed in s.44(3) [of the Arbitration Ordinance].

不容反悔法是英國衡平法發展而產生的一個術語，與強制執行公約裁決的情形格格不入。它並非《紐約公約》締約國之間一個到處通行的法律理念。假如**不容反悔法**所主張的僅止於此，即援引〔《仲裁條例》〕第44(3)條的一方必須秉誠行事；絕對不能對申索人糾纏不休，先針對程序上的問題對裁決提出爭辯，倘不得逞時才首次試圖提出公共政策這一論點來抗拒強制執行，那麼，正如〔《仲裁條例》〕第44(3)條所陳述者，這樣做只不過是表達公共政策的另一面。

b. *Hebei Import and Export Corporation vs. Polytek Engineering Company Limited*
Case Number: FACV000010_1998

In my view **estoppel** as such cannot be an answer to the seller's application to refuse enforcement in this case, and it is fruitless to inquire whether the "issues" now raised are the same as, or similar to, the ones put before the Beijing Court.

本席認為這種**不容反悔法**不能解決本案中賣方申請拒絕強制執行的問題。同時，去究查現在所提出的「爭論點」是不是跟向北京法院所提出的一樣或相類似，也是徒勞無功的。

c. *Direk Mahadumrongkul vs. Lau Chun Keung and others*
Case Number: CACV000133_1998

The other defendants maintain that they have a clear right to park cars on the true interpretation of the conveyancing documents, or otherwise they enjoy the same right by reason of implied easements, adverse possession, **estoppel**, waiver and prescription under the fiction of a lost modern grant or the Prescription Act 1832.

其餘的被告人堅稱根據財產轉易的文件的真正詮釋，他們明顯擁有泊車權，不然的話，他們根據隱含的地役權、逆權管有、**不容反悔法**、放棄權利，以及根據「遺失近期所簽立授予書」

這個虛構情況從而假設獲得時效歸益的原則（即因為長期使用土地而可以推定，曾於某一追憶可及的時刻，獲得授予該土地的使用權，只是有關授予書已告遺失而已），或1832年的時效歸益條例，同樣享有這個權利。

d. Section 98(4), Copyright Ordinance (Cap. 528)

Nothing in this Division is to be construed as excluding the operation of the general law of contract or **estoppel** in relation to an informal waiver or other transaction in relation to any of the rights mentioned in subsection (1).

本分部不得解釋為摒除與任何關乎第（1）款提及的權利的非正式放棄或其他處理有關的一般合約法或**不容反悔法**的施行。

使用百分比	ELDoS:	33.33%
	BLIS:	100.00%

3. 禁制

Mui Foon and others vs. Land Development Corporation
Case Number: HCMP006219_1998

Further, the Plaintiffs here have not sought to dispute the observation of the Privy Council in *Attorney General and anor v Humphreys Estate (Queen's Gardens) Ltd.* [1987] HKLR 427, 435 that it was possible, but unlikely, that in circumstances the Privy Council could not foresee, a party to negotiations set out in a document expressed to be "subject to contract" would be able to satisfy a court that the parties had subsequently agreed to convert the document into a contract, or that some form of estoppel had arisen to prevent both parties from refusing to proceed with the transaction envisaged by the document. In any event, no case of **estoppel** has been pressed on behalf of the Plaintiffs.

再者，本案的原訴人沒有尋求就律政司與另一人對堪富利士房產（皇后花園）有限公司（*Attorney General and anor v*

Humphreys Estate (Queen's Gardens) Ltd. [1987] **HKLR** 427,
435) 一案中樞密院的評析提出異議；該評析說有可能在樞密院
不能預見的情況下，參與談判的一方在一份文件中明確寫下
「以合約為準」而能夠使法庭信納雙方其後同意了把該檔轉換
為一份合約，或者某種形式的**禁制**已經產生，使雙方不能拒絕
進行該文件原先設想的交易，但是這個可能性卻很微。

使用百分比	ELDoS:	3.70%
	BLIS:	0.00%

ex debito justitiae *adv.*

/ˌeks ˈdebətəʊ dʒəsˈtɪʃiːiː/

Latin from a debt of justice

【中譯】 香港法庭判詞 ELDoS：**1** 有當然權利；香港法例 BLIS：—；其他 Others：**1** 公正所欠；**2** 應得權利；**3** 根據正當權利；**4** 法所應然者；**5** 屬於權利者；**6** 法定補償權；**7** 應得的補救權利

Interpretations 釋義

Remedies to which a claimant is entitled and that the court is bound to give "as required by justice".

申索人有權得到法庭為了維護司法公義而必須給予的補償。

Examples 例句

1. 有當然權利

Redland Concrete Limited vs. Hing Lee Construction Company Limited and another

Case Number: HCA008140_1998

Ms. Wong, for the defendant…argues that the legal position on setting aside irregular judgments has always been that the defendant is entitled to have an irregular judgment set aside **ex debito justitiae** – as of right, regardless of the merits of his defence or the conduct of the parties….

代表被告人的大律師黃女士……回應謂一直以來，在將不合規範判決的案件作廢中，不論被告人的抗辯理據充分與否；訴訟各方的行徑如何，被告人皆**有當然權利**，也就是其應得的補救權利，不接受將該不合規範的判決，要求將其作廢……。

使用百分比	ELDoS: 100.00%
	BLIS: 0.00%

ex facie adj./adv.

/ˌeks ˈfeɪʃiːiː/   /ˌeks ˈfeɪsiːiː/

Latin from the face

【中譯】 香港法庭判詞 ELDoS: **1** 表面上；香港法例 BLIS: **1** 形式上
的；其他 Others: **1**（文件）從表面看；**2** 顯然地

> **Interpretations 釋義**
>
> Apparently; evidently; from the face (of a document)
> 顯而易見的；明顯地；從（文件）表面看得出來的

Examples 例句

1. 表面上

Li Pui Wan vs. Wong Mei Yin
Case Number: CACV000049X_1997

In my view, the agreement between the plaintiffs and the defendant
is merely an agreement for sale and purchase of real estate and is
therefore not **ex facie** illegal.

本席認為，原告人和被告人之合約，只是一宗房地產買賣合
約，**表面上**絕非不合法。

使用百分比	ELDoS: 100.00%
	BLIS: 0.00%

2. 形式上的

Section 2(1), Royal Bank of Scotland Ordinance (Cap. 1138)

"security"（抵押）includes any mortgage or charge (whether legal
or equitable), assignment, debenture, fixed security, floating charge,

personal bond, bill of exchange, promissory note, trust receipt, warehouse warrant, guarantee, indemnity, lien, right of retention, hypothec, pledge (whether actual or constructive), mandate, hypothecation, right of set-off, right of compensation or undertaking, any standard security, any assignation or disposition **ex facie** absolute and any agreement or other deed, instrument or document qualifying the same, any bond and disposition or assignation in security, any bond of cash credit, any bond of cash credit and disposition or assignation in security, any assignation in security, any real right or burden of whatever kind in the nature of a security and any other deed, document, conveyance, instrument, arrangement or means (in each case made, granted, arising or subsisting under any applicable law) for securing the payment or discharge of any liability and also includes any agreement or undertaking (whether in writing or not) to give or execute any of the foregoing whether upon demand or otherwise

「抵押」（security）包括任何按揭或押記（不論是法律上的或衡平法上的）、轉讓、債權證、固定抵押、浮動押記、個人債券、匯票、承付票、信託收據、倉單、擔保、彌償、留置權、保留權、押物預支、質押（不論是實有的或法律構定的）、委託、押貨預支、抵銷權、補償權或承諾、任何標準抵押、任何**形式上的**絕對轉讓或絕對產權處置及規限該轉讓或產權處置的任何協議或其他契據、文書或文件、任何債券連抵押產權處置書或債券連抵押轉讓書、任何現金信貸債券、任何現金信貸債券連抵押產權處置書或現金信貸債券連抵押轉讓書、任何抵押轉讓書、屬抵押性質的各種土地權利或負擔，以及用作保證就任何法律責任付款或解除任何法律責任的任何其他契據、文件、轉易、文書、安排或方式（全部根據任何適用的法律而訂立、批出、產生或存續），並包括任何協議或承諾（不論是否書面形式），其內規定在接獲要求時或在其他情況下須發出或簽立前述任何一項

| 使用百分比 | ELDoS: | 0.00% |
| | BLIS: | 100.00% |

ex gratia *adj./adv.*

31

/ˌeks ˈɡreɪʃɪə/ /ˌeks ˈɡreɪʃə/

Latin as a favour

【中譯】 香港法庭判詞 ELDoS: **1** 特惠；香港法例 BLIS: **1** 特惠；**2** 恩恤；其他 Others: **1** 作為優惠的；**2** 通融的；**3** 出自恩惠的；**4** 寬限的

Interpretations 釋義

As a matter of grace or favour; without obligations; not as of right

一種寬限或優待；並非基於法律責任而作出的行為，也並非必然的權利

Examples 例句

1. 特惠

a. *Section 7, Pensions Ordinance (Cap. 89)*

Where an officer leaves the public service and a pension or gratuity cannot, except by the application of section 20A, be granted to him under this Ordinance, the Chief Executive may, if he thinks fit, grant such **ex gratia** payment to the officer as he thinks just and proper.

凡某人員離開公職，而根據本條例（除非引用第20A條）是不能將退休金或酬金批予該人員的，行政長官如認為適當，可將他認為是公正和恰當的**特惠**金批予該人員。

b. Section 11(1), Hong Kong Council on Smoking and Health Ordinance (Cap. 389)

The Council may – (a) provide allowances and benefits for its employees; (b) make payments, whether **ex gratia** or legally due, to the personal representative of a deceased employee or to any person who was dependent on such employee at his death.

委員會可——（a）為其僱員提供津貼及利益；（b）支付**特惠**金或在法律上應得的款項予去世僱員的遺產代理人，或在該僱員去世時受其供養的人。

c. Tong Tim Nui and others vs. Hong Kong Housing Authority
Case Number: CACV000281_1998

The Hong Kong Housing Authority did promise to make **ex gratia** payments of compensation, but persisted with its plans for redevelopment of the whole area (including Rennie's Mill) and, in 1995, started to serve notices to quit on the residents.

香港房屋委員會承諾會給予**特惠**補償金，但堅持實行整個地區（包括調景嶺在內）的重建計劃，並於1995年開始將遷出通知書送達調景嶺居民。

d. Tong Tim Nui and others vs. Hong Kong Housing Authority
Case Number: CACV000281_1998

Many of them, unhappy with the decision to turn them out of their premises, or with the amount of the **ex gratia** payments offered, or both, instituted proceedings for a judicial review of the Hong Kong Housing Authority's decision to serve them with notices to quit.

許多居民因不滿房委會要他們遷出的決定，或不滿房委會提出的**特惠**補償金額，又或既不滿該決定又不滿補償金額，遂提出訴訟要求法庭司法覆核香港房屋委員會要把遷出通知書送達他們的決定。

e. Section 4(3), Pneumoconiosis (Compensation) Ordinance (Cap. 360)

No compensation shall be payable – (a) where **ex gratia** compensation has been or will be paid by the Government for any incapacity or death resulting from pneumoconiosis diagnosed before the date of commencement of this Part....

無須在下列情況或向下列的人支付補償——（a）如政府已經或將會就在本部生效日期之前經診斷的肺塵埃沉着病所引致的任何喪失工作能力或死亡，支付**特惠**補償⋯⋯。

f. Section 16(1), Protection of Wages on Insolvency Ordinance (Cap. 380)

...where it appears to the Commissioner that an employer has failed to pay any wages, wages in lieu of notice or severance payment, as the case may be, or all or any of them to an applicant and that – ...(b) in the case of an employer who is a company, a winding-up petition has been presented against that employer, he may make an **ex gratia** payment to the applicant out of the Fund of the amount of the wages, wages in lieu of notice or severance payment, as the case may be, or all or any of them.

如處長覺得僱主未有將工資、代通知金或遣散費（視屬何情況而定）或上述各項、其中一項或多於一項付給申請人，而——⋯⋯（b）如僱主是一間公司，且已有人針對僱主提出清盤呈請⋯⋯則處長可從基金中撥出數額相等於該工資、代通知金或遣散費（視屬何情況而定）或上述各項、其中一項或多於一項的**特惠**款項支付給申請人。

使用百分比	ELDoS:	100.00%
	BLIS:	91.85%

2. 恩恤

a. Section 17(1), Pensions Ordinance (Cap. 89)

Without restricting the generality of subsection (1) the Board may –
...(b) make or provide **ex gratia** payments to any employee of the
Board, or to the personal representative of a deceased employee
of the Board or to any other person who was dependent on such
employee at his death....

在不局限第（1）款的一般性的原則下，管理局可——……（b）支
付或提供特惠或**恩恤**付款予任何僱員、去世僱員的遺產管理
人、或去世僱員在去世時所供養的人……。

b. Regulation 16(1), Traffic Wardens (Discipline) Regulations (Cap. 374j)

Where a tribunal has found a traffic warden guilty of a disciplinary
offence, the tribunal may, in addition to or in lieu of any punishment
he is by these regulations empowered to award, order the defaulter
to pay in full or in part – ...(c) the compensation paid, **ex gratia** or
otherwise, by the Government to any person in respect of the loss or
damage of that person's property by the defaulter....

凡審裁小組裁定一名交通督導員犯有一項違反紀律罪行，則該
審裁小組除根據本規例授權可裁決的懲罰外，尚可命令該犯規
人員支付以下全部或部分費用，或以支付該等費用來代替根據
本規例授權可裁決的懲罰——……（c）政府向任何人所作**恩恤**
補償或以其他方式所作補償的費用，而該項補償是就該犯規人
員遺失或損壞該人財物而作出的……。

c. Section 13(1), Industrial Training (Clothing Industry) Ordinance (Cap. 318)

The Authority may – ...(c) make payments, whether **ex gratia** or legally due, to the personal representative of a deceased employee or to any person who was dependent on such employee at his death.

訓練局可——……（c）向已故僱員的遺產代理人或該僱員死亡時所供養的人，支付款項，而不論其為**恩恤**性質或法律上應付的。

d. Section 5(2), Employees Compensation Assistance Ordinance (Cap. 365)

Without restricting the generality of subsection (1) the Board may – ...(c) make or provide **ex gratia** payments to any employee of the Board, or to the personal representative of a deceased employee of the Board or to any other person who was dependent on such employee at his death....

在不局限第（1）款的一般性的原則下，管理局可——……（c）支付或提供**恩恤**付款予該局僱員、去世僱員的遺產管理人或去世僱員在去世時所供養的人……。

e. Section 30, Employees Compensation Assistance Ordinance (Cap. 365)

Where it appears to the Board that a person is unable to establish entitlement to payment from the Fund pursuant to section 16 by reason, and by reason only, of the operation of a period of limitation in respect of a claim against an employer, the Board may, if it sees fit and in such amount as it considers appropriate in the circumstances, determine to make an **ex gratia** payment to the person from the Fund.

凡管理局認為有人純粹因為針對僱主的聲請的訴訟時效問題，以致不能確立他依據第16條獲得基金付款的權利，管理局如認為合適，可決定由基金對該人作出該局視乎情況認為數額適當的**恩恤**付款。

f. *Section 18(1), Volunteer and Naval Volunteer Pensions Ordinance (Cap. 202)*

...where a qualified person dies when he has been paid under this Ordinance or is otherwise entitled under this Ordinance to the payment of a grant payable by way of constant attendance allowance under section 10 in respect of any period of time ending with his death, there shall, apart from any other grant payable under this Part, be payable by way of **ex gratia** allowance a grant comprising....

……如任何合資格人士去世時，他已根據本條例獲支付根據第10條須以經常照顧津貼方式而就截至其去世為止的任何期間支付的撫恤金，或根據本條例另有權獲支付上述撫恤金，則除根據本部須支付的任何其他撫恤金外，須以**恩恤**津貼的方式支付撫恤金，該撫恤金包括以下各項付款……。

| 使用百分比 | ELDoS: | 0.00% |
| | BLIS: | 8.15% |

ex hypothesi *adv.*

/ˌeks haɪˈpɒθəsaɪ/   /ˌeks haɪˈpɒθəsi/

Latin hypothetically

【中譯】 香港法庭判詞 ELDoS: **1** 根據假定；香港法例 BLIS: 一；其他 Others: **1** 就假定來説

Interpretations 釋義

Based upon a hypothesis; according to something that is assumed to be real or true.

基於某項假設而作出的見解，而該等假設中的事情已假定為實在或真確。

Examples 例句

1. 根據假定

Leung Sai Lun Robert vs. Leung May Ling
Case Number: FACV000005_1998

A marriage pursuant to s. 38 [of the Marriage Ordinance] effects no relevant alteration in status, so the argument runs, because **ex hypothesi** the parties have celebrated a previous customary marriage which, in any event, is not invalidated by s. 38 [of the Marriage Ordinance].

依據〔《婚姻條例》〕第38條而締結的婚姻，並沒有引起婚姻地位有任何相關的變化；而論據又指出，這是因為**根據假定**，雙方原先舉行的舊式婚禮，不論怎樣，是不會因〔《婚姻條例》〕第38條而失效的。

使用百分比	ELDoS: 100.00%
	BLIS: 0.00%

ex officio *adj./adv.*

/ˌeks əˈfɪʃiəʊ/ /ˌeks əˈfɪsiəʊ/

Latin from office

33

【中譯】　香港法庭判詞 ELDoS: **1** 當然；香港法例 BLIS: **1** 當然；**2** 當然地；其他 Others: **1** 官守；**2** 依據職權的；**3** 依職權；**4** 因職權上的；**5** 依官職的

Interpretations 釋義

By virtue of the office or position; implied in the office

依據職守或職位而當然享有的權利，而其所享有的權利已隱含在該職位內。

Examples 例句

1. 當然

a. Section 9(1), Probate and Administration Ordinance (Cap.10)

The Registrar shall be **ex officio** Official Administrator under this Ordinance.

根據本條例，司法常務官是**當然**官守遺產管理官。

b. Section 17(1), District Councils Ordinance (Cap. 547)

A person who is a Chairman of a Rural Committee does not become an **ex officio** member unless the person swears acceptance of office in Form 2 set out in Schedule 4 and lodges the form of acceptance with the Designated Officer.

身為鄉事委員會主席的人必須採用附表4內的表格2宣誓接受席位並將該接受席位書提交指定人員，方會成為**當然議員**。

c. *Section 9(3), Hong Kong Academy of Medicine Ordinance (Cap. 419)*

Where the number of **ex officio** members referred to in subsection (2) c exceeds 2, there shall be elected to the Council 1 member for every multiple of 3 of such **ex officio** members.

如第（2）（c）款所指的**當然**委員數目超過2人，則每有3名**當然**委員即須有1名委員獲選加入院務委員會。

d. *Secretary for Justice and others vs. Chan Wah and others*
Case Number: FACV0011_2000 & FACV000013_2000

They are elected from among village representatives (or such other persons as may be approved by the Secretary [for Home Affairs]) by the **Ex-officio** Councillors.

他們由**當然**議員從村代表（或從民政事務局局長所批准的其他人）之中選出。

e. *Secretary for Justice and others vs. Chan Wah and others*
Case Number: FACV0011_2000 FACV000013_2000

Ex-officio Councillors. They consist of the Chairmen and Vice-Chairmen of Rural Committees (who as mentioned above are elected by village representatives) and New Territories Justices of the Peace.

當然議員。他們包括各鄉事委員會的正副主席（他們如前所述是由村代表選出）及新界太平紳士。

f. Secretary for Justice and others vs. Chan Wah and others
Case Number: FACV0011_2000 & FACV000013_2000

The Chairmen of Rural Committees elected by the village representatives are **ex-officio** members of the relevant District Councils.

由村代表選出的鄉事委員會主席是有關的區議會的**當然**議員。

使用百分比	ELDoS: 100.00%
	BLIS: 99.17%

2. 當然地

Schedule Statute Xiii-2, University of Hong Kong Ordinance (Cap. 1053)

An Honorary or Emeritus Professor shall not **ex officio** be a member of the Court, Council, Senate or the Board of any Faculty.

名譽教授或榮休教授不得**當然地**成為校董會、校務委員會、教務委員會或任何學院院務委員會的成員。

使用百分比	ELDoS: 0.00%
	BLIS: 0.83%

ex parte _adj./adv._

34

/ˌeks ˈpɑːti/   /ˌeks ˈpɑːteɪ/

Latin from a party

【中譯】 香港法庭判詞 ELDoS: **1** 單方面；**2** 單方；**3** 單方面的；香港法例 BLIS: **1** 單方面；**2** 單方面的；**3** 缺席時；其他 Others: **1** 一造

Interpretations 釋義

By, for or on one side of a case or dispute. A proceeding, order, injunction, application to court, etc is said to be ex parte when it is taken, made or granted on the request and for the benefit of one party only, and without notice to or contestation by, or in the absence of any other party who may be adversely affected by the court's decision. In general, the court will only hear the arguments from the party initiating the ex parte action.

在訴訟或爭議中，只由單方面發起行動或得益，即是指訴訟其中一方在沒有通知另一方、或另一方沒有爭議或缺席的情況下，向法庭申請某程序、進行聆訊、取得命令或禁制令等，而另一方則可能會因這個對申請一方有利的法庭判決而受到嚴重影響。一般而言，在單方面的申請程序中，法院只會聽取申請一方的論據。

Examples 例句

1. 單方面

a. Section 67(4), Legal Practitioners Ordinance (Cap. 159)

If after due notice of any taxation either party thereto fails to attend, the taxing officer may proceed with the taxation **ex parte**.

如在任何評定的通知已妥為發出後，其中一方沒有出席，則訟費評定人員可**單方面**繼續進行評定。

b. Rule 63(1), Companies (Winding-Up) Rules (Cap. 32H)

Any application for leave to disclaim any part of the property of a company pursuant to section 268(1) of the Ordinance shall be by **ex parte** summons.

依據本條例第268（1）條提出，要求獲得許可卸棄公司任何部分財產的申請，須以**單方面**傳票提出。

c. Section 3(1), Organized and Serious Crimes Ordinance (Cap. 455)

The Secretary for Justice may, for the purpose of an investigation into an organized crime, make an **ex parte** application to the Court of First Instance for an order under subsection (2) in relation to a particular person or to persons of a particular description.

為偵查有組織罪行，律政司司長可向原訟法庭提出**單方面**申請，就某人或某類別的人根據第（2）款發出命令。

d. Section 14(1), Trade Mark (Border Measures) Rules (Cap. 362F)

Any notice or other document required to be served by the Commissioner or an authorized officer under section 30D(5) of the Ordinance or these Rules shall be deemed to have been duly served on the person concerned if it is – (a) in the case of the owner – (i) delivered to him personally; or (ii) addressed to him and left at the address for service given in the **ex parte** originating summons referred to in rule 6….

根據本條例第30D（5）條或本規則須由關長或獲授權人員送達——（a）商標擁有人的任何通知或其他文件，如經——（i）面交該人；或（ii）致予該人並放置於在第6條所提述的**單方面**原訴傳票上的送達地址……。

e. Liu Sung Wai vs. HKSAR
Case Number: FACC000002_1998

On 15 January 1996 the prosecution, upon its **ex parte** application, obtained an order from Burrell J which ordered, pursuant to s.77E(1) of the Evidence Ordinance, that a letter of request be issued to an American court, namely the United States District Court for the Central District of California.

在一九九六年一月十五日，控方作出**單方面**申請。就該項申請，高等法院大法官貝偉和命令依據證據條例第77E（1）條，向美國法庭，即加利福尼亞州Central District的United States District Court發出請求書。

f. Chan Mei Yee vs. Director of Immigration
Case Number: HCAL000077A_1999

Leave to apply for judicial review is usually granted **ex parte**.

一般來說，准以申請司法覆核的許可，都是在**單方面**申請下批予的。

g. Section 17(1), Prevention of Bribery Ordinance (Cap. 201)

Any investigating officer may, for the purposes of an investigation into, or proceedings relating to, an offence suspected to have been committed under this Ordinance, make an **ex parte** application to a court for the issue of a warrant under subsection (1A).

為調查懷疑犯了的本條例所訂罪行或為進行與該罪行有關的法律程序，任何調查人員可向法庭提出**單方面**申請，要求根據第（1A）款發出手令。

h. *Liu Sung Wai vs. HKSAR*
Case Number: FACC000002_1998

To this end, it went before Wong **J ex parte** on 24 July 1996 and obtained from him an order identical to the one which it had obtained from Burrell J on 15 January 1996.

為了取得證據，控方於一九九六年七月二十四日在高等法院大法官王見秋席前作**單方面**申請，從而得到他發出一個與高等法院大法官貝偉和在一九九六年一月十五日所發的一樣的命令。

使用百分比	ELDoS: 60.00%
	BLIS: 91.87%

2. 單方

Hebei Import and Export Corporation vs. Polytek Engineering Company Limited
Case Number: FACV000010_1998

The appellant obtained an order **ex parte** by Leonard J. on 23 July 1996 granting leave to enforce the Award and the appellant entered judgment on that date.

上訴人在1996年7月23日獲得李安霖大法官頒下**單方**命令授予許可強制執行該裁決，而上訴人在當日已登錄判決。

使用百分比	ELDoS: 20.00%
	BLIS: 0.00%

3. 單方面的

a. *Section 11(3), Drug Trafficking (Recovery of Proceeds) Ordinance (Cap. 405)*

A charging order – (a) may be made only on an application by the prosecutor; (b) may be made on an **ex parte** application to a judge in chambers....

抵押令──（a）只可在檢控官提出申請後發出；（b）可由法官在內庭應**單方面的**聆訊形式申請而發出⋯⋯。

b. *Section 99(2), Bankruptcy Ordinance (Cap. 6)*

The Registrar shall in cases of urgency have power to make interim orders and to hear and determine unopposed or **ex parte** applications and any order so made shall, subject to an appeal to the court, be deemed to be an order of the court.

司法常務官在緊急情況下有權作出臨時命令，亦有權聆訊及裁定無人反對的或**單方面的**申請。任何如此作出的命令，除非有人就其向法院上訴，否則須當作法院的命令。

c. *Section 36(3), Broadcasting Ordinance (Cap. 562)*

In a case of urgency, the Chief Secretary may, under subsection (2), make an application for an interim order, **ex parte** and on affidavit, but otherwise the application shall be made by motion or summons.

在緊急情況下，司長可藉誓章以**單方面的**法律程序申請根據第（2）款作出臨時命令，但在其他情況下，申請須藉動議或傳票提出。

d. *Order 59 rule 14(1), The Rules of the High Court (Cap. 4A)*

Unless otherwise directed, every application to the Court of Appeal or a single judge which is not made **ex parte** must be made by summons and such summons must be served on the party or parties affected at least 2 clear days before the day on which it is heard or, in the case of an application which is made after the expiration of the time for appealing, at least 7 days before the day on which the summons is heard.

除非另有指示，否則所有並非**單方面的**向上訴法庭或單一名法官提出的申請，均必須藉傳票提出，而該傳票必須在其聆訊之日前2整天或之前送達受影響的一方或各方；或如申請是在上訴時限屆滿後提出，則傳票必須在其聆訊之日前7天或之前送達。

e. *Section 53(6C)(a), Landlord and Tenant (Consolidation) Ordinance (Cap. 7)*

Where a landlord believes that a tenant may have, without breach of the contractual tenancy, sublet the whole or any part of the premises and the landlord is unable, with reasonable diligence, to ascertain the identity of any such sub-tenant, the Tribunal may, on an **ex parte** application by the landlord, make an order calling upon any sub-tenant to give notice to the landlord of his interest in the premises and may give directions regarding the service of that order.

凡業主相信其租客可能已將處所的全部或部分分租而沒有違反合約下的租賃，而業主經過合理的努力後，仍未能確定分租客是何人，則應業主**單方面的**申請，審裁處可作出命令，要求分租客就其對處所所具有的權益向業主發出通知書，審裁處並可就該命令的送達作出指示。

| 使用百分比 | ELDoS: 20.00% |
| | BLIS: 7.72% |

4. 缺席時

Section 39(2), Labour Tribunal Ordinance (Cap. 25)

The powers conferred by subsection (1) may be exercised – ...(c) if an award is made **ex parte** against the defendant.

第（1）款所授的權力——⋯⋯（c）如判決被告人敗訴的裁斷是在被告人**缺席時**作出的，亦可行使。

| 使用百分比 | ELDoS: 0.00% |
| | BLIS: 0.41% |

ex tempore *adj./adv.*

/ɪk ˈstempəri/　/ek ˈstempəri/

Latin　from time

【中譯】　香港法庭判詞 ELDoS: **1** 即席；香港法例 BLIS: 一；其他 Others: 一

Interpretations 釋義

Without preparation

在沒有準備的情況下

Examples 例句

1. 即席

a. *Common Luck Investment Limited vs. Cheung Kam Chuen*
Case Number: FACV000022_1998

Common Luck's appeal against Deputy Judge Whaley's judgment was dismissed by the Court of Appeal in an **ex tempore** judgment, without examination of the legal effect of a New Territories Form B mortgage.

上訴人提出上訴，以推翻高等法院暫委法官韋理義的判決。上訴法庭未經查明《新界條例》表格B按契文書的法律意義，便**即席**宣判。

b. *Ruud Klinsman vs. The Secretary for Security and another*
Case Number: HCAL000052_1999

The principles have come to be known as the Hardial Singh principles, though I do not suppose that Lord Woolf M.R. (as he now is) realised that his short **ex tempore** judgment in the Hardial Singh case would be remembered in the way it has been.

自此以後，該原則便通常叫作Hardial Singh原則。雖然我並不以為Lord Woolf M. R.（他現在是上訴法院保管案卷的大法官）意識到他在庭上就Hardial Singh案**即席**説出的簡短判詞使人一直作為常規般牢記。

使用百分比	ELDoS: 100.00%
	BLIS: 0.00%

fieri facias *n.*

36

/ˈfaɪərɪ ˈfeɪʃɪəs/

Latin that you cause to be made

【中譯】　香港法庭判詞 ELDoS:　一；香港法例 BLIS: **1** 扣押債務人
財產令；**2** 財物扣押令；**3** 扣押債務人動產令；其他 Others:
1 應辦事宜；**2** 債務人動產扣押令

> **Interpretations 釋義**
>
> A writ of execution directing a bailiff to levy on the goods and
> chattels of the judgment debtor.
>
> 指示執達主任扣押判定債務人貨品及實產的執行令狀。

Examples 例句

1. 扣押債務人財產令

a. *Section 21C(1), High Court Ordinance (Cap. 4)*

Subject to subsection (2), a writ of **fieri facias** or other writ of
execution against goods issued from the Court of First Instance shall
bind the property in the goods of the execution debtor as from the
time when the writ is delivered to the bailiff to be executed.

除第（2）款另有規定外，原訟法庭發出的**扣押債務人財產令**狀
或其他針對貨物的執行令狀，由交付執達主任執行之時開始，
即對執行債務人的貨物的產權具約束力。

b. *Order 46 rule 1, The Rules of the High Court (Cap. 4A)*

In this Order, unless the context otherwise requires, "writ of
execution"（執行令狀）includes a writ of **fieri facias**, a writ of

possession, a writ of delivery, a writ of sequestration and any further writ in aid of any of the aforementioned writs.

在本命令中，除文意另有所指外，（執行令狀）（writ of execution）包括**扣押債務人財產令狀**，管有令狀、交付令狀、暫時扣押令狀及任何為協助任何前述令狀的進一步令狀。

c. Order 47 rule 3(1), The Rules of the High Court (Cap. 4A)

Where only the payment of money, together with costs to be taxed, is adjudged or ordered, then, if when the money becomes payable under the judgment or order the costs have not been taxed, the party entitled to enforce that judgment or order may issue a writ of **fieri facias** to enforce payment of the sum (other than for costs) adjudged or ordered and, not less than 8 days after the issue of that writ, he may issue a second writ to enforce payment of the taxed costs.

凡只判決或命令須支付一筆款項及須予評定的訟費，而當該筆款項根據判決或命令到期須予支付時訟費仍未評定，則有權強制執行判決或命令的一方，可發出**扣押債務人財產令**狀以強制執行該筆經判決或命令的款項（訟費除外）的支付，並可在已發出令狀8天或之後，發出第二份令狀以強制執行經評定的訟費的支付。

d. Order 13 rule 8, The Rules of the High Court(Cap. 4A)

Where judgment for a debt or liquidated demand is entered under this Order against a defendant who has returned to the Registry an acknowledgment of service containing a statement to the effect that, although he does not intend to contest the proceedings, he intends to apply for a stay of execution of the judgment by writ of **fieri facias,** execution of the judgment by such a writ shall be stayed for a period of 14 days from the acknowledgment of service and, if within that time the defendant issues and serves on the plaintiff a summons for such a stay supported by an affidavit in accordance with Order 47, rule 1, the stay imposed by this rule shall continue until the summons is heard or otherwise disposed of, unless the Court after giving the parties an opportunity of being heard otherwise directs.

凡根據本命令登錄被告人敗訴須繳付一筆債項或經算定的索求款項的判決，而該被告人已向登記處交回送達認收書，其中載有一項陳述，表明被告人雖不擬就法律程序提出爭辯，卻擬申請擱置藉**扣押債務人財產**令狀而作的判決執行，則藉該令狀而作的判決執行須予擱置，為期14天，由認收送達時起計；如被告人在該段時限內根據第47號命令第1條規則，向原告人發出並送達由誓章支持的傳票以作出該項擱置，則除非法庭在給予有關各方獲聆聽的機會後另有指示，否則藉本條規則而施加的擱置須持續，直至該傳票已作聆訊或以其他方法處置為止。

使用百分比	ELDoS:	0.00%
	BLIS:	88.10%

2. 財物扣押令

Rule 86(2), Matrimonial Causes Rules (Cap. 179A)

Except with the leave of the registrar, no writ of **fieri facias** or warrant of execution shall be issued to enforce payment of any sum due under an order for ancillary relief or as order made under the provisions of section 8 of the Matrimonial Proceedings and Property Ordinance (Cap 192) where an application for a variation order is pending.

除獲司法常務官許可外，不得在要求作出更改令的申請待決期間發出**財物扣押令**或執行令，以就任何根據附屬濟助命令或根據《婚姻法律程序與財產條例》（第192章）第8條條文所作命令而應繳付的款項，強制執行付款責任。

使用百分比	ELDoS:	0.00%
	BLIS:	9.52%

3. 扣押債務人動產令

Annex, The Rules of the High Court (Cap. 4A)

Writ of **fieri facias**

扣押債務人動產令狀

使用百分比	ELDoS:	0.00%
	BLIS:	2.38%

forum *n. pl. forums*

37

/ˈfɔːrəm/

Latin

【中譯】　香港法庭判詞 ELDoS: **1** 訴訟地；香港法例 BLIS: **1** 訴訟地；
　　　　其他 Others: **1** 公堂；**2** 審裁場所；**3** 管轄法院；**4** 法庭；**5** 法
　　　　院；**6** 訴訟地方；**7** 管轄地

Interpretations 釋義

A court; a judicial tribunal; the place where judicial or administrative
remedy is sought; the country in which a case is heard

法庭；司法審裁的地方；提供司法或行政濟助的地方；案件
聆訊的國家

Examples 例句

1. 訴訟地

a. *Schedule Article 16, Recognition of Trusts Ordinance (Cap. 76)*

The Convention does not prevent the application of those provisions
of the law of the **forum** which must be applied even to international
situations, irrespective of rules of conflict of laws.

不論法律衝突規則有何規定，本公約不妨礙**訴訟地**連在國際情
況下也必須引用的法律條文的適用。

b. *Schedule Article 11(d), Recognition of Trusts Ordinance (Cap. 76)*

However, the rights and obligations of any third party holder of the
assets shall remain subject to the law determined by the choice of law
rules of the **forum**.

但該資產如有協力廠商持有人，則該持有人的權利和義務仍受
由**訴訟地**法律選擇規則所確定的法律所限制。

c. *Schedule Article 15, Recognition of Trusts Ordinance (Cap. 76)*

The Convention does not prevent the application of provisions of the
law designated by the conflicts rules of the **forum**, in so far as those
provisions cannot be derogated from by voluntary act, relating in
particular to the following matters ....

訴訟地的法律衝突規則指定的法律條文，尤其是與以下事項有
關的，只要該等條文不能被故意行為排除其適用，本公約不妨
礙該等條文的適用……。

d. *Hebei Import and Export Corporation vs. Polytek Engineering Company Limited*
Case Number: FACV000010_1998

Proceedings to set aside are governed by the law under which the
award was made or the law of the place where it was made, while
proceedings in the court of enforcement are governed by the law of
that **forum**.

將裁決作廢的法律程序受作出裁決所根據的法律管轄或受作出
裁決地方的法律管轄，而執行法院進行的法律程序則受**訴訟地**
的法律管轄。

e. *Hebei Import and Export Corporation vs. Polytek Engineering Company Limited*
Case Number: FACV000010_1998

No doubt, in many instances, the relevant public policy of the **forum**
coincides with the public policy of so many other countries that the
relevant public policy is accurately described as international public
policy.

毫無疑問，在很多個案中，**訴訟地**的公共政策與很多其他國家
的公共政策相符合，因而把有關公共政策描述為國際公共政策
並沒有不對。

f. *Hebei Import and Export Corporation vs. Polytek Engineering Company Limited*
Case Number: FACV000010_1998

It has been generally accepted that the expression "contrary to the public policy of that country" in Article V. 2 (b) means "contrary to the fundamental conceptions of morality and justice" of the **forum**.

已普遍接受的是《紐約公約》第 V 2（b）條內「違反該國公共
政策」一語意指「違反**訴訟地**的道德和公義的根本理念」。

使用百分比	ELDoS: 100.00%
	BLIS:　100.00%

functus officio *pl. functi officio*

/ˈfəŋktəs əˈfiʃiːəʊ/   /ˈfəŋktəs əˈfisiːəʊ/

Latin having performed his function

【中譯】 香港法庭判詞 ELDoS: **1** 履行職責；香港法例 BLIS: 一；其他 Others: **1** 權責已完；**2** 職分已完；**3** 職責已盡

Interpretations 釋義

Refers to an officer who has discharged his duty or has finished his task and therefore has no further authority to act. Also applied to an instrument that has fulfilled its purpose and therefore has spent it force and is of no further effect.

一位官員在履行其責任或完成工作之後，不再有許可權行事。同樣，文書的使用目的達到後，其效力則告喪失，不再具有任何效用。

Examples 例句

1. 履行職責

Francis CheunG and another vs. Insider Dealing Tribunal
Case Number: CACV000157_1999

He being **functus officio**, this is but a basic rule of evidence.

他是在**履行職責**，而且這不過是基本證據規則。

使用百分比	ELDoS: 100.00%
	BLIS: 0.00%

habeas corpus *n. pl. habeas corpora*

/ˌheɪbɪəs ˈkɔːpəs/ /ˌheɪbiæs ˈkɔːpəs/

Latin that you have the body

【中譯】 香港法庭判詞 ELDoS: **1** 人身保護令；**2** 人身保護令狀；香港法例 BLIS: **1** 人身保護令；**2** 解交被拘押者……令；其他 Others: 一

Interpretations 釋義

A writ of habeas corpus is one that orders a person detaining another to bring the detainee to court and explain why he has been held. The process is meant to test the legality of the detention. The court commands the release of the detainee if it is satisfied that the detention has been wrongful.

此令狀命令拘留他人的一方把被拘留者帶到法庭，並解釋對其作出拘留的原因，此舉是要驗證該項拘留是否合法。如果法庭認為是項拘留錯誤不當，則會指令釋放被拘留者。

Examples 例句

1. 人身保護令

a. Section 13D(1C), Immigration Ordinance (Cap. 115)

Where a judge has ordered the release of a person detained under this section in proceedings for **habeas corpus**, the Director may, with the consent of the person so released, require him to enter into a recognizance under section 36(1) as though he were being detained under section 32.

凡法官在申請**人身保護令**的法律程序中，已命令釋放根據本條被羈留的人，則處長可在該名如此獲得釋放的人的同意下，要求該人根據第36 (1)條作出擔保，猶如他是根據第32條正被羈留一樣。

b. Section 24, High Court Ordinance (Cap. 4)

An appeal shall lie as of right to the Court of Appeal from any decision of the Court of First Instance on an application for **habeas corpus,** whether the Court of First Instance orders the release of the person detained or refuses to make such an order.

向上訴法庭提出來自原訟法庭對一項**人身保護令**申請所作決定的上訴，乃屬當然權利，不論原訟法庭是命令釋放被羈留的人或是拒絕作出上述命令。

c. Section 12(4), Fugitive Offenders Ordinance (Cap. 503)

On an application for **habeas corpus** made in the case of a person in relation to whom an order of committal has been made, the Court of First Instance may receive additional evidence relevant to the exercise of its jurisdiction under section 5.

如已就某人作出拘押令，則當**人身保護令**的申請在該情況下提出後，原訟法庭即可收取關於行使其在第5條下的司法管轄權的其他證據。

d. N vs. O
Case Number: HCMP004204_1998

While, in the absence of oral evidence tested under cross-examination, it is not for me to make any findings of fact, I am constrained to say that I find it a little strange that the process servers in New York apparently had no difficulty in locating the mother in order to serve the **habeas corpus** papers.

由於案中並無人提供口述的證供（更無曾接受盤問以考驗其真
實性的口述證供），故此本席不能作出事實的裁斷。可是，本
席也得指出：奇怪的是派送紐約法庭文書的人員在尋找男童母
親以便送達**人身保護令**文件時，顯然沒有遇到任何困難。

e. *Francis Cheung and another vs. Insider Dealing Tribunal*
Case Number: CACV000157_1999

In ex p. Rahman, an illegal entrant from Bangladesh who claimed
to be the son of a British citizen sought leave to apply for judicial
review and a writ of **habeas corpus** against a removal order.

在ex p. Rahman一案中，一名來自孟加拉的非法入境者，聲稱
其父親為英國公民，並尋求許可申請司法覆核，以及針對遣送
離境令申請**人身保護令**。

f. *N vs. O*
Case Number: HCMP004204_1998

In addition to the New York **habeas corpus** proceedings, after the
departure of mother and child from Luxembourg, the father sought a
review of the earlier order of the Luxembourg courts giving interim
custody of the child to the mother.

在他們母子離開盧森堡後，男童的父親不但在紐約提起**人身保
護令**的法律程序，而且還在盧森堡要求法庭覆核較早時將暫時
管養權判給男童母親的命令。

g. *Section 2, High Court Ordinance (Cap. 4)*

"writ of **habeas corpus**" (人身保護令狀) means a writ of **habeas
corpus** ad subjiciendum

「**人身保護令狀**」（writ of habeas corpus）指**解交被拘押者**並說
明其拘押日期及原因令狀

h. Section 81(3), Evidence Ordinance (Cap. 8)

Such prisoner or person shall be brought under the same care and custody, and be dealt with in like manner in all respects, as a prisoner required by any writ of **habeas corpus** awarded by the Court of First Instance to be brought before the said court to be examined as a witness in any cause or matter depending before the said court is by law required to be dealt with.

該囚犯或該人所得到的照顧及看管,以及處置的方式,須在各方面與獲原訟法庭判給**人身保護令**而須被帶到該法院席前,在上述法院席前的未審決的任何訟案或事宜中以證人身分接受訊問的囚犯,依法律所得的照顧及看管以及須予處置的方式一樣。

使用百分比	ELDoS: 85.71%
	BLIS: 71.67%

2. 人身保護令狀

a. In the Matter of Yung Kwan Lee and others
Case Number: FACV000001_1999

This is a **habeas corpus** case which involves a constitutional challenge.

這是一宗關於**人身保護令狀**之案件,涉及對憲法的質疑。

b. In the Matter of Yung Kwan Lee and others
Case Number: FACV000001_1999

On 5 December 1997 **habeas corpus** proceedings were commenced on the appellants' behalf seeking their release.

1997年12月5日,為了上訴人等能獲得釋放,為他們提起了申請**人身保護令狀**的訴訟。

使用百分比	ELDoS: 14.29%
	BLIS: 0.00%

3. 解交被拘押者⋯⋯令

a. Section 2GC(4), Arbitration Ordinance (Cap.341)

The Court or a judge of the Court may also order a writ of **habeas corpus** ad testificandum to be issued requiring a prisoner to be taken for examination before an arbitral tribunal.

法院或法院法官亦可命令發出**解交被拘押者**到庭作證令狀，規定將某囚犯帶到仲裁庭席前接受訊問。

b. Order 54 rule 5, The Rules of the High Court (Cap. 4A)

Where a writ of **habeas corpus** ad subjiciendum is ordered to issue, the judge by whom the order is made shall give directions as to the judge before whom, and the date on which, the writ is returnable.

凡已命令發出**解交被拘押者**並說明其拘押日期及原因令狀，發出命令的法官，須就該令狀所須向其回報的法官及回報的日期作出指示。

使用百分比	ELDoS:	0.00%
	BLIS:	28.33%

in limine *adv.*

/ɪn ˈlɪmɪnɪ/

Latin on the threshold

【中譯】　香港法庭判詞 ELDoS: **1** 一開始；**2** 自一步起；香港法例
　　　　BLIS: 一；其他 Others: 一

> **Interpretations 釋義**
> At the beginning; preliminarily
> 開始時期；最初階段

Examples 例句

1.　一開始

*Guangdong Foodstuffs Import & Export (Group) Corporation
and another vs. Tung Fook Chinese Wine (1982) Co. Ltd. and
another*
Case Number: HCA007759_1995

Nevertheless, if the plaintiff cannot prove the association or
identification of the disputed mark or get-up in this country with
goods in fact of his manufacture, the action fails **in limine**.

總之，原訴人假如不能證明在這個國家引起爭議的該標記或裝
璜能識別其製造的貨物或與他的貨物有關聯，則一**開始**就會敗
訴。

使用百分比	ELDoS: 50.00%
	BLIS:　 0.00%

2. 自一步起

To Kan Chi and others vs. Pui Man Yau and others
Case Number: HCMP000562_1992

The Plaintiffs submitted that the 2nd Defendant would fail **in limine** (i.e. on the threshold or at the outset) if the 2nd Defendant could not establish all the terms of this trust.

原告人陳詞説如果第二被告無法證實該信託所包含的各項條款，第二被告**自一步起**（in limine）已註定失敗。

使用百分比	ELDoS: 50.00%
	BLIS: 0.00%

in personam *adj.*

/ɪn pɜːˈsəʊnæm/

Latin against a person

41

【中譯】 香港法庭判詞 ELDoS: **1** 對人；香港法例 BLIS: **1** 對人；其他 Others: **1** 對人；**2** 對人的；**3** 對人訴訟

Interpretations 釋義

An action instituted to enforce rights against an individual or a person.

指對人或個別人仕提出的訴訟

Examples 例句

1. 對人

a. *"Resource 1" and the Owners of the Ship or Vessel "Tian Sheng No.1" vs. the Owners of Cargo Lately Laden on Board the Ship or Vessel "Tian Sheng No.8"*
Case Number: FACV000006_2000

The point is that s.12B(4) goes not to the existence of jurisdiction at all, but to the exercise of jurisdiction, limiting the situations in which in rem actions may be brought, notwithstanding that the Court will be exercising jurisdiction in **in personam** actions when the in rem limits are exceeded.

本席想指出的是：第12B（4）條和司法管轄權存在與否的問題完全無關，它只是和行使司法管轄權的問題有關，它限制了可以提出對物訴訟的情況，儘管法庭在對物訴訟的限制被超逾的情況下可行使**對人**訴訟的司法管轄權。

b. *"Resource 1" and the Owners of the Ship or Vessel "Tian Sheng No.1" vs. the Owners of Cargo Lately Laden on Board the Ship or Vessel "Tian Sheng No.8"*
Case Number: FACV000006_2000

They said that the person who would be liable on the claim in an action **in personam** was the owner of the Ship when the bills of lading were issued because the bills of lading had been signed for and on behalf of the master of the Ship and therefore evidenced a contract between them as cargo owners and the shipowner.

他們指出在提單發出時身為船東的人須就**對人**訴訟中的申索負上法律責任，因為提單是為或代船的主人所簽署的，因此證明了他們（以貨主的身分）和船東之間的合約關係。

c. *Section 12B(5), High Court Ordinance (Cap. 4)*

In the case of a claim in the nature of towage or pilotage in respect of an aircraft, an action in rem may be brought in the Court of First Instance against that aircraft if, at the time when the action is brought, it is beneficially owned by the person who would be liable on the claim in an action **in personam**.

就性質屬於航空器的拖曳或領港的申索而言，如在提出對物訴訟時，有關航空器是由若該申索是在**對人**訴訟中提出則會負上法律責任的人所實益擁有的，則可在原訟法庭針對有關航空器提出對物訴訟。

d. *Section 12C(3), High Court Ordinance (Cap. 4)*

The Court of First Instance shall not entertain any action **in personam** to enforce a claim to which this section applies until any proceedings previously brought by the plaintiff in any court outside Hong Kong against the same defendant in respect of the same incident or series of incidents have been discontinued or otherwise come to an end.

在原告人先前在香港以外的任何法院就同一事件或同一系列事件針對同一被告人提出的任何法律程序已中止或以其他方式完結之前，原訟法庭不得受理任何用以強制執行本條適用的申索的**對人訴訟**。

使用百分比	ELDoS: 100.00%
	BLIS: 100.00%

in re *prep.*

/ɪn ˈriː/

Latin in the matter of

【中譯】 香港法庭判詞 ELDoS: —；香港法例 BLIS: —；其他 Others:
1 對於；**2** 關於某事項；**3** 案由

Interpretations 釋義

In the matter of; concerning; regarding

有關某事情；關於⋯

Examples 例句

1. In re

a. *To Kan Chi and others vs. Pui Man Yau and others*
Case Number: HCMP000562_1992

Mr Patrick Fung S.C. for the 2nd Defendant relied on two cases in order to support that the Attorney General should get her costs. They are : **In re** Macduff [1896] 2 Ch. 451 and **In re** Rymer [1894] 1 Ch. 19.

代表第二被告人之資深大律馮柏棟先生援引兩個判例作為律政司可獲訟費之理據 **In re** Macduff一案（1896）2 Ch. 451和**In re** Rymer一案（1894）1 Ch. 19。

b. *Leung Sai Lun Robert vs. Leung May Ling*
Case Number: FACV000005_1998

For many years Chinese people in Hong Kong had in fact been executing Wills and in **In re** Tse Lai-chiu (Supra) it was held that the section implicitly recognised the testamentary capacity of Chinese persons in accordance with English laws.

多年來，香港的華人其實一直有簽立遺囑；而在**In re** Tse Lai-Chiu（如上）一案中，法庭裁定該條法例隱含地承認華人根據英國法律有立遺囑的能力。

使用百分比	ELDoS: —
	BLIS: —

in rem *adj.*

/ɪn ˈrem/

Latin against a thing

【中譯】 香港法庭判詞 ELDoS: **1** 對物；香港法例 BLIS: **1** 對物；其他 Others: **1** 對物權；**2** 對物訴訟

Interpretations 釋義

Refers to an action instituted to enforce rights in an object or a property (the thing) "against the whole world" as distinct from one instituted to enforce rights against an individual person. A right or an action of this kind binds other people generally and everyone is obliged to respect it.

對物或財產行使的權利而提出的訴訟。這個對物的行使權並非只針對個別人士，而是針對所有人。訴訟雙方以外的人士均受此對物權或對物訴訟結果約束。因此每個人也須尊重物主的對物權。

Examples 例句

1. 對物

a. *Section 6(2), Foreign Judgments (Reciprocal Enforcement) Ordinance (Cap. 319)*

For the purposes of this section, the courts of the country of the original court shall, subject to the provisions of subsection (3), be deemed to have had jurisdiction – ...(b) in the case of a judgment given in an action of which the subject matter was immovable property or in an action **in rem** of which the subject matter was movable property, if the property in question was at the time of the proceedings in the original court situate in the country of that court ....

就本條而言，除第(3)款另有規定外，在以下情況下原訟法院
的國家的法院須當作具有司法管轄權——⋯⋯(b)判決是在一
宗訴訟中作出，訴訟的標的物是不動產，或在一宗**對物**的訴訟
中作出，訴訟的標的物是動產，而在法律程序於原訟法院進行
時，有關的財產是位於該法院的國家內⋯⋯。

b. Section 25(1), Crown Proceedings Ordinance (Cap. 300)

Nothing in this Ordinance shall authorize proceedings **in rem** in
respect of any claim against the Crown, or the arrest, detention or sale
of any ships or aircraft belonging to Her Majesty or the Government,
or of any cargo or other property belonging to the Crown, or give to
any person any lien on any such ship, aircraft, cargo or other property.

本條例並無授權就任何針對官方提出的申索進行**對物**法律程
序，或授權扣留、扣押或出售屬於女皇陛下或政府的船舶或航
空器或屬於官方的貨物或其他財產，或就該等船舶、航空器、
貨物或其他財產而給予任何人留置權。

c. Order 14 Rule 1(2), The Rules of the High Court (Cap. 4A)

Subject to paragraph (3) this rule applies to every action begun by
writ other than – ... (c) an Admiralty action **in rem**.

除第(3)款另有規定外，本條規則適用於每一宗藉令狀開展的
訴訟，但屬以下情況者除外——⋯⋯(c)海事**對物**訴訟。

d. Section 18(1), Merchant Shipping (Liability and Compensation For Oil Pollution) Ordinance (Cap. 414)

Where – (a) any oil is discharged or escapes from a ship but does not
cause any pollution damage in Hong Kong; or (b) any relevant threat
of contamination arises in Hong Kong but no preventive measures
are taken to prevent or minimize such threat, no action (whether **in
rem** or in personam) shall be brought in any court in Hong Kong to

enforce a claim arising from – (i) pollution damage resulting from such discharge or escape; or (ii) a relevant threat of contamination, in the area of a Liability Convention country other than Hong Kong.

凡——（a）任何油類從船舶排出或逸出，但沒有在香港造成污染損害；或（b）在香港發生有關的污染威脅，但沒有採取預防措施以防止該威脅或將該威脅減至最小，則任何人均不得在香港法院就——（i）該宗排放或逸漏在香港以外的另一公約地區的範圍內造成的污染損害；或（ii）在香港以外的另一公約地區的範圍內的有關的污染威脅，提起索償訴訟（不論是**對物**訴訟或對人訴訟）。

e. Section 6, Merchant Shipping (Collision Damage Liability and Salvage) Ordinance (Cap. 508)

Any enactment which confers on a court Admiralty jurisdiction in respect of damage or loss shall have effect as though references in that enactment to such damage or loss included references to damages for loss of life or personal injury, and accordingly proceedings in respect of such damages may be brought **in rem** or in personam.

任何就損害或損失授予任何法院海事司法管轄權的成文法則，須猶如該成文法則對該等損害或損失的提述已包括提述喪失生命或身體受傷方面的損害賠償般具有效力，而關於該等損害賠償的法律程序可據此而**對物**或對人提起。

f. Section 4(6), Limitation Ordinance (Cap. 347)

Subsection (1) shall apply to an action to recover seamen's wages, but save as aforesaid this section shall not apply to any cause of action within the Admiralty jurisdiction of the High Court which is enforceable **in rem**.

第（1）款適用於追討海員工資的訴訟，但除此之外，本條並不適用於在高等法院海事司法管轄權範圍以內，並可**對物**強制執行的訴訟因由。

g. Section 12B(3), High Court Ordinance (Cap. 4)

In any case in which there is a maritime lien or other charge on any ship, aircraft or other property for the amount claimed, an action **in rem** may be brought in the Court of First Instance against that ship, aircraft or property.

在任何案件中，如就所申索的款額而在任何船舶、航空器或其他財產上有海上留置權或其他押記，則可在原訟法庭針對該船舶、航空器或財產提出**對物**訴訟。

h. Direk Mahadumrongkul vs. Lau Chun Keung and others
Case Number: CACV000133_1998

Upon securing possession under O113, a possessor would then appear to acquire a right **in rem** to the detriment of the other persons who might also be in occupation of the land of which the right to possession is disputed.

根據第113號命令得到管有之後，管有人似乎取得了**對物**權，而佔用該牽涉管有權爭議的土地的人士，便會受這個對物權影響。

使用百分比	ELDoS: 100.00%
	BLIS: 100.00%

in specie *adv.*

/ˌɪn ˈspiːʃiːiː/

Latin in kind

【中譯】 香港法庭判詞 ELDoS: **1** 不折不扣地；香港法例 BLIS: **1** 實物形式；**2** 原樣；**3** 屬性不變；其他 Others: **1** 特定；**2** 同式樣；**3** 同形式；**4** 按照說明

Interpretations 釋義

Specifically; in the way specified; without any form of substitution

明確具體地、以指明的方式進行；在無其他取代的方法下進行

Examples 例句

1. 不折不扣地

To Kan Chi and others vs. Pui Man Yau and others
Case Number: HCMP000562_1992

Since the son sold the land after 13 years of the death of the father, this would give rise to a factual inference that after the lapse of time the estate of the father had been fully administered and the son was entitled to the land **in specie** by implied assent.

兒子在父親死後13年將該地賣出。這種情況，可作以下事實推斷：事隔多年父親的遺產已全部落實執行，亦預設兒子有權**不折不扣地**享有這塊土地。

使用百分比	ELDoS: 100.00%
	BLIS: 0.00%

2. 實物形式

a. Section 36, Estate Duty Ordinance (Cap. 111)

The following shall be treated as benefits accruing to the deceased from the company, that is to say – (a) any profits of the company, and any periodical payment out of the resources or at the expense of the company, which the deceased received for his own benefit whether directly or indirectly, and any enjoyment **in specie** of land or other property of the company or of a right thereover which the deceased had for his own benefit whether directly or indirectly....

以下各項須視為死者從公司所獲的應累算利益，即──（a）死者直接或間接為使其本身受益而收受的任何公司利潤，及從公司資源中付出或由公司負擔的任何按期付款，及死者為使其本身受益而直接或間接以**實物形式**享用該公司的土地或其他財產，或享用這方面的權利⋯⋯。

b. Schedule 2-1, (7), Estate Duty Ordinance (Cap. 111)

The amount to be taken into account in respect of a benefit consisting of any enjoyment **in specie** of land or buildings or land and buildings or other property of the company or of a right thereover shall be the value of the enjoyment thereof for the period during which the benefit subsisted, and that value shall be calculated in the case of leasehold property situate in Hong Kong by reference to the annual assessment as ascertained for the purposes of section 5 of the Inland Revenue Ordinance (Cap 112), and in the case of other land or buildings or land and buildings by such method as the Commissioner may consider just and reasonable.

有關某項由公司的土地或建築物、土地連建築物、或其他財產的**實物形式**享用所構成的利益，或由前述各項享用權的權利所構成的利益，須予計算在內的款額須為上述各項享用在上述利益存在期間的價值，而該價值，如屬位於香港的批租土地財產時，須按照為《稅務條例》（第112章）第5條的目的而確定的每

年評估值以作計算，如屬其他土地或建築物或土地連建築物的
情況時，以署長認為公正合理的方法計算。

使用百分比	ELDoS:	0.00%
	BLIS:	50.00%

3. 原樣

a. Schedule 1 PART 1-2(b), Solicitors (General) Costs Rules (Cap. 159G)

For the purpose of ascertaining the costs payable on assignments by a liquidator distributing **in specie** leasehold property or interests therein to a shareholder, the value, as assessed by the Collector of Stamp Revenue, of the leasehold property or interests therein assigned shall be taken as the consideration for the assignment.

為確定清盤人將批租土地財產或其中權益按**原樣**分發給任何股東的轉讓契所須支付的事務費，經印花稅署署長評估的已轉讓批租土地財產或其中權益的價值，須視為該項轉讓的代價。

b. Schedule 3(Y), Hong Kong and China Gas Company (Transfer of Incorporation) Ordinance (Cap. 1022)

To distribute any of the property of the Company among its creditors and Members **in specie** or kind.

將本公司的任何財產按其**原樣**或原物分發予本公司的債權人及成員。

c. Schedule 1 Part I-136, Companies Ordinance (Cap. 32)

If the company shall be wound up the liquidator may, with the sanction of a special resolution of the company and any other sanction required by the Ordinance, divide amongst the members **in specie** or kind the whole or any part of the assets of the company (whether they shall consist of property of the same kind or not) and may, for such purpose, set such value as he deems fair upon any property to be divided as aforesaid and may determine how such division shall be carried out as between the members or different classes of members.

如公司須予清盤，清盤人在獲得公司特別決議的認許及本條例所規定的任何其他認許下，可將公司的全部或任何部分資產（不論此等資產是否包含同一類財產）按其**原樣**或原物在成員之間作出分配，並可為此目的而對於按前述方法將予分配的財產訂出其認為公平的價值，以及決定如何在成員或在不同類別的成員之間進行分配。

| 使用百分比 | ELDoS: 0.00% |
| | BLIS: 37.50% |

4. 屬性不變

Section 56(5), Marine Insurance Ordinance (Cap. 329)

Where goods reach their destination **in specie**, but by reason of obliteration of marks, or otherwise, they are incapable of identification, the loss, if any, is partial, and not total.

凡貨品抵達目的地而**屬性不變**，但由於標記經塗掉或由於其他原因以致貨品無法識別，則損失（如有的話）屬於部分損失而非全損。

| 使用百分比 | ELDoS: 0.00% |
| | BLIS: 12.50% |

in toto　*adv.*

/ɪn ˈtəʊtəʊ/

Latin　wholly

【中譯】　香港法庭判詞 ELDoS: **1** 全部；香港法例 BLIS: —；其他
　　　　　Others: **1** 全然；**2** 完全

Interpretations 釋義

Completely; entirely; as a whole

完全地；全面地；總括來說

Examples 例句

1. 全部

Poon Hau Kei vs. Hsin Cheong Construction Co. Limited
Taylor Woodrow International Limited Joint Venture
Case Number: FACV000012A_1999

On its face, the offers in the two letters, if accepted, would have satisfied Mr Poon's claim **in toto**, as if he had won all the way in these interlocutory proceedings and had final judgment made in full in respect of his claim.

表面上，在該兩函件中的提議，若獲接納，應可了結Poon先生全部的申索，就像他在這些非正審法律程序都**全部**勝訴了，以及他的申索也全部獲得最終判決。

| 使用百分比 | ELDoS: 100.00% |
| | BLIS:　　0.00% |

inter alia *adv.*

46

/ˌɪntə ˈeɪliə/ /ˌɪntə ˈælɪə/
Latin among other things

【中譯】 香港法庭判詞 ELDoS: **1** 主要；**2** 其中；**3** 當中；**4** 其中主
要；**5** 尤其是；**6** 除其他事情外；香港法例 BLIS: **1** 除其他事
項外；**2** 下列事項；**3** 其中包括；**4** 其中包括下述各方面的情
況；**5** 其他事宜；**6** 包括；**7** 即是；**8** 在連同其他事宜的情況
下；**9** 除其他外；**10** 除其他形式外；**11** 除在其他方面作出規
定外；**12** 除為其他事宜外；其他 Others: **1** 除了其他；**2** 除了
別的以外；**3** 在其他事物中；**4** 特別是

Interpretations 釋義

Among other things
把其他因素或事項排除在外，只留意續述的一項或多項。

Examples 例句

1. 主要

Golden Harvest (Hk) Limited vs. Tsui Man Kwong
Case Number: Hca016220_1998

The 2nd Defendant's counterclaims for, **inter alia**, the sum of
$4,574,374.23. [sic]

第二被告人的反申索**主要**是一筆為數 4,574,374.23 港元的款
項。

使用百分比	ELDoS: 30.00%
	BLIS: 0.00%

2. 其中

a. *Liu Kin Leung vs. Tsang Mi Ling*
Case Number: Hcmp007660_1999

Before the parties signed the Agreement and on or about 21 December 1998, the Purchaser's solicitors had noticed from the land search records that the Property was subject to, **inter alia**, two encumbrances....

雙方簽署正式合約之前，約於1998年12月21日，買方律師在土地查冊紀錄中發現該物業乃受多項產權負擔所規限，**其中**兩項為……。

b. *Direk Mahadumrongkul vs. Lau Chun Keung and others*
Case Number: CACV000133_1998

By an assignment dated 24th May 1968, Madam Chan Yuen Wah assigned to the plaintiff, Mr. Direk Mahadumrongkul, one equal undivided half share of Lot A with exclusive rights to the ground floor and garden of the Front Block subject to, **inter alia**, the following....

藉着一份日期為1968年5月24日的轉讓契，陳婉華女士將A地段二分之一相等的不分割分數，連同前座的地下和花園的獨有權利，轉讓予原告人吳多福先生（DIREK MAHADUMRONGKUL），但須符合一些條件，而**其中**有以下的……。

使用百分比	ELDoS: 20.00%
	BLIS:　 0.00%

3. 當中

Leung Sai Lun Robert vs. Leung May Ling
Case Number: FACV000005_1998

In *China Pride*, Godfrey JA held that the court will uphold provisions for the forfeiture of a deposit, **inter alia**, where it is shown that the deposit did not exceed a conventional percentage of the purchase price even if it in no way represents a genuine pre-estimate of the vendor's loss , stating that while this is anomalous, it is the law: see *China Pride* [1994] 2 HKC at 358F.

在 *China Pride* 一案中，上訴法院大法官高奕暉裁定謂倘若證據顯示按金並無超逾樓價的常規百分比，那麼即使按金完全不代表抵償賣方損失的真正預計數額，法庭也會維持**當中**包括沒收按金的條文。高奕暉大法官謂雖然這樣做異於平常，但法律確是如此：見案例 *China Pride* [1994] 2 HKC 第 358 頁 F 行。

使用百分比	ELDoS: 20.00%
	BLIS:　　0.00%

4. 其中主要

Zhou Cui Hao vs. Ting Fung Yee
Case Number: HCA007558Y_1996

The statutory compensation payable in respect of the resumption of the said Property amounted, **inter alia**, to the sum of HK$597,000.00 together with interest thereon.

因「該物業」被收回而獲法定賠償，**其中主要**包括597,000港元及賠償額的利息。

使用百分比	ELDoS: 10.00%
	BLIS:　　0.00%

5. 尤其是

Leung Sai Lun Robert vs. Leung May Ling
Case Number: FACV000005_1998

Fourthly, there is the slew of Ordinances relating, **inter alia**, to customary marriage and its incidents which came into effect mostly on 7th October, 1971.

第四個困難是，有很多的條例，**尤其是**與舊式婚姻及其附帶權利義務有關的，於1971年10月7日生效。

使用百分比	ELDoS: 10.00%
	BLIS:　 0.00%

6. 除其他事情外

Novatel Communications (Far East) Limited vs. Canadian Imperial Bank of Commerce and another
Case Number: HCA008052_1999

On the memo, a handwritten note, possibly by Mr Leung, dated 15 April 1993, stated, **inter alia**, that "the B & H arrangement is now off and working on a different arrangement to coincide with the financial planning of Pudwill in relation to his NovAtel business."

該便箋內有一段可能是由梁先生在 1993年4月15日手寫的批註說明，**除其他事情外**，也說「該B & H安排現已告吹，並正另作安排以便與Pudwill先生的NovAtel業務所定財務計劃一致。」

使用百分比	ELDoS: 10.00%
	BLIS:　 0.00%

7. 除其他事項外

Schedule Article 18-2, Fugitive Offenders (Torture) Order (Cap. 503I)

The Committee shall establish its own rules of procedure, but these rules shall provide, **inter alia**, that: (a) Six members shall constitute a quorum; (b) Decisions of the Committee shall be made by a majority vote of the members present.

委員會應制定自己的議事規則，但這些規則**除其他事項外**應規定（a）六位成員為法定人數；（b）委員會的決定以出席成員的過半數票作出。

使用百分比	ELDoS:	0.00%
	BLIS:	15.38%

8. 下列事項

Schedule 1 Article 19, Fugitive Offenders (Internationally Protected Persons and Hostages) Order (Cap. 503H)

The Secretary-General of the United Nations shall inform all States, **inter alia**: (a) of signatures to this Convention, of the deposit of instruments of ratification or accession in accordance with articles 14, 15 and 16 and of notifications made under article 18; (b) of the date on which this Convention will enter into force in accordance with article 17.

聯合國秘書長尤應將**下列事項**通知所有國家：（a）依照第十四條對本公約的簽署，依照第十五條和第十六條交存批准書或加入書，以及依照第十八條所作的通知；（b）依照第十七條本公約發生效力的日期。

使用百分比	ELDoS:	0.00%
	BLIS:	7.69%

9. 其中包括

Rule 5D, Solicitors' Practice Rules (Cap. 159H)

Where a firm acts for a client in relation to that client's criminal litigation the solicitor in charge of that matter shall take the following steps – ...(e) as soon as practicable, and in any event both before the relevant hearing and not more than 7 days after counsel has been instructed, the firm shall deliver a backsheet or other written instruction to counsel on which shall be endorsed (**inter alia**) – (i) the name and personal signature of the solicitor in charge of the matter; (ii) the name of the firm; (iii) the name of the case (and the court number if known at the time); (iv) the name of counsel; and (v) the agreed fee and any agreed refreshers....

凡任何律師行就某當事人的刑事訴訟而代該當事人行事，則負責該事件的律師須採取以下步驟——……（e）律師行須在切實可行範圍內儘快，並在任何情況下於有關聆訊前以及在大律師獲得聘用後不超過7天，向大律師交付一份背頁或其他書面指示，並須在其上批註（**其中包括**）以下資料——（i）負責該事宜的律師的姓名及他的個人簽名；（ii）律師行的名稱；（iii）案件的名稱（如當時已得悉法庭編號，則連同法庭編號）；（iv）大律師的姓名；及（v）已協定的費用及任何已協定的額外聘用費……。

使用百分比	ELDoS:	0.00%
	BLIS:	7.69%

10. 其中包括下述各方面的情況

Section 17(2), Land Survey (Disciplinary Procedure) Regulation (Cap. 473B)

The Disciplinary Board shall decide the disciplinary action to be taken against the defendant having regard, **inter alia**, to – (a) any decision on disciplinary action previously made in respect of the defendant; (b) the address of the defendant and the evidence adduced under subsection (1)(b); and (c) any other information it considers relevant.

紀律審裁委員會須在顧及**其中包括下述各方面的情況**後，決定對被告人作出的紀律制裁——（a）過往就被告人作出的任何紀律制裁決定；（b）根據第（1）（b）款作出的被告人發言及所援引的證據；及（c）紀律審裁委員會認為屬有關的任何其他資料。

| 使用百分比 | ELDoS: | 0.00% |
| | BLIS: | 7.69% |

11. 其他事宜

Section 2(1), Mizuho Corporate Bank, Ltd. (Hong Kong Consolidation) Ordinance (Cap. 1169)

consolidation agreement （合併協議） means the consolidation agreement dated 22 December 1999, governed by the laws of Japan and entered into by DKB, Corporate Business Bank and IBJ in relation, **inter alia**, to the reorganization and consolidation of the businesses carried on by DKB, Corporate Business Bank and IBJ according to customer segments and business functions (as amended or supplemented from time to time, including by implementing documents and agreements from time to time entered into)

「合併協議」（consolidation agreement）指第一勸業、實業商務銀行與日本興業於1999年12月22日簽訂、由日本法律管轄的合併協定（經不時的修訂或補充，包括實施文件及不時簽訂的協定），該合併協定是就第一勸業、實業商務銀行及日本興業經營的業務根據客戶組成和營業功能進行的重組和合併及**其他事宜**而簽訂的

| 使用百分比 | ELDoS: | 0.00% |
| | BLIS: | 7.69% |

12. 包括

Section 4(3), Insurance Companies (Determination of Long Term Liabilities) Regulation (Cap. 41E)

Without prejudice to the generality of subsections (1) and (2), the amount of the long term liabilities shall be determined in compliance with each of sections 5 to 16 and shall take into account, **inter alia**, the following factors – (a) all guaranteed benefits, including guaranteed surrender values; (b) vested, declared or allotted bonuses to which policy holders are already either collectively or individually contractually entitled; (c) all options available to the policy holder under the terms of the contract; and (d) expenses, including commissions.

在不損害第（1）及（2）款的概括性的原則下，長期負債額須遵從第5至16條每條的規定而厘定，並須顧及**包括**以下各項在內的因素——（a）所有保證利益，包括保證退保現金價值；（b）保單持有人根據合約已集體或個別地有權得到的既得的、已宣佈的或已分派的紅利；（c）保單持有人根據合約條款而可行使的所有選擇權；及（d）開支，包括佣金。

| 使用百分比 | ELDoS: | 0.00% |
| | BLIS: | 7.69% |

13. 即是

Section 2(1), Mizuho Corporate Bank, Ltd. (Hong Kong Consolidation) Ordinance (Cap. 1169)

appointed day （指定日期） means such day as may be appointed and notified pursuant to section 3, being the day on which, **inter alia**, the merger of IBJ into Corporate Business Bank and the change in the name of Corporate Business Bank to Mizuho Corporate Bank, Ltd. are to be effected under the laws of Japan pursuant to the consolidation agreement

「指定日期」（appointed day）指依據第3條指定及公佈的日期，**即是**依據合併協議在日本法律下日本興業合併入實業商務銀行及實業商務銀行更改名稱為 Mizuho Corporate Bank, Ltd. 生效的一天

使用百分比	ELDoS:	0.00%
	BLIS:	7.69%

14. 在連同其他事宜的情況下

Section 14(3), Hong Kong Reunification Ordinance (Cap. 2601)

Subsection (1) shall not be construed as affecting – (a) any power which is for the time being conferred (either exclusively or **inter alia**) by or under the law of a country or territory outside Hong Kong on notaries outside the jurisdiction of that country or territory....

第（1）款不得解釋為影響——（a）在當其時由香港以外的某國家或地區的法律或根據該等法律賦予（單獨或**在連同其他事宜的情況下**）在該國家或地區的司法管轄區以外的公證人的任何權力⋯⋯。

使用百分比	ELDoS:	0.00%
	BLIS:	7.69%

15. 除其他外

Schedule Article 14 – 4, Fugitive Offenders (Drugs) Order (Cap. 503J)

The Parties shall adopt appropriate measures aimed at eliminating or reducing illicit demand for narcotic drugs and psychotropic substances, with a view to reducing human suffering and eliminating financial incentives for illicit traffic. These measures may be based, **inter alia**, on the recommendations of the United Nations, specialized agencies of the United Nations such as the World Health

Organization, and other competent international organizations, and on the Comprehensive Multidisciplinary Outline adopted by the International Conference on Drug Abuse and Illicit Trafficking, held in 1987, as it pertains to governmental and non-governmental agencies and private efforts in the fields of prevention, treatment and rehabilitation. The Parties may enter into bilateral or multilateral agreements or arrangements aimed at eliminating or reducing illicit demand for narcotic drugs and psychotropic substances.

締約國應採取適當措施，消除或減少對麻醉藥品和精神藥物的非法需求，以減輕個人痛苦並消除非法販運的經濟刺激因素。**除其他外**，這些措施可參照聯合國、世界衛生組織等聯合國專門機構及其他主管國際組織的建議，以及1987年麻醉品濫用和非法販運問題國際會議通過的《綜合性多學科綱要》，該綱要涉及政府和非政府機構及個人在預防、治療和康復領域應作出的努力。締約國可達成旨在消除或減少對麻醉藥品和精神藥物的非法需求的雙邊或多邊協定或安排。

使用百分比	ELDoS:	0.00%
	BLIS:	7.69%

16. 除其他形式外

Schedule Article 14-3.(a), Fugitive Offenders (Drugs) Order (Cap. 503J)

The Parties may co-operate to increase the effectiveness of eradication efforts. Such co-operation may, **inter alia**, include support, when appropriate, for integrated rural development leading to economically viable alternatives to illicit cultivation. Factors such as access to markets, the availability of resources and prevailing socio-economic conditions should be taken into account before such rural development programmes are implemented. The Parties may agree on any other appropriate measures of co-operation.

縮約國可相互合作，以增強根除活動的有效性。這種合作**除其他形式外**，可酌情包括支援農村綜合發展，以便採用經濟上可行的辦法取代非法種植。在實施這種農村發展方案前，應考慮到諸如進入市場、資源供應和現有的社會經濟條件等因素。締約國可商定任何其他適當的合作措施。

使用百分比	ELDoS:	0.00%
	BLIS:	7.69%

17. 除在其他方面作出規定外

Preamble, Chinese Permanent Cemeteries Ordinance (Cap. 1112)

WHEREAS – ...(c) the said rules and regulations provided, **inter alia**, that the former Board should be composed of not less than 12 nor more than 20 members of whom the Director of Public Works, the Secretary for Chinese Affairs (then styled Registrar General) and the Director of Urban Services (then styled the Head of the Sanitary Department) were ex officio members and the remaining members were to be selected from and elected by those who subscribed as mentioned in paragraph (b) and were, subject to certain exceptions, to hold office for life....

鑒於——……（c）上述的規則及規例，**除在其他方面作出規定外**，亦規定前度委員會須由不少於12名但不多於20名的委員組成，其中工務司、撫華道（當時亦稱為撫華道）及市政事務署署長（當時稱為清淨局總辦）為當然委員，其餘的委員則從曾作（b）段所述的捐款的人當中挑選和選出，並且除在某些例外情況下，可終身擔任委員……。

使用百分比	ELDoS:	0.00%
	BLIS:	7.69%

18. 除為其他事宜外

Long title, Hong Kong Reunification Ordinance (Cap. 2601)

The Preparatory Committee for the Hong Kong Special Administrative Region of the People's Republic of China, exercising powers delegated to it by the National People's Congress of the People's Republic of China, established the Provisional Legislative Council of the Hong Kong Special Administrative Region by resolution passed on 24 March 1996, **inter alia**, for the purpose of considering and passing legislation particularly in anticipation of the reunification and during the transition period immediately before and immediately after that event and for the proper administration of the Hong Kong Special Administrative Region including the confirmation of anticipatory acts done prior to 1 July 1997

中華人民共和國香港特別行政區籌備委員會行使中華人民共和國全國人民代表大會所授予的權力，藉在1996年3月24日通過的決議，**除為其他事宜外**，亦特別為因應香港回歸而在緊接回歸前後的過渡期審議及通過法例，以及為香港特別行政區的有效管治，包括確認在1997年7月1日之前在預期回歸下作出的作為，而設立香港特別行政區臨時立法會

使用百分比	ELDoS:	0.00%
	BLIS:	7.69%

inter partes *adv.*

47

/ˈɪntə ˈpɑːtiːz/

Latin between the parties

【中譯】 香港法庭判詞 ELDoS: 一；香港法例 BLIS: **1** 在各方之間；
2 各方之間的；**3** 在各方之間的；**4** 各方之間；**5** 各方；其他
Others: **1** 訴訟各方；**2** 訴訟多方之間的；**3** 當事人之間

Interpretations 釋義

Between or among the parties
當事人之間；訴訟多方之間

Examples 例句

1. 在各方之間

    a. Order 59 rule 14(1A), The Rules of the High Court (Cap. 4A)

In support of any application (whether made ex parte or **inter partes**) the applicant shall lodge with the Registrar such documents as the Court of Appeal or a single judge may direct, and rule 9(3) and (4) shall apply, with any necessary modifications, to applications as they apply to appeals.

為支持任何申請（不論是單方面或是**在各方之間**提出），申請人須將上訴法庭或單一名法官所指示的文件遞交司法常務官；而第9（3）及（4）條規則在加以任何必要的變通後，即適用於申請，一如其適用於上訴。

b. Section 69(2), Registered Designs Rules (Cap. 522A)

In **inter partes** proceedings – (a) any party who wishes to be heard shall give notice in writing to the Registrar; (b) any party who intends to refer at the hearing to any document (other than a report of a decision of any court or of the Registrar) not already mentioned in the proceedings shall, unless the Registrar consents and the other parties agree, give at least 14 days' notice of his intention to do so and shall include with the notice details of, or a copy of, the document concerned.

在各方之間進行的法律程序中──（a）要求陳詞的任何一方，須向處長發出書面通知；（b）如任何一方擬在聆訊時提述任何在該等法律程序中不曾提述的文件（任何法院或處長的決定的報告除外），則除非處長同意且另一方同意，否則該方須就其擬如此做一事發出最少為期14天的通知，並須在該通知內包括有關文件的詳情或文本。

c. Section 82A(1), Bankruptcy Rules (Cap. 6A)

An application by the Official Receiver under section 19 of the Ordinance for the public examination of a bankrupt shall be made **inter partes** and the evidence in support of the application may be in the form of a report to the court setting out the reasons why such an examination is needed.

由破產管理署署長根據本條例第19條提出對破產人進行公開訊問的申請，須是**在各方之間**提出的申請，而支持該申請的證據可採用向法院作出報告的形式，列出為何需要作出該項訊問的理由。

d. Section 128B(2), Bankruptcy Rules (Cap. 6A)

The trustee's application under this rule shall be made **inter partes**.

受託人根據本條提出的申請，須是**在各方之間**提出的申請。

使用百分比	ELDoS:	0.00%
	BLIS:	33.33%

2. 各方之間的

a. *Section 89(3), Interpretation and General Clauses Ordinance (Cap. 1)*

Unless a judge otherwise directs, proceedings **inter partes** under this Part shall be held in open court.

除非法官另有指示，否則根據本部進行的**各方之間的**法律程序，均須在公開法庭進行。

b. *Clause 3, Schedule 3, Police Force Ordinance (Cap. 232)*

A magistrate, on receiving the application, may – ...(b) order that an **inter partes** hearing shall be conducted in private for the purposes of determining whether the approval should be given or not if he considers that it is necessary in the interest of justice to do so; or...

3. 裁判官在接獲申請後——⋯⋯（b）如認為為公正起見，有需要為裁定應否批予該項核准而以非公開形式進行**各方之間的**聆訊，他可下令以該形式進行上述聆訊；或⋯⋯

c. *Section 87(5), Interpretation and General Clauses Ordinance (Cap. 1)*

An application for an order under subsection (1) shall be made **inter partes**.

第（1）款下的命令的申請須屬**各方之間的**申請。

使用百分比	ELDoS:	0.00%
	BLIS:	25.93%

3. 在各方之間的

a. *Order 59 rule 14(2B), The Rules of the High Court (Cap. 4A)*

If an application under paragraph (2) is granted otherwise than after a hearing **inter partes**, notice of the order shall be served on the party or parties affected by the appeal and any such party shall be entitled, within 7 days after service of the notice, to apply to have the grant of leave reconsidered inter partes in open court.

如根據第（2）款提出的申請獲准，但不是**在各方之間的**聆訊後獲准的，關於有關命令的通知書須送達受上訴影響的一方或各方，而任何上述各方均有權在通知書送達後7天內，申請在公開法庭上在各方之間對該批予的許可重新考慮。

b. *Section 82(4), Patents (General) Rules (Cap. 514C)*

In **inter partes** proceedings, any party who intends to refer at the hearing to any document not already mentioned in the proceedings shall, unless the Registrar consents and the other party agrees, give at least 10 days notice of his intention with details of, or a copy of, the document to the Registrar and the other party.

在各方之間的法律程序中，除非處長同意而另一方亦贊成，否則任何一方如擬在聆訊中提述任何未曾在該法律程序中述及的文件，須將擬作該項提述的意向，向處長及另一方給予至少10天通知，通知並須連同該文件的細節或副本。

c. *Section 21(1), United Nations (Anti-Terrorism Measures) Ordinance (Cap. 575)*

Subject to subsection (2), proceedings **inter partes** in respect of applications mentioned in section 20(1)(a) shall be held in open court unless the court otherwise orders, upon application made by any party to the proceedings, that all or part of the proceedings shall be held in chambers or in camera.

在不抵觸第（2）款的條文下，除非法庭應就第20（1）（a）條所述的申請而進行的**在各方之間的**法律程序的任何一方的申請命令該等法律程序的全部或部分須在內庭或以非公開形式進行，否則該等法律程序須在公開法庭進行。

使用百分比	ELDoS:	0.00%
	BLIS:	18.52%

4. 各方之間

a. Section 2(6), United Nations (Anti-Terrorism Measures) Ordinance (Cap. 575)

Without prejudice to the powers of the Court of First Instance under the Rules of the High Court (Cap 4 sub. leg.), the Court of First Instance may of its own motion or on application order that any person who may be affected by an application – (a) under section 5 in the case of an application under section 5(1) made **inter partes**; or(b) under section 13, 17 or 18, be joined as a party to the proceedings.

（6）在不損害原訟法庭在《高等法院規則》（第4章，附屬法例）下的權力的原則下，原訟法庭可主動或應申請，命令——（a）任何受第5條所指的申請（如屬在**各方之間**提出的第5（1）條所指的申請）所影響的人；或（b）任何受第13、17或18條所指的申請所影響的人，加入成為有關法律程序的一方。

b. Schedule Item 7, Lands Tribunal (Fees) Rules (Cap. 17B)

Interlocutory application ex parte or **inter partes**

單方面或**各方之間**提出非正審申請

c. Section 18A(3A), Legal Aid Ordinance (Cap. 91)

Where the property recovered or preserved is land or an interest in land, a charge under subsection (1) shall vest in the Director who may register the charge under the Land Registration Ordinance (Cap 128) and may enforce the charge in any manner which would be available to a chargee in respect of a charge given **inter partes**.

凡所收回或保留的財產是土地或土地權益，第（1）款所指的押記須歸屬署長，署長可根據《土地註冊條例》（第128章）將有關押記註冊，並可使用任何可就**各方之間**作出的押記而由承押記人使用的方式強制執行該押記。

| 使用百分比 | ELDoS: | 0.00% |
| | BLIS: | 14.81% |

5. 各方

a. Rule 7(3), District Councils (Election Petition) Rules (Cap. 547C)

Subject to subrule (4), all applications under subrule (1) shall be made by **inter partes** summons, the return day of which shall be not later than 5 days after the lodgement of the election petition or the expiry of such other period as the Court may direct for giving security under section 54(1) of the Ordinance.

除第（4）款另有規定外，所有根據第（1）款提出的申請，須採用**各方**傳票提出，而該傳票的回報日須在提交選舉呈請書後5天內或原訟法庭就根據本條例第54（1）條提供保證金而指示的其他限期內。

b. Rule 7(3), Legislative Council (Election Petition) Rules (Cap. 542F)

Subject to subrule (4), all applications under subrule (1) shall be made by **inter partes** summons, the return day of which shall be not later than 5 days after the lodgement of the petition or the expiry of such other period as the Court may direct for giving security under section 66(1) of the Ordinance.

除第（4）款另有規定外，所有根據第（1）款提出的申請，須藉提交**各方**傳票而提出，而該傳票的回報日須在提交呈請書後5天內或原訟法庭就根據本條例第66（1）條提供保證金而指示的其他限期內。

使用百分比	ELDoS:	0.00%
	BLIS:	7.41%

inter se *adv.*

/ˌɪntə ˈseɪ/ /ˌɪntə ˈsiː/

Latin among themselves

【中譯】 香港法庭判詞 ELDoS: **1** 他們自己之間；**2** 彼此之間；香港法
例 BLIS: **1** 相互之間的；**2** 他們之間的；**3** 各人之間的；其他
Others: **1** 在們之間；**2** 在一組成員之間

Interpretations 釋義

Among or between themselves

他們之間

Examples 例句

1. 他們自己之間

Sky Heart Limited vs. Lee Hysan Estate Company Limited

Case Number: FACV000009_1998

She found as a fact that the covenants affecting each of the
subsections of Section Q were intended to be enforceable by the
owners of the respective properties **inter se**, as the covenants
gave effect to a building scheme devised by the plaintiff for the 16
interlocking dwelling houses covering the whole of Section Q.

法官就案件事實作出裁斷——由於契諾使原告人在整個Q段築
起16幢相連樓房的建屋計劃得以實現，故此裁斷該等影響遍及
Q段每一分段的契諾的用意，是使之可在各物業擁有人**他們自
己之間**強制執行。

使用百分比	ELDoS:	50.00%
	BLIS:	0.00%

2. 彼此之間

Sky Heart Limited vs. Lee Hysan Estate Company Limited
Case Number: FACV000009_1998

If the assignees are to have rights and obligations inter se with regard to the covenants, transcending the ordinary common law rules precluding the parties from suing in these circumstances, it must be because, first of all, there was a common intention that it should be so, and the circumstances are such that an equity arises which enables the assignees to enforce the covenants **inter se**.

故此，各承讓人欲在他們自己之間主張契諾下的權利和義務，便須超越一般普通法（即在此情況下，契諾各方不得興訟）的規則。也就是說，首先，各承讓人要有共同的意向，認為應該如此。其次，須具備可獲衡平法權利（即有權獲得衡平法濟助）的情節，使各承讓人得藉着衡平法權利在**彼此**之間強制執行契諾。

使用百分比	ELDoS: 50.00%
	BLIS: 0.00%

3. 相互之間的

a. *Section 73(1)(a), Legal Practitioners Ordinance (Cap. 159)*

The Council may make rules – (a) providing for – ...(iii) for the purpose of harmonizing the relationship of solicitors **inter se** and, with the prior approval of the Bar Council, governing the relationship of solicitors and barristers...

理事會可訂立規則──（a）規定──……（iii）為了協調律師**相互之間的**關係，在獲得執委會的事先批准後，對律師與大律師之間的關係予以管限……

b. *Section 72AA, Legal Practitioners Ordinance (Cap. 159)*

Subject to the prior approval of the Chief Justice, the Bar Council may make rules – ...(b) for the purpose of harmonizing the relationship of barristers **inter se** and, with the prior approval of the Council, governing the relationship of solicitors and barristers…

在獲得終審法院首席法官的事先批准下，執委會可就以下事宜訂立規則——……（b）協調大律師**相互之間的**關係，在獲得理事會的事先批准下，執委會並可為管限律師與大律師之間的關係而訂立規則……

使用百分比	ELDoS: 0.00%
	BLIS: 50.00%

4. 他們之間的

Section 4(1), Cremation and Gardens of Remembrance Regulation (Cap. 132M)

Application for a permit to cremate any human remains may be made in Form 1 in the First Schedule to the Director of Health by any of the following persons taking priority **inter se** in the order set out in this section…

下述任何人均可按本條所列**他們之間的**優先次序，以附表1的表格1向衛生署署長申請將遺骸火化的許可證……

使用百分比	ELDoS: 0.00%
	BLIS: 25.00%

5. 各人之間的

Section 4(3), Stamp Duty Ordinance (Cap. 117)

If any instrument chargeable with stamp duty is not duly stamped, the person or persons respectively specified in section 13(10), 19 or 20 or the First Schedule as being liable for stamping such instrument, and any person who uses such instrument, shall be liable, or jointly and severally liable, as the case may be, civilly to the Collector for the payment of the stamp duty and any penalty payable under section 9, and may be proceeded against without reference to any civil liability of such person **inter se** for the payment thereof.

如任何可予徵收印花稅的文書並無加蓋適當印花,則第13(10)、19或20條或附表1所分別指明須就有關文書負法律責任加蓋印花的人,以及任何使用該文書的人,均須在民事上負法律責任或在民事上共同及個別負法律責任(視屬何情況而定)向署長繳付有關印花稅以及根據第9條須繳付的罰款,而不論上述**各人之間的**繳付印花稅及罰款的民事法律責任為何,各人均可被起訴。

| 使用百分比 | ELDoS: | 0.00% |
| | BLIS: | 25.00% |

inter vivos *adv.*

49

/ˌɪntə ˈvaɪvəʊs/   /ˌɪntə ˈviːvəʊs/

Latin between the living

【中譯】 香港法庭判詞 ELDoS: **1** 生前；香港法例 BLIS: **1** 生前；**2** 生者之間的；**3** 生者之間；**4** 在世時；其他 Others: 一

Interpretations 釋義

From one living person to another.

在生人士之間進行的。

Examples 例句

1. 生前

a. Lau Leung Chau and others vs. Lau Yuk Kui and others
Case Number: FACV000015_1999

Thus by the very nature of ancestral worship trusts, the only kind of disposition that can create an ancestral worship trust is an **inter vivos** disposition.

換言之，按照祭祖信託的本義，只有在**生前**處置財產才可設立祭祖信託。

b. Section 10(2), Intestates' Estates Ordinance (Cap. 73)

Trusts declared by reference to any Statutes of Distribution in an instrument **inter vivos** made, or in a will coming into operation, before the commencement of this Ordinance shall, unless the contrary thereby appears, be construed as referring to the law relating to the distribution of effects of intestates which was in force immediately before the commencement of this Ordinance.

凡宣佈設立任何信託，如是參照在本條例生效日期前由死者於
生前訂立的文書內所述的遺產分配法規，或是參照在本條例生
效日期前開始實施的遺囑內所述的遺產分配法規，則除非該文
書或遺囑內出現相反情況，否則須解釋為參照在緊接本條例生
效日期前已實施的關於無遺囑者物件分配事宜的法律。

使用百分比	ELDoS: 100.00%
	BLIS: 2.94%

2. 生者之間的

a. Section 27(1), Stamp Duty Ordinance (Cap. 117)

Any conveyance of immovable property operating as a voluntary disposition **inter vivos** shall be chargeable with stamp duty as a conveyance on sale, with the substitution of the value of the property conveyed for the amount or value of the consideration for the sale.

任何不動產的轉易契，如其作用是作出**生者之間的**無償產權處
置者，則須作為售賣轉易契而予以徵收印花稅，但售賣代價的
款額或價值須由被轉易的不動產的價值代替。

b. Section 9(1), Estate Duty Ordinance (Cap. 111)

Where any shares in or debentures of a company are comprised in a gift **inter vivos** and the donee is, as the holder of those shares or debentures, issued with shares in or debentures of the same or any other company, or granted any right to acquire any such shares or debentures, then, unless the issue or grant is made by way of exchange for the first mentioned shares or debentures, the shares or debentures so issued, or the right granted, shall be treated for the purposes of this Ordinance as having been comprised in the gift in addition to any other property so comprised.

如**生者之間的**贈予包含某公司的股份或債權證，而受贈人作為
該等股份或債權證的持有人，獲發給同一公司或任何其他公司
的股份或債權證，或獲授予取得任何該等股份或債權證的任何

權利，在此情況下，除非上述的發給或授予是以首述的股份或
債權證作為交換的，否則如此發給的股份或債權證或授予的權
利，就本條例而言，須視為包含在該項贈予內並與任何其他財
產一起包含在內。

c. Section 6(7), Estate Duty Ordinance (Cap. 111)

Notwithstanding paragraphs (b), (c) and (h) of subsection (1) and
notwithstanding subsection (4), property passing on the death of
the deceased shall not be deemed to include property the subject of
any surrender, assurance, divesting, disposition, forfeiture, disposal,
donatio mortis causa, gift **inter vivos** or determination of an interest
made, effected or suffered to or for the benefit in Hong Kong of
any charitable institution or trust of a public character, or to the
Government, for charitable purposes.

即使第(1)款(b)、(c)及(h)段及第(4)款另有規定，凡對
財產作出、實行或容受作出放棄、轉易、脫除、處置、沒收、
處理、臨終贈予、**生者之間的**贈予，或作出、實行或容受某項
權益的終結，將財產給予香港任何慈善機構或公眾性質的信託
或使其受益，或為慈善的目的而給予政府的，則作為標的物的
該等財產，不須當作為包括在死者去世時轉移的財產內。

d. Section 29G(2), Stamp Duty Ordinance (Cap. 117)

In subsection (1) a reference to the amount or value of the
consideration shall be construed in relation to stamp duty chargeable
on a chargeable agreement for sale operating as a voluntary
agreement **inter vivos** as a reference to the value of the immovable
property subject to the agreement.

在第(1)款中，凡提述代價款額或價值之處，如該份可予徵收
印花稅的買賣協議的作用是作為**生者之間的**無償協議，則就該
份買賣協議可予徵收的印花稅而言，須解釋作提述受該份協議
規限的不動產的價值。

e. Section 44(5), Estate Duty Ordinance (Cap. 111)

…Provided that, in the case of shares or debentures falling to be valued on the death by virtue of a gift **inter vivos** made by the deceased, or by virtue of a disposition or determination, in relation to which subsection (1)(h) and subsection (2) of section 6 have effect, of an interest limited to cease on the death, the above conditions shall not apply….

……但如股份或債權證屬須在死者去世時予以估值,而該項估值是憑藉死者所作**生者之間的**贈予而須作出的,或是憑藉就一項限定於死者去世時終止的權益所作出的產權處置或終結(而對此第6條第(1)(h)款及(2)款具有效力)而須作出的,則以上各條件均不適用……。

使用百分比	ELDoS:	0.00%
	BLIS:	70.59%

3. 生者之間

a. Section 2, Legitimacy Ordinance (Cap. 184)

In this Ordinance, … "disposition" (產權處置) means an assurance of any interest in property by any instrument whether **inter vivos** or by will.

在本條例中,……「產權處置」(disposition)指藉任何文書,在**生者之間**或以遺囑作出的對財產上任何權益的轉易。

b. Section 15, Perpetuities and Accumulations Ordinance (Cap. 257)

Where a disposition **inter vivos** would fall to be treated as void for remoteness if the rights and duties thereunder were capable of transmission to persons other than the original parties and had been so transmitted, it shall be treated as void as between the person by whom it was made and the person to whom or in whose favour it was made or any successor of his, and no remedy shall lie in contract or otherwise for giving effect to it or making restitution for its lack of effect.

在**生者之間**作出的產權處置，其下的權利及責任如屬能夠傳轉予原來各方以外的其他人，並且若已如此傳轉是會使該產權處置被視作因時間久遠而無效者，則在作出該產權處置的人，與該產權處置是向其作出或是使其受惠的人或其任何繼承人兩者之間，該產權處置須視作無效，而在合約上或其他方面均不得有任何補救，以使該產權處置生效，或因該產權處置缺乏效力而作出任何返還。

c. Section 15(2), Adoption Ordinance (Cap. 290)

In any disposition of property made, whether by instrument **inter vivos** or by will (including codicil), after the date of an adoption order…

作出領養令的日期後進行的任何財產處置中，無論是藉**生者之間**作出的文書或是藉遺囑（包括遺囑更改附件）進行……

d. Section 10(1), Intestates' Estates Ordinance (Cap. 73)

References to any Statutes of Distribution in an instrument **inter vivos** made, or in a will coming into operation, after the commencement of this Ordinance shall, unless the context otherwise requires, be construed as references to this Ordinance; and references in such an instrument or will to statutory next-of-kin shall, unless the context otherwise requires, be construed as referring to the persons who take beneficially on an intestacy under this Ordinance.

於本條例生效日期後在**生者之間**所訂立的文書內，或在本條例生效日期後開始實施的遺囑內，凡提及任何遺產分配法規時，除非文意另有所指，否則須解釋為提及本條例；而在上述文書或遺囑內，凡提及法定最近親時，則除非文意另有所指，否則須解釋為提及根據本條例承受無遺囑遺產的實益權益的人士。

e. Section 6(1)(c), Estate Duty Ordinance (Cap. 111)

Provided that this paragraph shall not apply to gifts **inter vivos** which are made in consideration of marriage, or which are proved to the satisfaction of the Commissioner to have been part of the normal expenditure of the deceased, and to have been reasonable having regard to the amount of his income or to the circumstances, or which in the case of any donee do not exceed in the aggregate $200000 in value or amount.

但本段的規定，不適用於因婚姻而作出的**生者之間**贈予，亦不適用於經向署長證明而令其信納為死者正常開支的一部分，並於考慮死者的入息額及有關情況後，信納為合理的生者之間贈予；亦不適用於任何受贈人所獲贈的總值或總款額不超逾$200000的生者之間贈予。

使用百分比	ELDoS:	0.00%
	BLIS:	23.53%

4. 在世時

a. Schedule Article 2, Recognition of Trusts Ordinance (Cap. 76)

For the purposes of this Convention, the term "trust" refers to the legal relationship created-**inter vivos** or on death-by a person, the settlor, when assets have been placed under the control of a trustee for the benefit of a beneficiary or for a specified purpose.

在本公約中，「信託」一詞指財產授予人為了受益人的利益或指明的目的，將資產置於受託人的控制下而設立的法律關係，不論該關係是在財產授予人**在世時**或死亡時生效的。

使用百分比	ELDoS:	0.00%
	BLIS:	2.94%

intra vires *adj./adv.*

50

/ˈɪntrə ˈvaɪriːz/

Latin within the powers

【中譯】 香港法庭判詞 ELDoS: **1** 在許可權內；**2** 權力範圍以內；香港法例 BLIS: 一；其他 Others: **1** 權力之內；**2** 正當職權之內；**3** 在法定許可權內

> ## Interpretations 釋義
> Describing an act performed within the authority under the law or some other governing document.
>
> 在法律或其他規管文件賦予許可權內所作出的作為。

Examples 例句

1. 在許可權內

Fu Kin Chi, Willy vs. The Secretary for Justice
Case Number: FACV000002_1997

Plainly reg.3(2) lays down an **intra vires** scheme which is crucial to the maintenance of discipline within the Hong Kong Police Force.

明顯地第3（2）條規例訂立了**在許可權內**的體制，對維持香港警務處的紀律有關鍵性的作用。

使用百分比	ELDoS: 50.00%
	BLIS: 0.00%

2. 權力範圍以內

Novatel Communications (Far East) Limited vs. Canadian
Imperial Bank of Commerce and another
Case Number: HCA008052_1999

Unless he is put on notice to the contrary, a person dealing in good faith with a company which is carrying on an **intra vires** business is entitled to assume that its directors are properly exercising such powers for the purposes of the company as set out in its memorandum.

除非該名與公司真誠進行屬公司**權力範圍以內**交易的人士另行接獲通知，否則該人士有權假設公司董事是為了公司章程大綱所臚列的目的而恰當行使權力的。

使用百分比	ELDoS: 50.00%
	BLIS:　 0.00%

issue estoppel

51

/ˈɪʃuː ɪˈstɒpəl/   /ˈɪʃuː eˈstɒpəl/

French

【中譯】 香港法庭判詞 ELDoS: **1** 已決問題不得推翻；香港法例

BLIS: 一；其他 Others: 一

Interpretations 釋義

A form of estoppel under which the same parties are not allowed, in the present and all subsequent actions, to relitigate an issue that has been decided and was a critical and essential part of an earlier proceeding between them.

「不容反悔法」的其中一種形式。在此法則下，訴訟雙方在現時及其後的所有訴訟中，不得對法庭已經裁決的問題再提出訴訟，而該問題為早前法律訴訟程序中重要而必須的部分。

Examples 例句

1. 已決問題不得推翻

a. *Hebei Import and Export Corporation vs. Polytek Engineering Company Limited*
Case Number: FACV000010_1998

Nor is the difficulty lessened by the suggestion that the doctrine of **issue estoppel** should be applied flexibly, whatever that suggestion may be intended to mean.

有提議謂可彈性引用「**已決問題不得推翻**」這個法則，但不論該提議原意作用為何，這樣的提議也不能減低困難度。

b. *Hebei Import and Export Corporation vs. Polytek Engineering Company Limited*
Case Number: FACV000010_1998

In the Court of Appeal and in argument before this Court, reference was made to the possible application of the doctrine of **issue estoppel** arising from the decision and the proceedings in the Beijing Court and the similarity of the grounds on which an arbitration award can be set aside under PRC law and the grounds on which enforcement of an award can be resisted under the Ordinance. I have difficulty with the notion that the questions here are to be resolved by **issue estoppel**.

在上訴法庭和在本院席前提出論據時，曾提述及基於決定和在北京進行的法律程序因而可否引用「**已決問題不得推翻**」這個法則，並且提述及根據中華人民共和國法律可以撤銷仲裁裁決的理由與根據香港《仲裁條例》可以拒絕強制執行裁決的理由兩者之間的相同處。對於在本案中用「**已決問題不得推翻**」這法律概念來解決問題，本席有異議。

使用百分比	ELDoS: 100.00%
	BLIS:　　0.00%

jus soli *n.*

/ˈdʒʌs ˈsəʊlaɪ/

Latin law of the soil

【中譯】 香港法庭判詞 ELDoS: **1** 以出生地決定兒童的公民身分的原
則；香港法例 BLIS: 一；其他 Others: **1** 出生地主義；**2** 以出
生地的國籍為出生嬰兒的國籍的原則

Interpretations 釋義

The principle that the nationality of a person is determined by
his place of birth, irrespective of the citizenship of his parents.

此原則指一個人不論其父母的公民身分如何，他的國籍由是
其出生地所決定的。

Examples 例句

1. 以出生地決定兒童的公民身分的原則

The Director of Immigration vs. Master Chong Fung-Yuen
Case Number: FACA000026_2000

The United Kingdom had to deal with issues arising from the
perceived threat of large scale immigration into the United Kingdom
from British Commonwealth countries and this resulted in a policy
shift away from citizenship based on **jus soli**. (In English, "right of
the soil", that is, the principle that a child's citizenship is determined
by place of birth).

當時聯合王國意識到有大量移民從英聯邦國家進入聯合王國的
危機，為了要處理這危機所帶來的問題，便改變以 jus soli 決
定公民身分的政策。（jus soli 的英文意思是「土地的權利」，亦
即**以出生地決定兒童的公民身分的原則**）。

使用百分比	ELDoS:	100.00%
	BLIS:	0.00%

lis *n.*

/ˈlɪs/

Latin a suit

【中譯】 香港法庭判詞 ELDoS: **1** 聆訊；香港法例 BLIS: —；其他
Others: **1** 爭議；**2** 訴訟；**3** 訴訟案件；**4** 爭執；**5** 訴訟行為

> **Interpretations 釋義**
>
> A dispute; an action at law
>
> 爭執；法律訴訟

Examples 例句

1. 聆訊

a. *Apple Daily Limited vs. The Commissioner of the Independent Commission against Corruption*
Case Number: CACV000357A_1999

As for the first argument, I agree with the premise on which the argument is based, namely that an application for a search warrant is not a **lis** inter partes.

關於第一項論據，本席同意它所依據的前題，即申請搜查令並不是一項多方之間所進行的**聆訊**。

b. *Apple Daily Limited vs. The Commissioner of the Independent Commission against Corruption*
Case Number: CACV000357A_1999

(iii) I have given some thought to how this judgment should be headed. Para. 7 of the Practice Direction relating to Civil Appeals to the Court of Appeal requires such appeals to bear the same title as that which obtained in the court of first instance. However, the proceedings bore different titles there, as the application for the search warrants was not a **lis** inter partes, whereas the application to set them aside was. The heading which I have given to this judgment reflects the title to the application to set aside the warrants, because it was from the order made on that application that this appeal was brought.

本席曾考慮應在這份判案書的首頁中使用什麼名稱的問題，根據向上訴法庭提出民事上訴的實務指引的第7段規定，這類上訴應沿用在原訟法庭時法律程序中所使用的名稱。然而，在原訟法庭時法律程序使用過不同的名稱，原因是申請搜查令的程序並不是一項多方之間的**聆訊**，而申請把搜查令作廢的程序則屬這種聆訊。本席最後採用了在申請把手令作廢的聆訊中所使用的名稱，因為本上訴便是針對在上述申請中所作出的命令而提出的。

| 使用百分比 | ELDoS: 100.00% |
| | BLIS: 0.00% |

lis alibi pendens *n.*

/ˈlɪs ˈæləbaɪ ˈpenˌdenz/ /ˈlɪs ˈælɪbaɪ ˈpenˌdenz/

Latin a suit pending elsewhere

54

【中譯】 香港法庭判詞 ELDoS: **1** 另案進行；**2** 訴訟另案進行；香港法例 BLIS: 一；其他 Others: **1** 另案進行；**2** 訴訟另案進行

Interpretations 釋義

A lawsuit pending elsewhere.

That an action on a given matter between a plaintiff and defendant is pending in one court constitutes a plea that the defendant may use to stop the plaintiff bringing the same matter against him in another court.

訴訟在其他地方待決中。

即原告人與被告人在一法院就某事件提出的訴訟正在審訊中，被告人可把這點作為抗辯理由，阻止原告人在另一個法院就相同事件對他提出訴訟。

Examples 例句

1. 另案進行

a. *La Chemise Lacoste S.A. vs. Crocodile Garments Limited*
Case Number: CACV000011_1996

Although, therefore, there is some overlap, the issues and their nature in the two proceedings are so significantly different that I reject CG's contention that they are similar or sufficiently similar to sustain its plea of **lis alibi pendens**.

因此，雖然這兩項訴訟有部分重疊，但很明顯兩項訴訟的爭議及性質都極為不同，故本席不接納CG的論點——指兩項訴訟相似或大致相似而足以構成**另案進行**。

b. Collections Interior Limited vs. Jin Jiang Dickson Centre Co. Ltd. and another
Case Number: HCCT000007_1995

On 25 March 1995, the second defendant issued a summons applying for an order that the action against it be stayed on the grounds of forum conveniens, lack of jurisdiction and the existence or likelihood of **lis alibi pendens**.

一九九五年三月二十五日，第二被告以便利法庭、沒有司法管轄權及訴訟現正或可能**另案進行**為理由，發出傳票申請一項命令，將針對被告人的訴訟暫緩執行。

| 使用百分比 | ELDoS: 66.67% |
| | BLIS: 0.00% |

2. 訴訟另案進行

Abundance Assets Limited vs. Sun Asia Pacific Hotels and another
Case Number: HCCL000019A_1994

On 6 July 1994, Allson filed a summons claiming a stay of proceedings in this action on the ground of **lis alibi pendens**.

於一九九四年七月六日，Allson以**訴訟另案進行**為理由，提交了要求延緩訴訟程序的傳票以供存檔。

| 使用百分比 | ELDoS: 33.33% |
| | BLIS: 0.00% |

lis pendens *n. pl. lites pendentes*

/ˈlɪs ˈpenˌdenz/

Latin a pending suit

【中譯】 香港法庭判詞 ELDoS: **1** 待決案件；**2** 待決案件的；香港法
例 BLIS: **1** 待決案件；**2** 待決案件的；其他 Others: **1** 待決訴
訟；**2** 懸案；**3** 未決訴訟；**4** 有待法律解決

Interpretations 釋義

Any action pending in court relating to land or any interest in
land. If registered in the Land Registry, it serves as a notice
that the property in question is the subject of an action. Any
purchaser or encumbrancer of the property shall be bound by the
final outcome of the case.

任何關於土地或與土地權益有關而等候法庭判決的訴訟。如
果該訴訟案件已在土地註冊處登記，便有效力通告其他人有
關財產已成為某訟案的主體。該財產的任何買家或產權負擔
人均須受該案件的最後結果約束。

Examples 例句

1. 待決案件

a. Section 14, Land Registration Ordinance (Cap. 128)

The provisions of this Ordinance relating to judgments (subject to the
provisions hereinafter contained) shall extend to **lites pendentes**.

本條例與判決有關的條文（在不抵觸下文所載的條文下）引伸
而適用於**待決案件**。

b. *Vankin Investments Limited vs. Wing Lung Bank Limited*
Case Number: HCA015962_1999

On the same day, Vankin issued this action and immediately caused the Writ of Summons to be registered in the Land Registry as a **lis pendens**.

Vankin在截止投標當日，即1999年10月8日展開本訴訟，並隨即以傳訊令狀將本訴訟在土地註冊處註冊為**待決案件**。

c. *Vankin Investments Limited vs. Wing Lung Bank Limited*
Case Number: HCA015962_1999

Because of the **lis pendens**, the Bank's application to strike out the original Writ of Summons and Statement of Claim was fixed to be heard before a judge as soon as possible.

正因Vankin將本案註冊為**待決案件**，故此銀行要求剔除原傳訊令狀及申索陳述書之申請獲編排儘早聆訊。

d. *Section 4(6)(a)(iii)(A), Land (Compulsory Sale for Redevelopment) Ordinance (Cap. 545)*

Where the Tribunal makes an order for sale, it may order, subject to section 8(3), (4) and (5), that compensation be paid to a tenant for termination of his tenancy under section 8(1)(b) and it may also give such directions as it thinks fit – (a) relating to – ...(iii) subject to section 11(5), the application of the proceeds of the sale including – (A) the holding by the trustees of such part of those proceeds as is specified by the Tribunal in view of any **lis pendens** affecting the lot; and...

凡審裁處作出售賣令，審裁處可在符合第8（3）、（4）及（5）條的規限下，命令對其租賃根據第8（1）（b）條終止的租客付予賠償，亦可發出審裁處認為合適並符合以下説明的指示——

（a）關乎——……（iii）（在不抵觸第11（5）條的條文下）售賣所得收益的運用，包括——（A）由受託人持有審裁處鑒於有任何影響該地段的**待決案件**而指明的售賣收益中的某部分；及……

e. Section 16, Land Registration Ordinance (Cap. 128)

No **lis pendens** shall be registered in the Registry of the High Court, or elsewhere than in the Land Registry; and a lis pendens not registered in the said office shall not bind any purchaser or mortgagee of the estate intended to be thereby affected.

所有**待決案件**，均只許在土地註冊處註冊，不得在高等法院登記處或其他辦事處註冊；凡沒有在上述辦事處註冊的待決案件，對擬受此影響的產業的任何買方或承按人均無約束力。

f. Section 115(3), Landlord and Tenant (Consolidation) Ordinance (Cap. 7)

No notice or application under this Part shall, for the purposes of the Land Registration Ordinance (Cap 128), be regarded as an instrument in writing by which any parcel of ground, tenement or premises may be affected or as creating a **lis pendens**.

就《土地註冊條例》（第128章）而言，根據本部發出的通知書或作出的申請書，均不得視為可影響任何一幅地、物業單位或處所的文書，亦不得視為產生**待決案件**。

g. Section 11(1), New Territories Ordinance (Cap. 97)

A memorial of any deed, will or other instrument, or any judgment, order or **lis pendens**, in respect of or affecting land, may be prepared and shall be received at such places in addition to a New Territories Land Registry as the Land Registrar shall approve: Provided that the registration of any such memorial shall be deemed to have been effected on the date and at the time that an acknowledgement of the receipt thereof shall be endorsed thereon at the appropriate New Territories Land Registry.

有關或影響土地的任何契據、遺囑或其他文書、或任何判決、命令或**待決案件**，均可擬備註冊摘要，並除須在新界區土地註冊處收取外，且須在土地註冊處處長所批准的其他地點收取：但任何該等註冊摘要的註冊，須當作已在有關的註冊摘要在適當的新界區土地註冊處被批署認收的日期及時間完成。

h. Section 20, Land Registration Ordinance (Cap. 128)

The application to vacate a lis pendens under section 19 may be in a summary way by petition or motion in court or by summons in chambers, and may be made by any person interested in the property against which the **lis pendens** has been registered, whether such person is a party to the **lis pendens** or not.

根據第19條申請撤銷待決案件，可藉向法庭提出呈請或動議，或藉內庭發出傳票，以簡易程序提出，以及可由任何對已就**待決案件**作出註冊的財產具有權益的人提出，而不論該人是否為**待決案件**的一方。

使用百分比	ELDoS: 66.67%
	BLIS: 81.25%

2. 待決案件的

a. Section 20, New Territories Ordinance (Cap. 97)

It shall not be necessary for the Land Registrar to keep an index of names of the several parties to deeds and other instruments, or of the devisors or devisees in the case of wills, or of the plaintiffs or defendants in the case of judgments, orders and **lites pendentes**.

土地註冊處處長無須就以下的人的姓名備存索引：契據及其他文書的各方當事人、遺囑的遺贈人或承遺贈人，或判決、命令及**待決案件的**原告人或被告人。

b. *Vankin Investments Limited vs. Wing Lung Bank Limited*
Case Number: HCA015962_1999

Counsel also gave an undertaking to amend the Statement of Claim by deleting prayers 1 and 2 and to vacate the **lis pendens**.

同時，該位大律師亦承諾修訂其申索陳述書，即刪除其中第1及第2項的請求，又承諾將有關**待決案件的**註冊取消。

c. *Section 11(2), New Territories Ordinance (Cap. 97)*

Notwithstanding anything in this or any other enactment, the registration of any deed, will, or other instrument, or any judgment, order or **lis pendens**, in respect of or affecting land, shall be deemed to have been validly effected if effected at any place approved for such purpose by the Land Registrar.

即使本條例或任何其他成文法則有任何規定，任何有關或影響土地的契據、遺囑、其他文書、判決、命令或**待決案件的**註冊，如是在土地註冊處處長批准作註冊用途的地點完成，即須當作已有效地完成。

d. *Section 21, Land Registration Ordinance (Cap. 128)*

If an order is made for vacating any such registration, the Land Registrar shall, on the filing with him of a memorial and an office copy of such order, enter a discharge of such **lis pendens** on the register, and may issue certificates of such entry.

如有撤銷任何上述註冊的命令作出，土地註冊處處長須於註冊摘要和該命令的正式文本提交予他存檔時，在登記冊上記入解除該**待決案件的**記項，並可就該記項發出證明書。

使用百分比	ELDoS: 33.33%
	BLIS:　18.75%

177

locus classicus *n. pl. loci classicus* 56

/ˈləʊkəs ˈklæsɪkəs/

Latin place belonging to the highest class of citizens

【中譯】 香港法庭判詞 ELDoS: **1** 最具權威；**2** 權威章節；香港法例
BLIS: 一；其他 Others: 一

Interpretations 釋義

A classical passage; a text that belongs to the highest class
經典篇章，屬權威性最高的作品。

Examples 例句

1. 最具權威

Vankin Investments Limited vs. Wing Lung Bank Limited
Case Number: HCA015962_1999

The **locus classicus** of that aspect of res judicata is the judgment of
Wigram V. C. in *Henderson v. Henderson* (1843) 3 Hare 100, 115…

關於「已成定案」在這方面的準則，以 Wigram V.C. 在
Henderson v. Henderson（1843）3 Hare 100, 115一案的判決書**最具權威**。

使用百分比	ELDoS:	50.00%
	BLIS:	0.00%

2. 權威章節

Chan Siu Lun vs. Hui Cho Yee and another
Case Number: CACV000171A_1999

The **locus classicus** of that aspect of res judicata is the judgment of Wigram V.-C. in *Henderson v. Henderson* (1893) 3 Hare 100, 115 where the judge says:…

對於已判事情這項法則的特點，可參看大法官Wigram V.-C. 於 *Henderson v. Henderson*（（1893）3 Hare 100 at 115）一案判詞中的一段**權威章節**。大法官這樣說：……

使用百分比	ELDoS: 50.00%
	BLIS:　0.00%

locus standi *n. pl. loci standi*

57

/ˈləʊkəs ˈstændaɪ/

Latin place to stand

【中譯】　香港法庭判詞 ELDoS: **1** 資格；香港法例 BLIS: 一；其他
Others: **1** 立足地位；**2** 陳述權；**3** 出庭資格；**4** 發言權；**5** 立
足點

Interpretations 釋義

A right to appear before and be heard by a court or any other
formal bodies.

出席法院或任何正式團體的聆訊與陳情的資格。

Examples 例句

1. 資格

a. *Ng Yat Chi vs. Max Share Limited and another*
Case Number: FACV000003A_1997

The Court of Appeal agreed that Mr Choy, not being a registered
shareholder, had no **locus standi**.

上訴法院同意由於蔡先生不是註冊股東因此沒有**資格**提出呈
請。

b. *Ng Yat Chi vs. Max Share Limited and another*
Case Number: FACV000003A_1997

These allegations have yet to be tried and the proceedings have not
proceeded beyond the Petition. This is because the Company and
China Resources then applied to strike it out on the ground that
neither Mr Ng nor Mr Choy had **locus standi** to present it.

這些指稱有待審理，而法律程序的進展尚未超越呈請階段，這是因為「該公司」及「華潤」後來申請剔除呈請書，而所持理據是吳先生或蔡先生均沒有**資格**提出呈請。

使用百分比	ELDoS: 100.00%
	BLIS: 0.00%

mala fide[1] *adj./adv.*

58

/ˈmeɪlə ˈfaɪdɪ/   /ˈmælə ˈfaɪdɪ/

Latin in bad faith

【中譯】 香港法庭判詞 ELDoS: **1** 惡意的；香港法例 BLIS: **1** 惡意；其
他 Others: **1** 不誠實地；**2** 不誠實的；**3** 心懷不軌；**4** 詐欺的；
5 蓄意

> ## Interpretations 釋義
>
> In bad faith; acting dishonestly
> 惡意、不誠實地行事

Examples 例句

1. 惡意的

Wong Yeung Ng vs. The Secretary for Justice
Case Number: CACV000161A_1998

Given that the attacks were **mala fide**, scurrilous, abusive, shocking
and reprehensible, he submits that the fundamental rights of freedom
of expression and freedom of the press given under Article 16 of
the Bill of Rights, Article 27 of the Basic Law and the International
Covenant of Civil and Political Rights as incorporated in the Basic
Law, protect the appellant unless it can be shown that the statements
and conducts were "necessary" exceptions to the rule. This cannot be
demonstrated unless on the evidence the risk to the administration of
justice was real, substantial and immediate.

雖然那些攻擊是**惡意的**、誹謗性的、惡言漫罵的、令人震驚
和應受指摘的，但是Kentridge先生陳詞說上訴人受到《人權法
案》第十六條、《基本法》第二十七條和被納入《基本法》內的

---

1. Please note that both *mala fide* and *mala fides* have different parts-of-speech.

《公民權利和政治權利國際公約》等保障，因為這些條文規定
人人皆享有發表自由和新聞自由這些基本權利。法庭只有在證
明有關的陳述或行為是法規中所指的「必要的」例外情況時才
可以裁定罪名成立，但是必須有證據顯示司法有真正的、實質
的和即時的危險會被干擾。

| 使用百分比 | ELDoS: 100.00% |
| | BLIS: 0.00% |

2. 惡意

a. Section 45(1), Landlord and Tenant (Consolidation) Ordinance (Cap. 7)

Any person who shall **mala fide** do any act whatsoever with intent to
induce the lessee of any premises to give up possession thereof shall
be liable on summary conviction to a fine of $2000.

任何人**惡意**作出任何作為，意圖誘使處所的承租人捨棄對處所
的管有，循簡易程序定罪後，可處罰款$2000。

b. Rule 24, Proof of Debts Rules (Cap. 6E)

If a creditor is dissatisfied with the decision of the trustee in respect
of a proof, the court may, on the application of the creditor, reverse
or vary the decision. The Official Receiver or trustee shall not be
personally liable for any costs in respect of the rejection by him in
whole or in part of any proof unless it is proved to the satisfaction of
the court that he has acted **mala fide** or with gross negligence.

如任何債權人不滿受託人就任何債權證明表而作出的決定，法
院可應該債權人的申請，推翻或更改該項決定。破產管理署署
長或受託人無須就其全部或部分拒絕接納任何債權證明表而個
人承擔有關費用，但如有證明使法院信納他行事時有**惡意**或嚴
重疏忽，則屬例外。

| 使用百分比 | ELDoS: 0.00% |
| | BLIS: 100.00% |

mala fides[1] *n.*

/ˈmeɪlə ˈfaɪdiːz/   /ˈmælə ˈfaɪdiːz/

Latin bad faith

59

【中譯】 香港法庭判詞 ELDoS: **1** 不真誠；**2** 惡意；香港法例 BLIS:
1 惡意；其他 Others: **1** 不誠實；**2** 歪意

Interpretations 釋義

Bad faith

惡意；不誠實；不軌之心事

Examples 例句

1. 不真誠

Mexon Holdings Limited vs. Silver Bay International Limited
Case Number: CACV000076_1999

The whole purpose of requisitions on title is that purchasers are afforded an opportunity of raising points on the abstract of title and any muniments of title which may have been delivered to the purchasers and if they fail to avail themselves of this opportunity they must abide the consequences. This observation is made when there is an absence of any **mala fides**.

就業權提出要求的整個目的是讓買方有機會，就可能已交付買方的業權摘要及任何產權證書，提出查詢業權的要求，假如買方不利用這個機會，本身便須承擔後果。本席有此看法是因為本席認為並不存在任何**不真誠**的情況。

使用百分比	ELDoS: 50.00%
	BLIS: 0.00%

---

1. Please note that both *mala fide* and *mala fides* have different parts-of-speech.

2. 惡意

a. Section 66, Bankruptcy Ordinance (Cap. 6)

Where the Official Receiver or trustee has seized or disposed of any goods, chattels, property or other effects in the possession or on the premises or under the control of a debtor against whom a bankruptcy order has been made and it is thereafter made to appear that the said goods, chattels, property or other effects were not at the date of the bankruptcy order the property of the debtor, the Official Receiver or trustee shall not be personally liable for any loss or damage arising from such seizure or disposal sustained by any person claiming such property nor for the costs of any proceedings taken to establish a claim thereto, unless the court is of opinion that the Official Receiver or trustee has been guilty of **mala fides** or of gross negligence in respect of the same.

凡已針對某債務人作出破產令，而破產管理署署長或受託人已檢取或處置該債務人所管有或在其處所內或在其控制下的任何貨品、實產、財產或其他物品，而其後情況使人覺得該貨品、實產、財產或物品於破產令的日期並非該債務人的財產，則對於任何申索該財產的人因該項檢取或處置而蒙受的損失或損害，或對於為確立該項申索而採取的任何法律程序的訟費，破產管理署署長或受託人無須承擔個人法律責任，但如法院認為破產管理署署長或受託人在該事上曾懷有**惡意**或曾有嚴重疏忽，則屬例外。

b. Keep Point Development Limited vs. Chan Chi Yim & Ngai Yuet Fong & 62 Other Defendants, Full Country Development Limited and Yuen Sung & Co
Case Number: HCMP006550A_1998

I have no hesitation in saying that there is no evidence here of any collusion between Mr Yuen and Full Country, and no suggestion of dishonesty or **mala fides** on his part. But the whole scenario, of the speed of these transactions, the attendance in groups, the presence of

Cheng Kwok Tung to immediately renegotiate any financial matter a client was not happy with, takes on the air of an automatic process to be dealt with as efficiently and quickly as possible, and partly at least for the benefit of Full Country.

本席毫不猶疑説，此處並無證據顯示：袁先生與Full Country 是有任何串通之舉；也無提示指出：他本人有不誠實或**惡意** 之處。但整個情況——這些交易完成的速度、出席人士分組處 理、鄭國棟在委託人一旦不滿意任何財務事項時便立即再行商 議等種種事情——顯示出這進行中的機械式程序，須要處理得 盡可能有效和快捷，部分原因至少就是為了Full Country的利 益。

使用百分比	ELDoS: 50.00%
	BLIS: 100.00%

mandamus *n. pl. mandamuses*

/mænˈdeɪməs/

Latin we command

60

【中譯】 香港法庭判詞 ELDoS: **1** 履行義務令；**2** 履行責任令；香港法例 BLIS: **1** 履行義務令；**2** 履行責任令；**3** 履行職務令；**4** 強制令；其他 Others: **1**（給下級法院的）命令書；**2** 命令狀；**3**（上級法院要求下級法院或官員採取某一特殊行為的）指令；**4** 執行令

Interpretations 釋義

An order issued by a court directing a corporation, or a public official or body, or an inferior court or tribunal to perform a duty as required by law. The usual practice is such an order will only be made when there are no alternative legal remedies.

由法院發出的令狀，指示法人團體、公職人員或團體、下級法院或審裁處必須根據法律規定履行任務。常見的做法是，只有在沒有其他法律補救方法的時候，法院才會發出此令狀。

Examples 例句

1. 履行義務令

a. Section 64(3), Interpretation and General Clauses Ordinance (Cap. 1)

The conferring by any Ordinance of a right of appeal or objection to the Chief Executive in Council shall not prevent any person from applying to the High Court for an order of **mandamus**, certiorari, prohibition, injunction or any other order, instead of appealing or making an objection to the Chief Executive in Council, where an application for such an order would lie....

任何條例授予向行政長官會同行政會議提出上訴或反對的權利，並不因此而阻止任何人向高等法院提出依法有權利提出的**履行義務令**、移審令、禁止令、強制令或其他命令的申請，以代替向行政長官會同行政會議提出上訴或反對⋯⋯。

b. Secretary For Justice and others vs. Chan Wah and others
Case Number: FACV0011_2000 FACV000013_2000

As a result of the Court of Appeal's judgment, a number of declarations stand and also in Mr Tse's case an order of **mandamus** directing the relevant Rural Committee to register him as a candidate.

基於上訴法庭的判決，多項宣告維持有效，而且就謝先生的案件而言，一項指示有關鄉事委員會讓他註冊成為候選人的**履行義務令**亦因此繼續生效。

c. Lau Kong Yung and others vs. The Director of Immigration
Case Number: CACV000108_1999

I would make no further order and refuse the applications for the various declarations relating to status and other matters, for **mandamus** to compel the Director to specify a new scheme by notice in the Gazette and for prohibition to prevent the execution of the removal orders.

本席不再發出其他命令，並拒絕申請人要求法庭就身分及其他事宜作出宣告的各項申請，拒絕申請人要求發出**履行義務令**強制入境處處長以憲報公告形式公佈一個新計劃的申請，以及拒絕申請人要求發出禁止令阻止入境處處長執行遣送離境令的申請。

d. Section 12(3), Public Health (Animals And Birds) Ordinance (Cap. 139)

No proceedings by way of **mandamus**, injunction, prohibition or other order shall be taken against the Chief Executive in Council in respect of anything arising out of this section.

任何人不得就本條引起的任何事情，針對行政長官會同行政會議採取要求**履行義務令**、強制令、禁止令或其他命令的法律程序。

e. Section 18, Quarantine and Prevention of Disease Ordinance (Cap. 141)

No matter or thing done by any health officer or by any public officer acting under his direction shall, if it were done bona fide for the purpose of executing this Ordinance, subject him or such public officer personally to any action, liability, claim or demand whatsoever: Provided that nothing herein contained shall exempt any person from any proceeding by way of **mandamus**, injunction, prohibition or other order.

任何衛生主任或任何在衛生主任的指示下行事的公職人員，凡在施行本條例時真誠地行事，則他所作的任何事宜或事情並不使他本人因此而承擔任何訴訟、法律責任、申索或要求：但本條所載條文並不豁免任何人承擔任何循**履行義務令**、強制令、禁止令或其他命令的途徑進行的法律程序。

f. Section 21I(3), High Court Ordinance (Cap. 4)

The power of the Court of First Instance under any enactment to require, magistrates or a judge or officer of a District Court to do any act relating to the duties of their respective offices, or to require a magistrate to state a case for the opinion of the Court of First Instance, in any case where the Court of First Instance formerly had by virtue of any enactment jurisdiction to make a rule absolute, or an order, for any of those purposes, shall be exercisable by order of **mandamus**.

就原訟法庭根據任何成文法則，規定裁判官或區域法院法官或人員須作出任何與其各別職位的職責有關的作為的權力而言，或規定裁判官須呈述案件以便原訟法庭給予意見的權力而言，如原訟法庭以前憑藉任何成文法則曾具有司法管轄權可就任何該等目的而使某項規令成為絕對規令或一項命令，原訟法庭即可以**履行義務令**行使該權力。

使用百分比	ELDoS: 88.89%
	BLIS:　80.56%

2. 履行責任令

a. Section 104(9), Magistrates Ordinance(Cap. 227)

No application for a review shall be granted and no exercise by a magistrate shall be made of the power conferred on him by subsection (5) subsequent to the commencement of proceedings by either party with a view to questioning the decision of the magistrate by way of appeal, **mandamus** or certiorari, unless such proceedings shall have been abandoned.

任何一方如為質疑裁判官的決定而以上訴、**履行責任令**或移審令的形式開始法律程序後，覆核的申請即不會獲得批准，而裁判官亦不得行使第（5）款授予的權力，但如該等法律程序已被放棄，則屬例外。

b. Lau Chi Fai and another vs. The Secetary for Justice and another
Case Number: HCMP001198_1999

If the authority fails or refuses to thus create "private law" rights for the employee, the employee will have "public law" rights to compel compliance, the remedy being **mandamus** requiring the authorities so to contract or a declaration that the employee has those rights.

假如該機關未能或拒絕因此而為僱員訂立「私法」權利，僱員便可行使「公法」權利迫使僱主遵從，補救方法是藉**履行責任令**規定該等機關要按該等條款立約，或藉一項宣告確認僱員享有該等權利。

c. Section 128, Magistrates Ordinance (Cap. 227)

In all cases where a magistrate refuses to do any act relating to the duties of his office, it shall be lawful for the party requiring the act to be done to apply to the Court of First Instance for an order of **mandamus**, and if the court make the order, no action or proceeding whatsoever shall be commenced or prosecuted against the magistrate for having obeyed the order.

在所有案件中，如裁判官拒絕作出與其職責有關的任何作為，則要求作出該作為的一方，可向原訟法庭申請**履行責任令**，而倘法庭作出該項命令，則不得因裁判官已遵守該項命令而對其展開或提出訴訟或法律程序。

d. Section 112, Magistrates Ordinance (Cap. 227)

Where a magistrate refuses to state a case or amend the case stated, the judge may, on the application of the person who applied for a case to be stated or the case stated to be amended, make an order of **mandamus** requiring the magistrate to state a case or amend the case stated.

凡裁判官拒絕呈述案件或拒絕修訂案件呈述，則在申請案件呈述的人提出申請後，或在申請將案件呈述修訂的人提出申請後，法官可發出**履行責任令**，規定裁判官呈述案件或修訂有關的案件呈述。

使用百分比	ELDoS: 11.11%
	BLIS:　　8.33%

3. 履行職務令

a. Section 53(2), Family Status Discrimination Ordinance (Cap. 527)

Subsection (1) shall not preclude the making of an order of certiorari, **mandamus** or prohibition.

第（1）款不阻止作出移審令、**履行職務令**或禁止令。

b. Section 71(2), Disability Discrimination Ordinance (Cap. 487)

Subsection (1) shall not preclude the making of an order of certiorari, **mandamus** or prohibition.

第（1）款不阻止作出移審令、**履行職務令**或禁止令。

c. Section 75(2), Sex Discrimination Ordinance (Cap. 480)

Subsection (1) shall not preclude the making of an order of certiorari, **mandamus** or prohibition.

第（1）款不阻止作出移審令、**履行職務令**或禁止令。

使用百分比	ELDoS:	0.00%
	BLIS:	8.33%

4. 強制令

Section 33(4), Land Survey Ordinance (Chapter 473)

Nothing in this Ordinance exempts any person from any proceeding by way of **mandamus**, injunction, prohibition or other order unless it is expressly so enacted.

本條例並不豁免任何人不受循**強制令**、禁制令、禁止令或其他命令的途徑進行的法律程序牽涉，但法律明文規定的除外。

使用百分比	ELDoS:	0.00%
	BLIS:	2.78%

mens rea *n.*

61

/ˈmens ˈreɪə/

Latin a guilty mind

【中譯】 香港法庭判詞 ELDoS: **1** 犯罪意圖；**2** 意圖；**3** 犯意；香港法
例 BLIS: 一；其他 Others: **1** 造意；**2** 犯意；**3** 犯罪心意；**4** 犯
罪意思；**5** 犯罪意圖

Interpretations 釋義

One of the elements of a crime that the prosecution must prove
before a court convicts a criminal defendant. A mens rea also
refers to the state of mind or intention of the accused person to
carry out the act of crime.

構成罪行的其中一個元素，控方需要證明被告人有「犯罪意
圖」，法庭才可以把他定罪。「犯罪意圖」亦指被告人有意圖／
目的去作出一些犯法行為。

Examples 例句

1. 犯罪意圖

a. *Lau Cheong, Lau Wong vs. Hong Kong SAR*
Case Number: FACC000006_2001

In this appeal, a challenge is made to the legal and constitutional
validity of two aspects of the offence of murder, namely, an intention
to cause grievous bodily harm as a sufficient form of **mens rea**; and
life imprisonment as the mandatory penalty under section 2 of the
Offences Against the Person Ordinance, Cap 212.

在本上訴案中，所提出的質疑是關乎謀殺罪的兩方面，並針對
其法律及憲法的有效性；這兩方面是：意圖引致身體受嚴重傷

害作為**犯罪意圖**的充分形式；以及終身監禁根據《侵害人身罪
條例》（香港法例第212章）第2條而作為強制性刑罰。

b. Lau Cheong, Lau Wong vs. Hong Kong SAR
Case Number: FACC000006_2001

The first two questions address the **mens rea** for murder. The
appellants seek first to challenge the sufficiency, as a matter of
common law, of an intention to cause grievous bodily harm as such
mens rea.

最先的兩個問題所針對的是謀殺罪的**犯罪意圖**。兩位上訴人首
先尋求質疑，就普通法而言，意圖引致身體受嚴重傷害作為謀
殺罪的意圖是否充分。

c. Lau Cheong, Lau Wong vs. Hong Kong SAR
Case Number: FACC000006_2001

Criminal liability at common law usually requires proof of relevant
prohibited conduct causing certain prohibited consequences (the
actus reus), accompanied by a defined state of mind on the part of the
accused in relation to that conduct and its consequences (the **mens
rea**).

根據普通法，刑事法律責任的構成，通常需要證明有關的禁制
行為造成某些禁制的後果（犯罪行為），連同被告人對有關的
行為及其後果所存有的心態（**犯罪意圖**）。

d. HKSAR vs. Wong Ping Shui Adam, Leung Chung Michael
Case Number: FAMC000001_2001

Section 24 therefore defines the actus reus of the offence as the
handling of goods which are "stolen" goods. It goes on to define the
mens rea as the dishonest knowledge or belief that the goods are
stolen. The quality or status of the goods being stolen is therefore an
element in both the actus reus and the **mens rea**.

因此，第24條界定了該罪行的犯罪行為是所處理的貨品屬於「被竊」的貨品。這條例進而界定罪行的**犯罪意圖**是不誠實地知悉或相信該些貨品是被竊貨品。所以，該些貨品作為被竊貨品的特質或狀況，對犯罪行為和**犯罪意圖**來說，都是一項要素。

使用百分比	ELDoS: 92.86%
	BLIS: 0.00%

2. 意圖

HKSAR vs. Pun Ganga Chandra, Gurung Santosh, Gurung Rajendra Bikram
Case Number: CACC000309_1999

Lord Hutton took a similar view in Powell. He recognised at p. 25F–G that "on one view it is anomalous that if foreseeability of death or really serious harm is not sufficient to constitute mens rea for murder in the party who actually carries out the killing, it is sufficient to constitute **mens rea** in a secondary party".

大法官Lord Hutton在Powell案中亦有同感。他認為（第25頁F–G）從某一方面來說，對於真正出手殺人的被告，如果他可預見會造成死亡，或真正嚴重傷害，這樣也不足以構成謀殺**意圖**的話，但卻足以構成從犯的謀殺意圖的話，那實在是反常的。

使用百分比	ELDoS: 5.34%
	BLIS: 0.00%

3. 犯意

HKSAR vs. Pun Ganga Chandra, Gurung Santosh, Gurung Rajendra Bikram
Case Number: CACC000309_1999

The rule represents a respectable view as to what the law of murder should embrace, even though views may differ on the topic, and even if it results in a different **mens rea** being required for a defendant charged with murder, and one charged with attempted murder.

這條規則提出了寶貴意見述明有關謀殺罪的法律所應涵蓋者為何。雖然有關這個主題的意見會個個不同，而這個規則亦有可能會導致被控謀殺的被告及跟被控企圖謀殺被告之兩者之間有不同的**犯意**。

使用百分比	ELDoS:	1.79%
	BLIS:	0.00%

minutia *pl. minutiae*

/maɪˈnjuːʃɪə/ /mɪˈnjuːʃɪə/

Latin a very small thing

62

【中譯】 香港法庭判詞 ELDoS: **1** 微小細節；香港法例 BLIS: —；其他 Others: —

Interpretations 釋義

A trivial matter; an unimportant thing

瑣碎事宜；不重要的事情

Examples 例句

1. 微小細節

a. *Bewise Motors Co. Ltd. vs. Hoi Kong Container Services Ltd.*
Case Number: FACV000004_1997

I have adverted to the foregoing **minutiae** of clause 4(a) and their implications not for their significant support of the Defendant's construction (which they clearly do provide) but to demonstrate that they do not undermine that construction.

本席先前提出對第4（a）條款的一些**微小細節**及其含意的看法，不是因為它們對被告人的釋義提供了重要的支援（它們顯然有此作用），而是想顯示它們並沒有破壞該釋義。

b. *HKSAR vs. Li Chung Yuk*
Case Number: CACC000214_1999

Of course, neither of these witnesses would have much cause to recall the **minutiae** of this matter which, in real terms, was a relatively routine operation – certainly in its early stages.

各證人都沒有什麼理由可令他們回想起這事上的每一**微小細節**，這是很自然的。何況這件事，相對而言，實際上只不過是他們其中一次的慣常行動——特別是在它的初段。

使用百分比	ELDoS: 100.00%
	BLIS: 0.00%

modus operandi *n. pl. modi operandi*

63

/ˌməʊdəs ˌɒpəˈrændiː/　/ˌməʊdəs ˌɒpəˈrændaɪ/

Latin method of operating

【中譯】　香港法庭判詞 ELDoS: **1** 手法；**2** 犯案手法；香港法例 BLIS:
　　　　一；其他 Others: **1** 行事手法；**2** 作案慣例；**3** 慣技；**4** 作案手
　　　　法；**5** 辦事方法；**6** 作法

Interpretations 釋義

Describes a characteristic way of committing crimes which suggests that the crime under investigation might have been committed by a person who committed crimes in the same distinctive way before.

形容犯案的特別慣技。該慣技顯示，正在調查的刑事罪行中，作案者可能是曾以相同顯著特徵的手法犯案的人。

Examples 例句

1. 手法

HKSAR vs. Wong Lo Tak
Case Number: CACC000652X_1997

Clearly, in cases where similar offences are involved, although the **modus operandi** for these offences are more or less the same, there must be some offences which are less serious and others which are more serious.

很明顯，在同一類別的案件中，雖然**手法**大同小異，但是總有一些是較輕微而另一些則較嚴重的。

使用百分比	ELDoS: 50.00%
	BLIS: 0.00%

2. 犯案手法

Tang Siu Man vs. HKSAR
Case Number: FACC000001_1997

And in support of that he may adduce evidence of a string of burglary convictions which reflect such a **modus operandi**.

為了支持他的講法，他可能提出證據，證明他有一連串的入屋犯法案底，反映這是他的**犯案手法**。

使用百分比	ELDoS: 50.00%
	BLIS:　　0.00%

mutatis mutandis

/muˌtɑːtɪs muˈtændɪs/   /mjuˌtɑːtɪs mjuˈtændɪs/

Latin with necessary changes in detail

【中譯】 香港法庭判詞 ELDoS: **1** 作出必要的修改；香港法例 BLIS:
1 在加以必要的變通後；**2** 加以必要的變通；**3** 加以必要的變
通後；**4** 在作出必要的變通後；**5** 經必要的變通後；**6** 可作必
要的變通；**7** 在加以必要的變通；**8** 比照；其他 Others: **1** 相
應變通；**2** 相應類推；**3** 准用；**4** 細節上作必要的修改

Interpretations 釋義

The necessary changes in details being made as required by the
circumstances.

按情況而對細節作必須的改動。

Examples 例句

1. 作出必要的修改

Ng Siu Chau vs. HKSAR
Case Number: FACC000002_1999

The charges were the same in each case, **mutatis mutandis** the
details, and alleged that he had offered advantages in 1996 to…

每一項控罪的指控都相同，只是在細節上**作出必要的修改**，都
是指稱上訴人於1996年曾提供利益予……

使用百分比	ELDoS: 100.00%
	BLIS: 0.00%

2. 在加以必要的變通後

a. Section 50(2), Professional Accountants Ordinance (Cap. 50)

The provisions of section 49(2)and(3)shall apply **mutatis mutandis** to an application under this section.

第49（2）及（3）條的條文**在加以必要的變通後**，適用於根據本條提出的申請。

b. Section 48, Federation of Hong Kong Industries Ordinance (Cap. 321)

The provisions of section 27 and 39 save and except subsections (1) and (5) of section 27 and subsection (2)(b) of section 39 shall apply, **mutatis mutandis**, to meetings of any scheduled group as they apply to meetings of the general committee, and the quorum for any such meeting of a scheduled group shall not be less than one-fourth of its full members present in person or by proxy.

除第27條第（1）及（5）款及第39條第2（b）款外，第27及39條的條文**在加以必要的變通後**，適用於列明組別的會議，一如其適用於理事會會議，而在列明組別的任何該等會議上，如有不少於四分之一該組別的正式會員親身或委任他人以投票代表身分代為出席會議，即構成法定人數。

c. Section 76, Magistrates Ordinance (Cap. 227)

The provisions with reference to summonses contained in Part II in relation to offences punishable on summary conviction shall apply equally, **mutatis mutandis**, to summonses under this Part.

第 II 部所載與可循簡易程序定罪而判罰的罪行有關並涉及傳票的條文，**在加以必要的變通後**，同樣適用於根據本部發出的傳票。

d. Section 6, International Organizations and Diplomatic Privileges Ordinance (Cap. 190)

Notwithstanding any provision to the contrary contained in any Ordinance, the international custom relating to the immunities and privileges as to person, property or servants of sovereigns, diplomatic agents, or the representatives of foreign powers for the time being recognized by the People's Republic of China shall, in so far as the same is applicable **mutatis mutandis**, have effect in Hong Kong.

即使任何條例載有相反條文，當其時獲中華人民共和國承認，並與君主、外交代表或外國代表的人身、財產或受僱人的豁免權及特權有關的國際慣例，**在加以必要的變通後**如適用於香港，則在香港具效力。

使用百分比	ELDoS:	0.00%
	BLIS:	62.26%

3. 加以必要的變通

a. Section 32(1), Employees' Compensation Ordinance (Cap. 282)

If the total or partial incapacity (whether of a permanent or temporary nature) or the death of an employee results from an occupational disease and is due to the nature of any employment in which the employee was employed at any time within the prescribed period immediately preceding such incapacity or death, whether under one or more employers, then, the employee or members of his family, as the case may be, shall be entitled to compensation under this Ordinance as if such incapacity or death had been caused by an accident arising out of and in the course of employment in respect of which the provisions of section 5 apply, and the provisions of this Ordinance (including in particular section 15) shall, **mutatis mutandis**, apply thereto, subject to the following modifications…

如職業病引致僱員完全或部分喪失工作能力（不論屬永久或暫時的）或引致僱員死亡，而該職業病的起因是由於在緊接該項喪失工作能力或死亡發生之前的訂明期間內任何時間僱員受僱從事的工作的性質所致，則不論他是受僱於一名或多於一名僱主，僱員或其家庭成員（視屬何情況而定）有權根據本條例獲得補償，猶如該項喪失工作能力或死亡是僱員在受僱工作期間因工遭遇意外所致，而該宗意外是第5條所適用者一樣；此外，本條例條文（特別是第15條）須**加以必要的變通**而適用，尤須作以下變通⋯⋯

b. Section 4(3), New Territories (Renewable Government Leases) Ordinance (Cap. 152)

Every new Government lease shall be deemed to be for a term of twenty-four years less three days from the 1st day of July 1973, and shall be deemed to contain – ... (d) the same covenants, exceptions, reservations, stipulations, provisos and declarations (including the right of re-entry) **mutatis mutandis** as are contained in the existing Government lease of the land to which the new Government lease relates other than – (i) the covenant to pay the Government rent; and (ii) the provision (if any) for fixing a new Government rent at the expiration of the first ten years of the term; and (iii) the right of renewal on the expiration of the term....

每份新政府租契均須當作年期為24年減3天，由1973年7月1日起計，此外——（d）除**加以必要的變通**外，須當作載有相同於新政府租契所關乎的土地的現行政府租契所載的契諾、原權益保留條款、新權益保留條款、約定條件、但書及聲明（包括重收權），但不包括——（i）繳交地稅的契諾；及（ii）在年期首10年屆滿時厘定新地稅的條文（如有的話）；及（iii）年期屆滿時的續期權利⋯⋯。

c. Section 8A(4), Magistrates Ordinance (Cap. 227)

If a person upon whom a notice under subsection (1) has been served appears before a magistrate in accordance with the notice, or is brought before a magistrate by a warrant issued under subsection (3), the magistrate may hear and determine the offence alleged in the notice as if a complaint has been made or an information has been laid against that person in respect of the offence and for such purposes, the provisions under this Ordinance relating to hearing of complaint or information and the proceedings thereon shall apply **mutatis mutandis**.

如根據第（1）款獲送達通知書的人，按照該通知書的指示到裁判官席前應訊，或藉根據第（3）款所發手令被帶到裁判官席前，裁判官可對通知書上所指稱的罪行進行聆訊及裁定，猶如該人因該罪行而遭人申訴或告發一樣；為此，本條例有關申訴或告發的聆訊及其法律程序的條文，須**加以必要的變通**而適用。

d. Section 21(1), Employees' Compensation Ordinance (Cap. 282)

Save as is provided in this Ordinance and any rules made thereunder, the District Court shall, upon or in connection with any question to be investigated or determined thereunder, have all the powers and jurisdictions exercisable by the District Court in or in connection with civil actions in such Court in like manner as if the Court had by the District Court Ordinance (Cap 336) been empowered to determine all claims for compensation under this Ordinance whatever the amount involved and the law, rules and practice relating to such civil actions and to the enforcement of judgments and orders of the Court shall **mutatis mutandis** apply.

除本條例另有規定及根據本條例訂立的規則另有規定外，區域法院在根據本條例及上述規則須作調查或裁定的問題上或在與該等問題有關的事宜上，具區域法院在該法院的民事訴訟中或在與該法院的民事訴訟有關的事宜上可以行使的一切權力及司法管轄權，猶如該法院已獲《區域法院條例》（第336章）授予權力對所有根據本條例提出的補償申索作出裁定，且不論所涉款額大小，而有關該等民事訴訟及強制執行該法院判決及命令的法律、規則及慣例，須**加以必要的變通**而適用。

使用百分比	ELDoS:	0.00%
	BLIS:	11.32%

4. 加以必要的變通後

a. Section 84, District Court Ordinance (Cap. 336)

An appeal shall lie at the suit of the Secretary for Justice to the Court of Appeal against a verdict or order of acquittal, which shall include any order quashing or dismissing a charge for any alleged defect therein or want of jurisdiction. Such an appeal shall relate to matters of law only and the following procedure shall apply thereto – (a) within 7 clear days after the reasons for a verdict have been recorded or after the order of acquittal, or within such further period as a judge of the High Court may, whether before or after the expiration of such period, allow, an application may be made in writing to the judge to state a case setting forth the facts and the grounds on which the verdict or order was arrived at or made and the grounds on which the proceeding is questioned for the opinion of the Court of Appeal; and the provisions of sections 106 to 109 inclusive of the Magistrates Ordinance (Cap 227) shall apply, **mutatis mutandis**, to the preparation, amendment and setting down of such case stated….

如律政司司長針對某裁定無罪的裁決或命令（包括因指稱控罪欠妥或缺乏司法管轄權而將控罪撤銷或駁回的任何命令）而提起訴訟，則可向上訴法庭提出上訴。該上訴只可關於法律事宜並須按以下程序——（a）在裁決的理由記錄後或裁定無罪的命令作出後7整天內，或在高等法院大法官於該期間屆滿之前或之後准許的較長期間內，可以書面方式提出申請，要求有關的法官對案件作呈述，以徵詢上訴法庭的意見。該呈述須列出達致或作出該裁決或命令所據的事實及理由，以及該法律程序受質疑的理由。對於擬備、修訂和排期聆訊該案件呈述，《裁判官條例》（第227章）第106至109條的條文（首尾兩條包括在內）經**加以必要的變通後**須予適用……。

b. *Section 7(3), Motor Vehicles Insurance (Third Party Risks) Ordinance (Cap. 272)*

The provisions of section 5 shall apply **mutatis mutandis** in relation to any deposit made under subsection (1)(a) of this section, subject to the modification that for paragraph (d) of the said section 5 there shall be substituted the following paragraph – "(d) subject to the provisions of paragraph (f) of this section, the deposit shall be retained by the Director of Accounting Services so long as the depositor carries on in Hong Kong the business in respect of which the deposit is made;".

第5條的條文**加以必要的變通**後適用於根據本條第（1）（a）款作出的繳存，但其中須作出一項變更，即以下段取代第5條（d）段──「（d）除本條（f）段條文另有規定外，繳存人在香港經營與其所作繳存有關的業務的期間，所作的繳存須由庫務署署長留存；」。

c. *Section 48, Apprenticeship Ordinance (Cap. 47)*

The following provisions of the Employment Ordinance (Cap 57) shall **mutatis mutandis**, and subject to any specific provisions to the contrary contained in this Ordinance or in a contract of apprenticeship, apply to employers, registered apprentices and registered contracts of apprenticeship under this Ordinance...

《僱傭條例》（第57章）的以下條文，**加以必要的變通後**，適用於本條例所述的僱主、註冊學徒及已註冊學徒訓練合約，但須受本條例或學徒訓練合約內任何相反的特定條文所規限……

d. *Section 55(2), Employment Ordinance (Cap. 57)*

Without prejudice to the generality of subsection (1), the grounds on which the Commissioner may withdraw an exemption shall include **mutatis mutandis** the grounds contained in section 53(1) on which he may refuse to issue or renew a licence or revoke a licence.

在不損害第(1)款的概括性的原則下，處長可撤回豁免所依據
的理由，須包括**加以必要的變通後**的第53(1)條所載他可拒絕
發牌或續牌或撤銷牌照所依據的理由。

使用百分比	ELDoS:	0.00%
	BLIS:	7.55%

5. 在作出必要的變通後

a. Section 36(1)(c), Volunteer and Naval Volunteer Pensions Ordinance (Cap. 202)

For the avoidance of doubt, it is hereby declared that – (i) subject to subparagraph (ii), the provisions of this Ordinance shall apply **mutatis mutandis** in respect of the payment of any sum of money payable by virtue of paragraph (a) or (b), as they apply to the payment of a grant which is payable under Part III or IV of this Ordinance and in respect of which a claim has, upon the commencement of the amending Ordinance, already been lodged in accordance with section 21(1) and admitted pursuant to a decision of the Board under section 21(4)....

為免生疑問，現宣佈——(i)除第(ii)節另有規定外，本條例
的條文**在作出必要的變通後**，適用於憑藉(a)或(b)段須支付
的任何付款的支付，一如該等條文適用於下述撫恤金的支付一
樣：該撫恤金是根據本條例第III或IV部所須支付的，並且在
修訂條例生效時，已有一項申索就該撫恤金而按照第21(1)條
呈交並依據第21(4)條所指的評議局的決定獲接納……。

b. Section 187(5), Copyright Ordinance (Cap. 528)

The defendant in an action under this section may apply, by way of counterclaim, for relief to which he would be entitled in a separate action in respect of an infringement by the plaintiff of the copyright to which the threats relate and, in any such case, the provisions of this Ordinance with respect to an action for infringement of copyright are, **mutatis mutandis**, applicable in relation to the action.

根據本條而提起的訴訟中的被告人，可藉反申索而申請他在就原告人侵犯關乎有關威脅的版權而提起的另一宗訴訟中，會有權獲得的濟助，而在任何該等個案中，本條例關於提起侵犯版權訴訟的條文**在作出必要的變通後**，即就該訴訟而適用。

c. Section 14C(3), Fire Services Ordinance (Cap. 95)

For the purpose of enabling due inquiry to be made as to whether a subordinate officer or member of other ranks should be required to pay any amount under subsection (2), affording him due opportunity to make representations and enabling any requirement under that subsection to be appealed against and reviewed, Part III shall apply **mutatis mutandis** to and in respect of such a requirement as it applies to and in respect of a finding of guilty of an offence against discipline in accordance with the provisions of the Third Schedule and an award of punishment.

為使任何部屬人員或員佐級成員是否鬚根據第（2）款繳付款項一事獲妥當調查，為使他獲得充分機會作申述，並為使根據該款所作的規定能予上訴或覆核，第III部**在作出必要的變通後**，適用於上述規定，並就該規定而適用，一如其適用於根據附表3的條文就違紀行為作出的裁斷及判處的懲罰，並就該裁斷及懲罰而適用。

d. Section 51(1)(c), Mental Health Ordinance (Cap. 136)

The Training Centres Ordinance (Cap 280) shall apply **mutatis mutandis** to any person remanded to a training centre under paragraph (a) for observation, investigation and treatment.

任何人如根據（a）段還押在教導所以接受觀察、調查和治療，則《教導所條例》（第280章）**在作出必要的變通後**，對該人適用。

使用百分比	ELDoS:	0.00%
	BLIS:	9.43%

6. 經必要的變通後

a. Section 100A(3), Bankruptcy Ordinance (Cap. 6)

Where a regulating order is made the Bankruptcy Rules (Cap 6 sub. leg.) shall apply **mutatis mutandis** to the Official Receiver, trustee and creditors' committee appointed or acting after the making of a regulating order, and to the conduct of any ballot or other proceedings ordered by the court under section 100B or 100F.

凡有規管令作出，則《破產規則》（第6章，附屬法例）**經必要的變通後**，適用於在規管令作出後獲委任或行事的破產管理署署長、受託人及債權人委員會，亦適用於法院根據第100B或100F條下令進行的任何投票或其他程序。

b. Section 227A(3), Companies Ordinance (Cap. 32)

Where a regulating order is made the Companies (Winding-up) Rules (Cap 32 sub. leg.) shall apply **mutatis mutandis** to the Official Receiver, liquidator and committee of inspection appointed or acting after the making of a regulating order, and to the conduct of any ballot or other proceedings ordered by the court under section 227C or 227D.

凡有規管令作出，《公司（清盤）規則》（第32章，附屬法例）**經必要的變通後**，適用於在規管令作出後獲委任或行事的破產管理署署長、清盤人及審查委員會，亦適用於法院根據第227C或227D條下令進行的任何投票或其他程序。

使用百分比	ELDoS:	0.00%
	BLIS:	3.77%

7. 可作必要的變通

Section 8, Government Leases Ordinance (Cap. 40)

Every new Government lease shall be deemed to contain – ...(c) the same covenants, exceptions, reservations, stipulations, provisos and declarations (including the right of re-entry) **mutatis mutandis** as are contained in the renewable Government lease of the lot or section to which the new Government lease relates....

每份新政府租契均須當作載有——……(c)在其所涉地段或分段的可續期政府租契內載有的相同(**可作必要的變通**)契諾、原權益保留條款、新權益保留條款、約定條件、但書及聲明(包括重收權)……。

使用百分比	ELDoS:	0.00%
	BLIS:	1.89%

8. 在加以必要的變通

Section 90(2), Magistrates Ordinance (Cap. 227)

The provisions of section 79 (which relates to a magistrate's power to remand an accused person) shall apply, **mutatis mutandis** and subject to the substitution in subsection (1) of that section of "20 clear days" for "8 clear days", in relation to the exercise by a magistrate of the powers conferred by subsection (1)(b), but the application of such provisions shall be without prejudice to any of the powers of the District Court to enforce the attendance of a person accused of an indictable offence in respect of which the charge or complaint has been transferred to that court.

第79條的條文(涉及裁判官將被控人還押的權力)**在加以必要的變通**並將該條第(1)款的「8整天」改為「20整天」之後,即就裁判官行使第(1)(b)款授予的權力而適用,但此等條文的應用並不損害區域法院就已轉交該法院處理的控罪或申訴強制被控可公訴罪行的人出庭的任何權力。

使用百分比	ELDoS:	0.00%
	BLIS:	1.89%

9. 比照

Article 5(4)(d), Schedule, Fugitive Offenders (Drugs) Order (Cap. 503J)

The provisions of article 7, paragraphs 6 to 19 are applicable **mutatis mutandis**. In addition to the information specified in article 7, paragraph 10, requests made pursuant to this article shall contain the following...

第七條第6至19款的規定可以**比照**適用。除第七條第10款所列情況外,按本條規定提出的請求書還應包含以下各項 ⋯⋯

使用百分比	ELDoS:	0.00%
	BLIS:	1.89%

nisi *adj.*

/ˈnaɪsaɪ/ /ˈniːsiː/

Latin unless

【中譯】 香港法庭判詞 ELDoS：**1** 暫准；**2** 暫時；**3** 臨時；**4** 暫時性
的；**5** 非絕對；香港法例 BLIS：**1** 暫准；其他 Others：**1** 不利
出者法則

Interpretations 釋義

Not final or absolute.

A term used to indicate that a decree, order, judgment, etc. is
valid and to take effect unless the party adversely affected by the
court's decision appears within a stated period and shows cause
why it should not take effect or be revoked.

非最終或絕對。

用以顯示判令、命令、判決書是暫時有效的。除非因法庭判
決而有不利影響的一方能在指定時間內到法庭陳請，並解釋
該文書不應生效或應予撤銷的原因，否則該文書絕對有效。

Examples 例句

1. 暫准

a. *Section 14(3), High Court Ordinance (Cap. 4)*

No appeal shall lie – …(d) from an order absolute for the dissolution
or nullity of marriage in favour of any party who, having had time
and opportunity to appeal from the decree **nisi** on which the order
was founded, has not appealed from that decree….

不得提出來自以下各項的上訴——……（d）一項判任何一方勝
訴的婚姻解除或無效的絕對命令，而該一方雖已有時間及機
會提出來自該項命令所依據的**暫准**判令的上訴卻並無如此上
訴……。

b. Rule 5B(3), Order 42, The Rules of the District Court (Cap. 336H)

Where a written judgment is handed down pursuant to this rule the Court may make therein an order **nisi** as to costs and, unless an application has been made to vary that order, that order shall become absolute 14 days after the decision is pronounced.

凡依據本條規則宣佈書面判決，區域法院可在該書面判決中作出關於訟費的**暫准**命令，而除非有人申請更改該命令，否則該命令在有關決定宣告後14天即成為絕對命令。

c. Section 18(3), Matrimonial Proceedings and Property Ordinance (Cap. 192)

If the court makes absolute a decree **nisi** of divorce or of nullity of marriage, or makes a decree of judicial separation, without having made an order under subsection (1) the decree shall be void but, if such an order was made, no person shall be entitled to challenge the validity of the decree on the ground that the conditions prescribed by subsections (1) and (2) were not fulfilled.

如法庭在未有根據第（1）款作出命令的情況下，將離婚或婚姻無效**暫准**判令轉為絕對判令，或作出裁判分居判令，則該等判令均屬無效；但如法庭已作出該等命令，則任何人均無權以第（1）及（2）款所訂明的條件尚未履行為理由而質疑該等判令的有效性。

d. Section 17(1), Matrimonial Causes Ordinance (Cap. 179)

Where a decree **nisi** of divorce has been granted but not made absolute, then, without prejudice to section 16, any person (excluding a party to the proceedings other than the Proctor) may show cause why the decree should not be made absolute by reason of material facts not having been brought before the court may…

凡離婚**暫准**判令已批出但未轉為絕對判令，在以不損害第16條的規定為原則下，任何人（不包括法律程序中代訴人以外的任何一方）可基於關鍵性的事實並未向法院提出的理由，而提出該判令不應轉為絕對判令的因由；在此情形下，法院可 ……

e. Order 59 rule 16(1), The Rules of the High Court (Cap. 4A)

The following provisions of this rule shall apply to any appeal to the Court of Appeal in a matrimonial cause against a decree **nisi** of divorce or nullity of marriage.

本條規則的以下條文適用於在一宗婚姻訴訟中針對離婚**暫准**判令或婚姻無效的暫准判令而向上訴法庭提出的上訴。

f. Walton Wai-Tati Li vs. Evelyn Man-York Li
Case Number: CACV000271_1998

For all of the foregoing reasons, I would dismiss the appeal with a costs order **nisi** giving the plaintiff its costs.

基於所有前述理由，本席駁回上訴並頒下**暫准**訟費令判給原告人其訟費。

g. Zhou Cui Hao vs. Ting Fung Yee
Case Number: HCA007558Y_1996

Since the Defendant is in person I will mention for her information that Order 42 rule 5B(6) of the Rules of the High Court provides in regard to orders **nisi** as to costs that "unless an application has been made to vary that order, that order shall become absolute 14 days after the decision is pronounced".

由於被告人沒有律師代表，本席在此告知被告人，《高等法院規則》第42號命令第5B（6）規則訂明，關於訟費的**暫准**命令，「除非有人提出申請更改該命令，否則該命令在決定宣告後14天即成為絕對命令。」

h. Leung Sai Lun Robert vs. Leung May Ling
Case Number: FACV000005_1998

For these reasons this appeal is dismissed with an order **nisi** that the costs here and in both courts below should be paid by the Defendants.

基於這些原因，本席駁回本上訴，並頒下**暫准**命令，被告人等須繳付本法院，上訴法庭及原訟法庭的訟費。

使用百分比	ELDoS:	58.82%
	BLIS:	100.00%

2. 暫時

a. Guangdong Foodstuffs Import & Export (Group) Corporation and another vs. Tung Fook Chinese Wine (1982) Co. Ltd and another
Case Number: HCA007759_1995

I will order costs **nisi** to the Plaintiffs in respect of their claims and the Defendants' counterclaim.

至於原訴方之訴訟請求及被訴方之反訴請求引起的訴訟費，現判予**暫時**命令，由被訴方承擔。

b. Chan Hau Hin and others vs. Wan Chung Construction Co. Ltd.
Case Number: HCLA000038X_1998

The above costs order **nisi** shall become absolute 14 days after this judgment is handed down.

上述訟費決定屬**暫時**決定，會在頒下本判案書後14天作實。

使用百分比	ELDoS:	17.65%
	BLIS:	0.00%

3. 臨時

a. Union Bank Of Hong Kong Limited vs. Chapol Limited and others
Case Number: HCMP002048_1997

The order on costs is an order **nisi** to be made absolute 14 days after the handing down of the judgment.

此項訟費令乃一**臨時**命令，將於本判案書發下日期14天后轉為正式命令。

b. *Gimex Development Limited vs. Cua Wai Tai*
Case Number: CACV000174_1999

The Plaintiff has never sought to obtain an award of its costs of the proceedings, and the order **nisi** which I would therefore make is that there be no order as to the costs of the proceedings or of the appeal.

原訴人從來沒有尋求取得這些法律程序的訟費，故此我將作出的**臨時**命令就是這些法律程序或是上訴的訟費，法庭均不作出任何命令。

| 使用百分比 | ELDoS: 11.76% |
| | BLIS: 0.00% |

4. 暫時性的

Roe Investment Limited vs. Prince Good Limited and others
Case Number: FACV000013_1999

As, in effect, Roe has finally emerged the winning party in these proceedings there should be an order **nisi** that Prince Good and Unionix should pay the costs on these appeals and in the Court of Appeal, to be made absolute unless, within 14 days of this judgment, either party should make written submissions (copied to the other party) as to why some other order should be made.

實際上，由於Roe在這些法律程序中，已最終勝訴，應有一**暫時性的**命令，要Prince Good和Unionix支付這些上訴和在高等法院上訴法庭的訟費；除非任何一方於本判案書日期起計14天內，以書面陳詞(副本送另一方)，説明應作出其他命令的原因，則該命令將成為絕對命令。

| 使用百分比 | ELDoS: 5.88% |
| | BLIS: 0.00% |

5. 非絕對

Roe Investment Limited vs. Prince Good Limited and others
Case Number: FACV000013_1999

As to the costs incurred in the two appeals, the Court of Appeal made an order **nisi** for 9/10th of the costs to be paid by Roe and Kowloon Development, with the remaining 1/10th of the costs to await outcome of the trial of Unionix's claim for damages in HCA 1034/97.

至於在兩宗上訴中招致的訟費，上訴法庭作出**非絕對**命令，命令Roe與Kowloon Development支付訟費的九成，餘下的一成訟費，待Unionix在高院民事訴訟1997年第1034號案中的損害賠償申索審訊有結果後，再作定奪。

使用百分比	ELDoS:	5.88%
	BLIS:	0.00%

non est factum pl. non est factums

66

/ˈnɒn ˌest ˈfæktəm/

Latin it is not his deed

【中譯】　香港法庭判詞 ELDoS: **1** 否認訂立契約；香港法例 BLIS:
　　　　一；其他 Others: **1** 非其所為；**2** 否認簽署；**3** 否認締結契
　　　　約；**4** 非被告契據的抗辯；**5** 否認作為原告請求基礎的蓋印證
　　　　書的抗辯；**6** 否認訂立合同的答辯

> ### Interpretations 釋義
> A plea alleging that the instrument sued on was not executed by the defendant or that he was mistaken as to the nature of the same.
> 被告人在因法律文書而導致的訴訟中，可使用的抗辯理由，指該法律文書並非由他簽立或他在錯誤理解該文書性質的情況下簽立。

Examples 例句

1. 否認訂立契約

   a. ***Union Bank of Hong Kong Limited vs. Chapol Limited and others***
   Case Number: HCMP002048_1997

In *Saunders v. Anglia Building Society* [1971] AC 1004, it was held that the plea of **non est factum** could not be argued unless it could be shown that the signatory thought that he was signing a document substantially different in nature or in kind and that the person raising the plea had acted reasonably and with due care.

在 *Saunders v Anglia Building Society* ［1971］AC 1004一案中，法庭認定，除非有證據顯示簽署人以為自己所簽署的是一份在性質或實質上和他理解很不同的文件，而提出爭辯的人又已合理及適當地小心行事，否則他不可提出「**否認訂立契約**」作為抗辯理由來爭辯。

b. *Union Bank of Hong Kong Limited vs. Chapol Limited and others*
Case Number: HCMP002048_1997

On the matters raised by Mr. Yan, his defence is basically two folded, namely **non est factum** and misrepresentation.

根據甄先生提出的事項，他的抗辯主要分為兩方面，即「**否認訂立契約**」及「**失實陳述**」。

c. *Union Bank of Hong Kong Limited vs. Chapol Limited and others*
Case Number: HCMP002048_1997

The burden of proof in relation to a defence of **non est factum** is indeed a heavy one which lays on the person pleading it (see *Union Bank of Hong Kong Ltd v. Ng Yiu Hung and another* [1975] HKLR 26).

事實上，以「**否認訂立契約**」作為抗辯理由的舉證責任非常重大，而且須由申辯一方負起（見 *Union Bank of Hong Kong Ltd v Ng Yiu Hung and another* ［1975］HKLR 26 一案）。

使用百分比	ELDoS: 100.00%
	BLIS: 0.00%

novus actus interveniens

67

/ˌnəʊvəs ˌæktəs ɪntəˈviːnɪənz/

Latin new intervening act

【中譯】　香港法庭判詞 ELDoS: **1** 新的干預行為；香港法例 BLIS: 一；
其他 Others: **1** 外因行為；**2** 新介入行為；**3** 新的干預因素；
4 新的干預行為；**5** 新行為的介入；**6** 新的妨害行為；**7** 新的
妨礙訴訟的行為

Interpretations 釋義

An intervening act that breaks the causal link between the
defendant's original wrongful act or omission and subsequent
events. It is a defence that the defendant may use to relieve
himself from the responsibility for the harm the victim has
suffered.

指一個干預的行動或動作。這干預動作切斷了被告人原本的
不合法行為或不作為與其後所發生事件之間的因果關係。被
告人可藉此作辯護，以解除自己對受害人所造成傷害的責
任。

Examples 例句

1. 新的干預行為

a. Ting Kwong Lun & Others vs. Secretary for Justice
Case Number: HCA001202_2002

However, if the chain has not been broken, or to use language
more familiar in the area of tort law, if there was no **novus actus
interveniens**, then the causal connection between the alleged wrong
and the alleged damage has not been broken, and Mr Fok's point will
be gone.

不過，若然這個連鎖關係沒有被打破，或套用侵權法中的詞彙，沒有**新的干預行為**的話，則原告人等所指稱的過失和損害之間的因果關係便沒有被打破，而霍大律師的論據也就不能成立。

b. *Ting Kwong Lun & others vs. Secretary for Justice*
Case Number: HCA001202_2002

In other words, one is really here concerned with when the intervening conduct of a third party will constitute a **novus actus interveniens** sufficient to relieve the defendant of liability for its original wrong-doing.

換言之，我們所真正關注的是：第三者的干預行為在什麼情況下會構成**新的干預行為**，使到被告人原本因犯錯而須負的法律責任得以免除。

c. *Ting Kwong Lun & others vs. Secretary for Justice*
Case Number: HCA001202_2002

As has been wisely pointed out by the learned editors of *Clerk & Lindsell on Torts* (18th ed), "no precise or consistent test can be offered to define when the intervening conduct of a third party will constitute a **novus actus interveniens**" and "the question of the effect of a novus actus 'can only be answered on a consideration of all the circumstances and, in particular, the quality of that later act or event'".

Clerk & Lindsell on Torts（第18版）一書的編者便有以下的至理名言：「關於第三者的干預行為在什麼情況下會構成新的干預行為，沒有任何準確或一致的驗證標準可供界定」；在「評估**新的干預行為**的影響時，『必須考慮所有情況，尤其是其後的有關作為或事件的性質。』」

使用百分比	ELDoS: 100.00%
	BLIS: 0.00%

officium *n.*

/əˈfɪʃɪəm/

Latin service

【中譯】 香港法庭判詞 ELDoS: **1** 職責；香港法例 BLIS: —；其他 Others: —

Interpretations 釋義

Duty or obligations arising from one's job, office or position

工作或職位所須承擔的任務或責任。

Examples 例句

1. 職責

Ultra Eternal Limited vs. Liu Tai Cheong
Case Number: HCMP001188_1996

Executors, no doubt can sell virtute officii, but that must be with a view to performing their **officium**.

毫無疑問，遺囑執行人可憑藉其身分作出售賣行為，但必須是以履行彼等之**職責**為目標。

使用百分比	ELDoS: 100.00%
	BLIS: 0.00%

onus　*n. pl. onuses*

69

/ˈəʊnəs/

Latin a burden or load

【中譯】　香港法庭判詞 ELDoS: **1** 責任；**2** 舉證責任；香港法例 BLIS:
1 責任；**2** 舉證責任；其他 Others: **1** 義務；**2** 負擔

> ## Interpretations 釋義
> A burden; an encumbrance; an obligation; a responsibility for
> doing something
> 須承擔的義務；負擔；履行某項事情的責任

Examples 例句

1. 責任

a. Section 29, Gas Safety Ordinance (Cap. 51)

In any proceedings for an offence against this Ordinance consisting
of a failure to comply with a requirement under this Ordinance
to do something so far as is practicable or so far as is reasonably
practicable, or to use the best practicable means to do something,
the **onus** is on the accused to prove that it was not practicable or not
reasonably practicable to do more than was in fact done to comply
with the requirement, or that he has used the best practicable means
to comply with the requirement, or done the appropriate thing to
comply with the requirement.

在根據本條例提出的檢控中，如控罪涉及沒有按本條例下的規
定，在可行或合理可行的範圍內儘量辦理事情或用最佳可行方
法辦理事情，則被告有**責任**證明要辦理比實際已辦理的更多的
事情以遵行有關規定，並不可行或不合理可行，或被告已採用
最佳可行方法或已辦理適當事情以遵行有關規定。

b. *Common Luck Investment Limited vs. Cheung Kam Chuen*
Case Number: FACV000022_1998

Taken in isolation, this passage may be thought to suggest that the judge had indeed placed the **onus** on the deceased to prove that he had not entered into the 1964 mortgage.

若單看這段文字，容或使人聯想到原審法官確是要承按人承擔**責任**，證明其本人並無訂立該1964年的按揭。

c. *Hebei Import and Export Corporation vs. Polytek Engineering Company Limited*
Case Number: FACV000010_1998

If, what the respondent seeks to do is to raise a specific ground under s.44(2) under the guise of public policy, then it is only right that it should bear the **onus** of establishing that ground.

假如答辯人所尋求的是以公共政策作為幌子從而提出第44(2)條的特定理由，那麼，答辯人就應該承擔確立該理由的**責任**，這樣做才算正確。

使用百分比	ELDoS: 61.54%
	BLIS: 90.48%

2. 舉證責任

a. *Common Luck Investment Limited vs. Cheung Kam Chuen*
Case Number: FACV000022_1998

The Defendant has not discharged the **onus** of satisfying me on a balance of probabilities that his signature to this Memorial was irregularly obtained and that he did not execute such mortgage in favour of the Bank in 1964.

以相對可能性來衡量，被告人（承按人）未能履行**舉證責任**，使本席信納是別人以不當手段使他在該註冊摘要上簽名，以及他並無簽立該1964年以銀行為承按人的按揭。

b. Chim Hon Man vs. HKSAR
Case Number: FACC000003_1998

For the reasons given by Brennan J in *S v The Queen* (at pp 271–272) it is inconceivable that the prosecution could discharge the **onus** of showing that a subsequent charge for an offence in a relevant period of time was other than for an offence for which he had been convicted or acquitted previously.

基於大法官Brennan J在*S v The Queen*一案中（第271–272頁）所述的理由，很難想像控方能夠履行**舉證責任**，證明被告人其後所被控告在有關時段內所犯的罪行，並不是他之前曾被裁定有罪或獲裁定無罪的罪行。

c. Tang Siu Man vs. HKSAR
Case Number: FACC000001_1997

That the **onus** is on the prosecution is common knowledge.

舉證責任在於控方這點是常識。

d. Section 6, Stowaways Ordinance (Cap. 83)

The **onus** of proving the consent of the owner shall lie upon the accused.

證明獲得船東同意的**舉證責任**，須由被控人承擔。

e. Section 140, Public Health and Municipal Services Ordinance (Cap. 132)

Where, under the provisions of this Ordinance, any person is required to be vaccinated, inoculated or otherwise immunized against disease, the **onus** of proving that such vaccination, inoculation or immunization has been performed shall rest upon the person required to be so vaccinated, inoculated or immunized, as the case may be.

凡任何人根據本條例條文須接種疫苗、接受防疫注射，或以其他方式獲得防疫，該人須負有**舉證責任**，證明已作有關疫苗接種、防疫注射或防疫措施（視屬何情況而定）。

f. Section 3(2), Employment Ordinance (Cap. 57)

In any dispute as to whether a contract of employment is a continuous contract the **onus** of proving that it is not a continuous contract shall be on the employer.

在僱傭合約是否連續性合約的爭議中，僱主須承擔證明該合約並非連續性合約的**舉證責任**。

使用百分比	ELDoS: 38.46%
	BLIS: 9.52%

parens patriac

70

/ˈpæˌrenz ˈpætriːiː/ /ˈpeˌrenz ˈpeɪtriːiː/

Latin parent of the country

【中譯】 香港法庭判詞 ELDoS: **1** 監護人；**2** 監護官員；香港法例
BLIS: 一；其他 Others: 一

Interpretations 釋義
Refers to the role of the state as the guardian of those who cannot legally take care of their own interests such as infants and the insane.
政府替法律上無法處理個人權益的人士（如未成年者及精神病患者）所擔任的監護人角色。

Examples 例句

1. 監護人

a. To Kan Chi and others vs. Pui Man Yau and others
Case Number: HCMP000562_1992

In this regard, I also consider that it does not matter which party should be the Plaintiff and which party should be the Defendant, although I entirely agree with J. Chan, J.'s direction that the To Ka Yi Tso and the To Clan should be the Plaintiffs whereas Rev. Sik and the Secretary for Justice as **parens patriae** should be the Defendants. It is just a matter of convenience and good case management.

就此，本席不接納第二被告人所說、第二被告人無需就青雲觀或青山禪院的擁有權提出申辯或提出確實證明的意見。就此點，本席亦不認為誰當原告人、誰當被告人關乎宏旨，當然本席亦完全同意陳振鴻大法官所令：陶嘉儀祖及陶族該當原告人

而釋大師及身分為**監護人**的律政司該當被告人，然而這不過是
審訊程序管理因時制宜之舉。

b. To Kan Chi and others vs. Pui Man Yau and others
Case Number: HCMP000562_1992

The 2nd Defendant, Secretary for Justice, appeared as the **parens patriae** for the charity.

本案第二被告人律政司司長作為慈善組織的**監護人**出庭答辯。

| 使用百分比 | ELDoS: 75.00% |
| | BLIS: 0.00% |

2. 監護官員

Hong Kong Housing Services for Refugees Limited vs. The Secretary for Justice
Case Number: HCMP006007_1999

It was clearly necessary for the Secretary for Justice to be served as the officer fulfilling the role previously played by the Attorney-General in representing the S.A.R. Government as **parens patriae** and so acting as protector of charities.

由於律政司（Attorney-General）代表政府作為監護官員，這身
分也令他成為慈善組織保護人。他過去肩負的職責既然現在由
律政司司長履行，所以原訴傳票有需要向作為特區政府**監護官
員**的律政司司長送達。

| 使用百分比 | ELDoS: 25.00% |
| | BLIS: 0.00% |

pari passu *adv.*

71

/ˌpæri ˈpæsuː/

Latin equally

【中譯】　香港法庭判詞 ELDoS: **1** 同時同等；香港法例 BLIS: **1** 同時同等；**2** 同等；**3** 同時及同等地；**4** 平等地；其他 Others: 一

Interpretations 釋義

Equally; by an equal progress; of the same rank.

A term used in a number of contexts but particularly in the situation of creditors sharing the assets of a debtor on a pro rata basis where none of them can have priority over the others.

平等地；同等步伐；在相同等級之上。

這個詞語可用於不同的情況，特別指債權人按比例分配債務人的資產，但他們當中沒有人享有優先權。

Examples 例句

1. 同時同等

a. Section 250, Companies Ordinance (Cap. 32)

Subject to the provisions of this Ordinance as to preferential payments, the property of a company shall, on its winding up, be applied in satisfaction of its liabilities **pari passu**, and, subject to such application, shall, unless the articles otherwise provide, be distributed among the members according to their rights and interests in the company.

除本條例中有關優先付款的條文另有規定外，公司財產在公司清盤時，須運用於公司債務的**同時同等**清償，而在符合該項運用原則下，除非章程細則另有訂定，否則須按照成員在公司所享有的權利及權益派發予成員。

b. *Hong Kong Housing Services for Refugees Limited vs. The Secretary for Justice*
Case Number: HCMP006007_1999

In the ordinary case, on a voluntary winding-up, section 250 of the Companies Ordinance would apply. That section provides as follows: – "Subject to the provisions of this Ordinance as to preferential payments, the property of a company shall, on its winding up, be applied in satisfaction of its liabilities **pari passu**, and, subject to such application, shall, unless the articles otherwise provide, be distributed among the members according to their rights and interests in the company."

《公司條例》第250條適用於處理一般自動清盤的申請。該條文規定如下：「除本條例中有關優先付款的條文另有規定外，公司財產在公司清盤時，須運用於公司債務的**同時同等**清償，而在符合該項運用原則下，除非章程細則另有訂定，否則須按照成員在公司所享有的權利及權益派發予成員。」

使用百分比	ELDoS: 100.00%
	BLIS: 10.00%

2. 同等

a. *Schedule 1 Table A Article 5, Companies Ordinance (Cap. 32)*

The rights conferred upon the holders of the shares of any class issued with preferred or other rights shall not, unless otherwise expressly provided by the terms of issue of the shares of that class, be deemed to be varied by the creation or issue of further shares ranking **pari passu** therewith.

持有發行時附有優先或其他權利的任何類別股份的人，所獲授予的權利，除非發行該類別股份的條款另有明文規定，否則不得當作因有產生或發行更多與其享有**同等**權益的股份而有所更改。

b. Section 75A(1), Companies Ordinance (Cap. 32)

Where in the case of – (a) debentures forming part of a series issued by a company and ranking **pari passu** with the other debentures of that series; or(b) debenture stock,the debentures or the trust deed or other document securing the debentures or stock provide for the holding of meetings of holders of debentures or stock, then subject to any provision so made, sections 113, 114B, 114C, 114D(2) and 114E shall apply in relation to such meetings and to the holders of the debentures or stock as they apply in relation to meetings of the company and members of the company.

凡屬——（a）構成公司所發行的一系列享有**同等**權益的債權證中的一部分的債權證；或（b）債權股證，而該等債權證或保證該等債權證或債權股證的信託契據或其他文件，就舉行債權證或債權股證持有人會議一事訂定條文，則在如此訂立的條文的規限下，第113、114B、114C、114D（2）及114E條適用於此等會議及該等債權證或債權股證持有人，一如適用於公司的會議及公司的成員。

c. Section 80(7), Companies Ordinance (Cap. 32)

Where a series of debentures containing, or giving by reference to any other instrument, any charge to the benefit of which the debenture holders of that series are entitled **pari passu** is created by a company, it shall for the purposes of this section be sufficient if there are delivered to or received by the Registrar within 5 weeks after the execution of the deed containing the charge or, if there is no such deed, after the execution of any debentures of the series, the following particulars….

凡公司設定一系列債權證，而該等債權證包含任何押記或藉提述任何其他文書而給予任何押記，並且由該系列債權證的持有人**同等**享有該項押記的利益，則若於載有該項押記的契據簽立後5個星期內，或（如無上述契據）於該系列任何債權證簽立後5個星期內，將下述詳情交付處長或由處長接獲，就本條而言，乃屬足夠⋯⋯。

d. Section 65A(2), Companies Ordinance (Cap. 32)

If at any time all the issued shares in a company, or all the issued shares therein of a particular class, are fully paid up and rank **pari passu** for all purposes, none of those shares need thereafter have a distinguishing number, so long as it remains fully paid up and ranks **pari passu** for all purposes with all shares of the same class for the time being issued and fully paid up.

如在任何時候，公司的全部已發行股份或公司某一類別的全部已發行股份，已全部繳足股款，並且在各方面均享有**同等**權益，則該等股份只要保持全部繳足股款及在各方面與當其時所有已發行並已全部繳足股款的相同類別股份享有**同等**權益的狀況，此後便無須具有一個識別號碼。

| 使用百分比 | ELDoS: | 0.00% |
| | BLIS: | 70.00% |

3. 同時及同等地

Section 38(8), Bankruptcy Ordinance (Cap. 6)

Subject to the provisions of this Ordinance, all debts proved in the bankruptcy shall be **paid pari** passu.

除本條例另有規定外，在破產案中經證明的所有債權均須**同時及同等地**予以償付。

| 使用百分比 | ELDoS: | 0.00% |
| | BLIS: | 10.00% |

4. 平等地

Section 56(1), Occupational Retirement Schemes Ordinance (Cap. 426)

Subject to subsections (2), (3) and (4), the assets of an occupational retirement scheme shall on its winding up be applied by the liquidator in satisfaction of its liabilities as at the date on which the winding up commenced **pari passu**.

在第（2）、（3）及（4）款的規限下，當某職業退休計劃清盤時，清盤人須運用該計劃的資產，**平等地**償還在計劃開始清盤當日的各項負債。

| 使用百分比 | ELDoS: 0.00% |
| | BLIS: 10.00% |

per capita *adj./adv.*

/pə ˈkæpɪtə/

Latin by the head

【中譯】 香港法庭判詞 ELDoS: **1** 人均；香港法例 BLIS: **1** 按每個人
計算；其他 Others: **1** 按人數；**2** 按人口平均計算；**3** 每人

Interpretations 釋義

Per head; for each person. Also a method of distribution of an
estate. Under this method every individual of a designated pool
of successors receives an equal share in his own right regardless
of the generation or the branch of family to which he belongs.

按每個人計算，亦指遺產分配的方法。根據此方法，每個合
資格繼承人，不論其輩分或所屬家族支系，各自取得應得的
遺產，每份分額相等。

Examples 例句

1. 人均

a. *To Kan Chi and others vs. Pui Man Yau and others*
Case Number: HCMP000562_1992

This case has not however resolved the situation as to how every
male member would agree to divide the property if the majority for
self-interest reason (as the majority Kans in the case) favoured the
per capita basis and would not have agreed to the division unless the
minority also agreed to such a basis.

然而該案並未解決以下問題：如果大多數男丁為自身利益着
想，既選擇**人均**基準，又除非少數派男丁遷就此基準，否則不
願分產（一如簡家訴訟的大多數男丁），試問要取得所有男丁
同意分產又談何容易。

b. *To Kan Chi and others vs. Pui Man Yau and others*
Case Number: HCMP000562_1992

This case is concerned with whether tso property should be divided on per stirpes basis as contended by the plaintiff who has only two sons, or on **per capita** basis as contended by the defendant who has seven sons and eight grandsons.

此案例涉及的問題為，祖之分產應否如僅有兩子之父的原告人所主張，以家系或房計算，抑由生有七子八孫的被告人所主張以**人均**或丁計算。

使用百分比	ELDoS: 100.00%
	BLIS: 0.00%

2. 按每個人計算

Schedule 1, Merchant Shipping (Limitation of Shipowners Liability) Ordinance (Cap. 434)

Notwithstanding paragraph 1 of this Article, the national law of any State Party to this Convention may fix, as far as carriers who are nationals of such State are concerned, a higher **per capita** limit of liability.

儘管有本條第1段的規定，本公約締約國的國家法律，可就身為該國國民的承運人，厘定較高的**按每個人計算**的責任限額。

使用百分比	ELDoS: 0.00%
	BLIS: 100.00%

per incuriam *adj.*

73

/ˌpɜː ɪnˈkjʊrɪəm/

Latin through the lack of care

【中譯】 香港法庭判詞 ELDoS：**1** 因失察所致；香港法例 BLIS：一；
其他 Others：**1** 出自失察；**2** 法庭失言；**3** 因不小心；**4** 疏忽所
致；**5** 疏忽引起；**6** 因失誤所致

Interpretations 釋義

Through carelessness; through inadvertence.

A court's decision is said to have been reached per incuriam
if the court ignored a relevant statutory provision or precedent
when adjudicating upon the case. Such a decision does not set a
precedent and need not be followed.

不小心或非故意引起的。

如果法庭在判案時忽略了相關的法例條文或案例，其判決則
屬因失察而得出的結果。該項判決不會成為案例，日後各級
法院也毋須依循。

Examples 例句

1. 因失察所致

a. *Mark Anthony Seabrook vs. HKSAR*
Case Number: FACC000006_1998

And when it eventually decided against the appellant, it did so (after
going into the merits of the case and deliberating for two months)
on the basis of its view on a point of sentencing principle, namely
that Humphries's case had been decided **per incuriam**, and that
sentencing guidelines which reduce sentences never benefit persons
who were sentenced before the guidelines were laid down.

可是上訴人上訴失敗並不是因為上訴法庭不願意將限期延長，而是——上訴法庭於聆訊完該案的理據及經過2個月的慎重考慮，最後決定將上訴人的申請駁回——基於判刑原則的問題。上訴法庭認定案例Humphries的決定是**因失察所致**，以及減輕刑罰的量刑指引永不惠及那些在該指引未訂立前已被判刑的人。

b. *Mark Anthony Seabrook vs. HKSAR*
Case Number: FACC000006_1998

HKSAR v. Humphries [1998] 2 HKLRD 520, condemned as **per incuriam** by the Court of Appeal in the present case, was itself a decision of the Court of Appeal (Power VP and Mayo and Stuart-Moore JJA).

案例*HKSAR v. Humphries*［［1998］2 HKLRD 520］本是上訴法庭（鮑偉華副庭長，上訴法庭法官梅賢玉及司徒冕組成）的決定。然而，卻在本上訴案被上訴法庭另一個審判庭宣告其決定是**因失察所致**。

c. *Mark Anthony Seabrook vs. HKSAR*
Case Number: FACC000006_1998

But one month later the division of the Court of Appeal from whose judgment this appeal is brought answered the same question in the negative, refused to reduce this appellant's sentence, and said that the other division's decision was **per incuriam**.

可是，在一個月後，上訴法庭的另一個審判庭，就同一問題作出的回應，卻是否定的結論；並且認為審判庭的先前決定是**因失察所致**，所以拒絕減輕本案上訴人的刑罰。本案上訴人不服其裁決，因此向本法院提出上訴。

使用百分比	ELDoS: 100.00%
	BLIS: 0.00%

per se *adj./adv.*

74

/ˌpɜː ˈseɪ/

Latin by itself

【中譯】 香港法庭判詞 ELDoS: **1** 本身；**2** 本質上；香港法例 BLIS：
1 本身；其他 Others: **1** 自身；**2** 唯因

> **Interpretations 釋義**
> Intrinisically; standing on its own
> 事物的本質；就事情本身而言。

Examples 例句

1. 本身

a. *Section 21, Defamation Ordinance Defamation Ordinance (Cap. 21)*

Heading: Words imputing unchastity to woman or girl **per se** actionable

意指婦人或少女不貞的言詞**本身**即可予以訴訟

b. *Lam Chi Keung vs. HKSAR*
Case Number: FAMC000012_1997

It is now said that the Court of Appeal erred in law because a statement of fact in a notice served under Schedule 2 cannot, **per se**, establish that fact as proved in a criminal court. It is, counsel says, a pure out-of-court statement.

現上訴一方指稱上訴法院犯了法律上的錯誤，因為（根據第二附表送達的）通知書內所載的事實陳述，其**本身**並不能確立該項事實已在刑事法院獲得證實。大律師指出這僅是庭外的陳述而已。

c. *Oriental Daily Publisher Limited vs. Commissioner for Television and Entertainment Licensing Authority*
Case Number: FACC000001_1998

I venture to suggest that if these photographs are considered indecent, the Tribunal would be coming close to holding that photographs of semi-naked females are **per se** indecent according to community standards.

恕本席大膽指出，假若這些照片被視為不雅，那麼審裁處便幾乎等如裁定半裸女子的照片（用社會的標準來衡量時），**本身**是不雅的。

使用百分比	ELDoS:	80.00%
	BLIS:	100.00%

2. 本質上

Hong Kong Housing Services for Refugees Limited vs. The Secretary for Justice
Case Number: HCMP006007_1999

The cases show that the mere existence of a power to alter objects does not **per se** affect the institution's charitable status. It is affected only if and when that power is exercised in such a way as to incorporate non-charitable objects.

種種的情況已表明了只具備更改宗旨的權力，**本質上**不會影響該機構的慈善組織地位，除非該機構行使權力收納非慈善宗旨，這才影響它的地位。

使用百分比	ELDoS:	20.00%
	BLIS:	0.00%

praecipe _n._

75

/ˈpriːsɪpɪ/ /ˈpresəpiː/

Latin command

【中譯】 香港法庭判詞 ELDoS: **1** 便箋；香港法例 BLIS: **1** 便箋；其他 Others: **1** 申請便箋

Interpretations 釋義

A written request filed in a court office by a party to a proceeding that contains the particulars of a document which he wishes to have prepared or issued.

訴訟其中一方送交法院辦公室的書面請求，內容為該方要求法院為其事先準備或發出文件的詳情。

Examples 例句

1. 便箋

a. Rule 16, Order 38, The Rules of the High Court (Cap. 4A)

Where there is a mistake in any person's name or address in a writ of subpoena, then, if the writ has not been served, the party by whom the writ was issued may have the writ re-sealed in correct form by filing a second **praecipe** under rule 14(5) endorsed with the words "Amended and re-sealed".

凡在任何傳召出庭令狀之上某人的姓名或名稱或位址出現錯誤，如該令狀尚未送達，則發出該令狀的一方可將該令以正確形式重新蓋章，方式是根據第14(5)條規則將第二份注有「Amended and re-sealed」字樣的**便箋**送交存檔。

b. Order 46 rule 6(2), The Rules of the High Court (Cap. 4A)

Before such a writ is issued a **praecipe** for its issue must be filed.

在令狀發出前，必須將關於發出該令狀的**便箋**送交存檔。

c. Order 75 rule 14(1), The Rules of the High Court (Cap. 4A)

Where a person claiming to have a right of action in rem against any property which is under arrest or the proceeds of sale thereof wishes to be served with notice of any application to the Court in respect of that property or those proceeds, he must file in the Registry a **praecipe** in Form No. 9 in Appendix B and, on the filing of the **praecipe**, a caveat shall be entered in the caveat book.

聲稱有權針對任何被扣押的財產或其出售所得收益提出對物訴訟的人，如希望獲送達關於任何就該財產或該等收益而向法庭提出的申請的通知書，則必須將一份採用附錄B表格9格式的**便箋**送交登記處存檔，該份**便箋**一經送交存檔，知會備忘即須登錄於知會備忘登記冊。

d. Walton Wai-Tati Li vs. Evelyn Man-York Li
Case Number: CACV000192_1997

Before a writ of subpoena is issued a **praecipe** for the issue of the writ must be filed in the Registry together with a note from a judge or master authorizing the issue of such writ and the sum of $500 shall be deposited in the Registry, in addition to any fee payable in respect of such issue, as a deposit in respect of the witness' reasonable expenses; and the **praecipe** must contain the name and address of the party issuing the writ, if he is acting in person, or the name or firm and business address of that party's solicitor and also (if the solicitor is the agent of another) the name or firm and business address of his principal.

在發出傳召出庭令狀前，必須將關於發出該令狀的**便箋**送交登記處存檔，該便箋須連同法官或聆案官授權發出該令狀的短簡送交存檔；除任何須就發出該令狀而繳付的費用外，亦須在登記處存放$500，作為就證人的合理開支而存放的款項；該**便箋**必須載有發出該令狀的一方的姓名或名稱及地址（如該一方是親自行事），或該一方的律師的姓名或事務所以及營業地址，並如該律師是另一律師的代理人，則亦須載有其委託人的姓名或事務所以及營業地址。

e. *Walton Wai-Tati Li vs. Evelyn Man-York Li*
Case Number: CACV000192_1997

In England and Wales, as in Hong Kong, a **praecipe** for the issue of the subpoena must first be filed in the office from which the subpoena is to issue.

在英格蘭及威爾斯，情況跟香港一樣，都必須先把要求發出傳召出庭令的**便箋**存交負責發出該令的辦事處。

使用百分比	ELDoS: 100.00%
	BLIS: 100.00%

prima facie 76

adj./adv.

/ˌpraɪmə ˈfeɪʃi/   /ˌpraɪmə ˈfeɪsi/

Latin at first sight

【中譯】 香港法庭判詞 ELDoS: **1** 表面；**2** 表面看來；**3** 表面上；**4** 表面成立；香港法例 BLIS: **1** 表面；**2** 表面看來；**3** 表面上；**4** 初步；**5** 表面證據；**6** 表面證據顯示；其他 Others: **1** 初步的；**2** 初步看來

Interpretations 釋義

On the face of it; unless disproved by evidence to the contrary

在沒有相反證據否定下，初步看來是成立的事物或理據等。

Examples 例句

1. 表面

a. Rule 40(2), Order 75, The Rules of the High Court (Cap. 4A)

The summons must be supported by an affidavit or affidavits showing that the defendant in question has a bona fide claim against the plaintiff in respect of the casualty in question and that he has sufficient **prima facie** grounds for the contention that the plaintiff is not entitled to the relief given him by the decree.

傳票必須由一份或多份表明下述事宜的誓章支持，即被告人就傷亡而針對原告人有真正的申索，以及被告人有充分的**表面**理由提出爭議，指原告人無權享有判令所給予他的濟助。

b. Section 69A(1), Companies Ordinance (Cap. 32)

The certification by a company of any instrument of transfer of shares in or debentures of the company shall be taken as a representation by the company to any person acting on the faith of the certification that there have been produced to the company such documents as on the face of them show a **prima facie** title to the shares or debentures in the transferor named in the instrument of transfer, but not as a representation that the transferor has any title to the shares or debentures.

任何公司對其股份或債權證的任何轉讓文書所作出的證明，須視作為該公司對基於信賴該項證明而行事的人作出一項表示，即該公司已獲出示文件，而該等文件**表面**顯示，該等股份或債權證的表面所有權屬於姓名或名稱載於該份轉讓文書的出讓人；但該項證明不得視作為就該名出讓人對該等股份或債權證具有任何所有權的一項表示。

c. Section 27(1), High Court Ordinance (Cap. 4)

If, on an application made by the Secretary for Justice under this section, the Court of First Instance is satisfied that any person has habitually and persistently and without any reasonable ground instituted vexatious legal proceedings, whether in the Court of First Instance or in any inferior court, and whether against the same person or against different persons, the Court of First Instance may, after hearing that person or giving him an opportunity of being heard, order that no legal proceedings shall without the leave of the Court of First Instance be instituted by him in any court and that any proceedings instituted by him in any court before the making of the order shall not be continued by him without such leave and such leave shall not be given unless the Court of First Instance is satisfied that the proceedings are not an abuse of the process of the Court and that there is **prima facie** ground for the proceedings.

如應律政司司長根據本條提出的申請，原訟法庭信納任何人曾慣常及經常在無合理理由的情況下提起無埋纏擾的法律程序（不論是在原訟法庭或任何下級法院，亦不論是針對同一人或針對不同的人），原訟法庭可在聆聽該人或在給予該人獲聆聽的機會後，命令在無原訟法庭許可的情況下，該人不得在任何法院提起法律程序，以及在無該許可的情況下，該人在該項命令作出前在任何法院所提起的法律程序不得繼續進行，而除非原訟法庭信納該等法律程序並非濫用法院程序及該等法律程序具有**表面**理由，否則不得給予該許可。

d. *Section 20(1), Bills of Exchange Ordinance (Cap. 19)*

Where a simple signature on a blank paper is delivered by the signer in order that it may be converted into a bill, it operates as a **prima facie** authority to fill it up as a complete bill for any amount, using the signature for that of the drawer, or the acceptor, or an indorser; and, in like manner, when a bill is wanting in any material particular, the person in possession of it has a prima facie authority to fill up the omission in any way he thinks fit.

凡空白紙張上的普通簽名，由簽名人交付予其他人，以將該紙張轉成為匯票，則該簽名所發揮的效用，是**表面**授權任何人在該紙張上填上任何款額，使其成為完成的匯票，而利用該簽名作為出票人、承兌人或背書人的簽名；同樣地，如匯票上漏填任何要項，則管有該匯票的人亦獲表面授權按其認為適當的方式填上漏填專案。

e. *Mui Foon and others vs. Land Development Corporation*
Case Number: HCMP006219_1998

Accordingly, I find that taking all the circumstances into account, and reading the parties' correspondence as a whole, this is not a case where the usual **prima facie** meaning did not apply.

考慮過所有的情況和整體地閱讀過雙方的書信往還後，相應地我的裁斷是此案並非一宗不可應用該通常**表面**意義的案件。

f. *Mui Foon and others vs. Land Development Corporation*
Case Number: HCMP006219_1998

The term "subject to contract" has acquired a definite ascertained legal meaning. Its clear **prima facie** meaning is that until there was an exchange of signed agreements between the parties, neither party was legally bound to buy or sell (as the case may be) – either party was at liberty to withdraw.

「以合約為准」一詞，已經有一個界定了的、確定的法律意義，其清楚的**表面**意義是除非雙方之間已交換了簽署了的協定，否則任何一方都毋須受法律約束而要購買或出售（視情況而定）——任何一方都有撤回的自由。

使用百分比	ELDoS: 46.67%
	BLIS: 55.56%

2. 表面看來

a. *Section 136(3), Copyright Ordinance (Cap 528)*

An application under subsection (1) must be in such form as is prescribed by rules of court and must be supported by an affidavit of the right holder which – ...(e) states the grounds for the application, including the facts relied upon by the deponent as showing that the article in question is **prima facie** an infringing copy....

根據第（1）款提出的申請，必須採用法院規則訂明的格式，並須有權利持有人作出的誓章支持，而該誓章須——……（e）述明提出申請的理由，包括宣誓人賴以顯示有關物品**表面看來**是侵犯版權複製品的事實……。

b. *Section 30B(3), Trade Descriptions Ordinance (Cap. 362)*

An application under subsection (1) shall be in such form as is prescribed by rules of court and shall be supported by an affidavit of the owner which – (Amended 35 of 2000 s. 98)...(c) states the grounds for the application, including the facts relied upon by the deponent as showing that the goods in question are **prima facie** infringing goods...

根據第（1）款提出的申請，須按法院規則指明的格式，並須由商標擁有人作出的誓章支持，而該誓章須——（由2000年第35號第98條修訂）……（c）述明提出申請的理由，包括宣誓人倚賴以顯示有關貨品**表面看來**是侵犯權利貨品的事實……

c. *Section 30C(1), Trade Descriptions Ordinance (Cap. 362)*

Where, on the hearing of an application made under section 30B, the owner presents adequate evidence to satisfy the Court of First Instance that the goods in question are **prima facie** infringing goods, the Court of First Instance may make an order directing the Commissioner or an authorized officer to take reasonable measures to seize or detain the goods on or after their importation.

凡於聆訊根據第30B條提出的任何申請時，商標擁有人出示充分的證據，使原訟法庭信納有關貨品**表面看來**是侵犯權利貨品，則原訟法庭可作出命令，指示關長或任何獲授權人員採取合理措施，於該等貨品進口時或進口之後檢取或扣留該等貨品。

d. *Secretary for Justice vs. Jerry Lui Kin Hong*
Case Number: FACC000003_1999

By this time someone had also noticed that, as some of the CYJ & Co. ledgers were computer print-outs, they were **prima facie** not within s.22 at all.

在當時已有人注意到有些陳盈仁公司的分類帳只是電腦列印本，所以這些分類帳**表面看來**根本不屬第22條所指的證據。

e. *Paul Chen and another vs. Lord Energy Limited*
Case Number: FACV000011_1998

It should be emphasised that on this approach, the matter is only **prima facie** and it may therefore be displaced on examination.

本席在此強調：只是在**表面看來**有上文所述情況的，才採用這個處理方法。故此，有關情況一經核證，處理手法或會有所不同。

f. *Poon Hau Kei vs. Hsin Cheong Construction Co. Limited Taylor Woodrow International Limited Joint Venture*
Case Number: FACV000012A_1999

Prima facie Mr. Poon should have all the costs incurred in this Court and in the Court of Appeal.

表面看來，Poon先生應獲得所有在本院及上訴法庭招致的訟費。

g. *Section 137(1), Copyright Ordinance (Cap. 528)*

Where, on the hearing of an application made under section 136, the right holder presents adequate evidence to satisfy the Court of First Instance that the article in question is **prima facie** an infringing copy, the Court of First Instance may make an order directing the Commissioner or an authorized officer to take reasonable measures to seize or detain the article on or after its importation.

凡有就根據第136條提出的申請而進行的聆訊，則如在進行該聆訊時權利持有人出示充分的證據，令原訟法庭信納有關物品**表面看來**是侵犯版權複製品，則原訟法庭可作出命令，指示關

長或任何獲授權人員採取合理措施,於該物品輸入時或輸入後
檢取或扣留該物品。

使用百分比	ELDoS: 26.67%
	BLIS: 16.67%

3. 表面上

a. Section 221, Companies Ordinance (Cap. 32)

The court may, at any time after making a winding-up order, require
any contributory for the time being on the list of contributories, and
any trustee, receiver, banker, agent or officer of the company to pay,
deliver, convey, surrender, or transfer forthwith, or within such time
as the court directs, to the liquidator any money, property, or books
and papers in his hands to which the company is **prima facie** entitled.

法院可在作出清盤令後的任何時間,要求任何當其時名列分擔
人列表的分擔人以及任何受託人、接管人、銀行、代理人或
公司的高級人員,立即或在法院所指示的時間內,將在其手中
而公司又在**表面**上有權享有的任何款項、財產或簿冊及文據支
付、交付、轉易、退回或轉讓予清盤人。

b. Section 72(1), Trade Marks Ordinance (Cap. 559)

The Registrar shall have the power to give to a person who proposes
to apply for the registration of a trade mark advice as to whether the
trade mark appears to the Registrar **prima facie** to be capable of
distinguishing goods or services of one undertaking from those of
other undertakings within the meaning of section 3(1) (meaning of
"trade mark").

處長有權向擬申請將某商標註冊的人,就處長覺得該商標**表面**
上是否屬第3(1)條(「商標」的涵義)所指能夠將某一企業的
貨品或服務與其他企業的貨品或服務作出識別的商標而給予意
見。

c. Section 73(1), Trade Marks Rules (Cap. 559A)

Any person who proposes to apply for the registration of a trade mark may apply to the Registrar for advice as to whether the trade mark appears to the Registrar **prima facie** to be capable of distinguishing goods or services of one undertaking from those of other undertakings within the meaning of section 3(1) of the Ordinance.

任何擬申請將某商標註冊的人，可向處長提出申請，徵求處長對他是否覺得該商標**表面**上屬本條例第3（1）條所指能夠將某一企業的貨品或服務與其他企業的貨品或服務作出識別的商標的意見。

d. Rule 67, Companies (Winding-Up) Rules (Cap. 32H)

The powers conferred on the court by section 211 of the Ordinance shall be exercised by the liquidator. Any contributory for the time being on the list of contributories, trustee, receiver, banker or agent or officer of a company which is being wound up under order of the court shall, on notice from the liquidator and within such time as he shall by notice in writing require, pay, deliver, convey, surrender or transfer to or into the hands of the liquidator any sum of money or balance, books, papers, estate or effects which happen to be in his hands for the time being and to which the company is **prima facie** entitled.

本條例第211條授予法院的權力，須由清盤人行使。任何公司如正根據法院命令進行清盤，當其時名列其分擔人列表的任何分擔人或該公司的任何受託人、接管人、銀行、代理人或高級人員，須在接獲清盤人的通知時及在清盤人藉書面通知而規定的期限內，將當其時恰巧在他手中而又是公司**表面**上有權享有的任何款項或結餘、簿冊、文據、產業或財物支付、交付、轉易、退回或轉讓予清盤人或清盤人手中。

e. Section 35, Evidence Ordinance (Cap. 8)

In civil proceedings – ...(c) the court may, on matters of public history, literature, science, or art, refer, for the purposes of evidence, to such published books, maps, or charts as the court may consider to be of authority on the subject to which they relate;...shall **prima facie** be deemed to be correct, and shall be admitted in evidence without further proof.

在民事法律程序中——⋯⋯（c）法庭可為證據方面的目的，就公眾歷史、文學、科學或藝術方面的事宜，參照法庭認為在有關的主題上具權威地位的已出版書本、地圖或圖表；⋯⋯須當作**表面**上正確，無須再加證明，即須接納為證據。

f. Chim Hon Man vs. HKSAR
  Case Number: FACC000003_1998

The ordinary rule is that a word should **prima facie** bear the same meaning in the same section.

根據通常的規則，任何字詞在同一條法例條文中應該**表面**上有相同的涵義。

g. Direk Mahadumrongkul vs. Lau Chun Keung and others
  Case Number: Cacv000133_1998

In those circumstances it seems to me that, **prima facie**, the three defendants must be regarded as being in sole occupation.

在這樣情況下，我認為，**表面**上3名被告人必須視為單獨佔用該等泊車位。

使用百分比	ELDoS: 20.00%
	BLIS: 19.44%

4. 表面成立

Redland Concrete Limited vs. Hing Lee Construction Company Limited and another

Case Number: HCA008140_1998

His Lordship said that the view expressed by Lord Justice Jenkins in *Grimshaw v. Dunbar* [1953] 1 QB 408, 416 was a long way from the view expressed by Sir Roger Omrod in Saudi Eagle where it was held that in dealing with the question of construction the real question was whether it was a "**prima facie**" defence (per Lord Atkins in *Evans v. Bartlam*, at p. 480), a "serious" defence (per Lord Russell of Killowen at p. 482) or had merits to which "the court should pay heed" (per Lord Wright at p. 489).

原審法官謂上訴法院法官Jenkins於*Grimshaw v. Dunbar*（[1953]1 QB 408, 416）一案發表的見解與Roger Omrod爵士在Saudi Eagle案所說的截然不同。 上訴法院法官Jenkins裁定，在詮釋方面，真正的問題是：這是否一項「**表面成立**」的抗辯（按 Atkins 勳爵於*Evans v. Bartlam*案（第480頁）所言）；「嚴正」的抗辯（按Russell 勳爵所言，見第482頁），或是具有法庭應當考慮的勝訴因由（按Wright勳爵所言，見第489頁）。

使用百分比	ELDoS:	6.67%
	BLIS:	0.00%

5. 初步

Schedule 1 Article 1–2, Fugitive Offenders (Internationally Protected Persons and Hostages) Order (Cup. 503H)

"alleged offender" means a person as to whom there is sufficient evidence to determine **prima facie** that he has committed or participated in one or more of the crimes set forth in article 2.

「嫌疑犯」是指有充分證據可以**初步**斷定為犯有或參與第二條所列舉的一項或數項罪行的人。

使用百分比	ELDoS:	0.00%
	BLIS:	2.78%

6. 表面證據

Schedule, Fugitive Offenders (Malaysa) Order (Cap. 503D)

ARTICLE 14 **PRIMA FACIE** RULE AND TERMS OF SURRENDER

第十四條**表面證據**規則及移交條件

使用百分比	ELDoS:	0.00%
	BLIS:	2.78%

7. 表面證據顯示

Section 26, Tramway Ordinance (Cap. 107)

If it be represented in writing to the Chief Executive in Council by the Commissioner for Transport or by 20 inhabitant ratepayers that the public are not afforded the full benefit of the tramway, the Chief Executive in Council may (if satisfied that **prima facie** the case is one for inquiry) appoint an officer to inquire into the matter and to hold an inquiry and report thereon, and if the truth of the representation be proved, the Chief Executive in Council may issue an order to the company requiring it to provide such a service of cars as will afford to the public the full benefit of the tramway, and such order may prescribe the number of cars which the company shall run upon the tramway and the mode and times in and at which such cars shall be run. Every such order shall be served upon the company within 48 hours after it has been made, and shall be published in the Gazette next following the making thereof…

如運輸署署長或有20名身為差餉繳納人的居民就公眾未獲得電車軌道的益處一事，以書面向行政長官會同行政會議申述，行政長官會同行政會議（如信納**表面證據顯示**該個案須作查訊）可委任一名人員調查該事，並進行查訊及提交查訊報告；如申述書的真實性得以證實，行政長官會同行政會議可向公司發出命令，要求其提供能使公眾充分獲得電車軌道益處的電車廂服務，而該命令亦可訂明公司須安排在電車軌道上行駛的電車廂數目，以及該等電車廂行駛的方式及時間。每一該等命令須於其發出後48小時內送達公司，並須於其發出後的下一期憲報上刊登……

使用百分比	ELDoS:	0.00%
	BLIS:	2.78%

prima facie case

n. pl. prima facie cases

77

/ˌpraɪmə ˈfeɪʃi keɪs/   /ˌpraɪmə ˈfeɪsi keɪs/

Latin prima facie = at first sight

【中譯】 香港法庭判詞 ELDoS: **1** 表面證據；香港法例 BLIS: **1** 表面
證據；**2** 表面的案；**3** 表面個案；其他 Others: **1** 表面案情；
2 有表面證據的案件；**3** 有初步證據的案件；**4** 有立案證據的
案件；**5** 有希望立案的案件

Interpretations 釋義

A case that has been established by sufficient evidence and will
prevail unless the other side adduces satisfactory evidence to
disprove it.

除非另一方援引令人信納的證據反駁，否則案件在充分及有
力的證據支持下得以成立。

Examples 例句

1. 表面證據

a. Section 43, Insurance Companies Ordinance (Cap. 41)

Provided that such a petition shall not be presented except by leave
of the Court, and leave shall not be granted until a **prima facie case**
has been established to the satisfaction of the Court and until security
for costs for such amount as the Court may think reasonable has been
given.

但此項呈請非經法庭許可不得提出，而法庭除非信納**表面證據**
經已確立，且法庭認為屬合理數額的訟費保證金經已付出，否
則不得給予許可。

b. Section 8(4), Juvenile Offenders Ordinance (Cap. 226)

If it appears to the court that a **prima facie case** is made out, the evidence of any witnesses for the defence shall be heard, and the child or young person shall be allowed to give evidence.

法庭如認為控罪的**表面證據**成立,則須聆聽辯方證人的證據,並須容許該兒童或少年人作證。

c. Section 38, Landlord and Tenant (Consolidation) Ordinance (Cap. 7)

Where a landlord establishes a **prima facie case** that there has been an apparent change in the occupancy of premises or of part thereof, the tenant shall be deemed to have parted with the possession of such premises or of such part unless he satisfies the Tribunal to the contrary.

凡業主能確立**表面證據**,證明處所或其部分的佔用情況表面上有改變,租客即當作已放棄對該處所或其部分的管有,但租客如能提供相反證據足以使審裁處信納,則屬例外。

d. Lau Suk Han and another vs. HKSAR
   Case Number: FAMC000005_1998

The question is essentially one of statutory construction of section 4(1)(a) and (3) of the Dangerous Drugs Ordinance. It was conceded by the applicants that if section 4(1)(a) is held to cover dangerous drugs in transit, a **prima facie case** is revealed against each applicant. The Court of Appeal concluded, reversing the trial judge, that section 4(1)(a) covered dangerous drugs in transit.

問題基本上是《危險藥物條例》第4(1)(a)及(3)條的法定釋義。申請人接納同意假若裁定第4(1)(a)條是包括過境途中的危險藥物,那針對每名申請人而言便有**表面證據**。上訴法庭推翻原審法官的結論,裁定第4(1)(a)條是包括過境途中的危險藥物。

e. *Mexon Holdings Limited vs. Silver Bay International Limited*

Case Number: FACV000016_1999

It seems to me that there was a **prima facie case** here that the sub-division of the floor might have resulted in an unauthorized partition because there had been no proper provision for adequate means of escape in case of emergency.

依本席看來，本案有**表面證據**證明將該層樓細分可能導致非法分劃，因為並沒有為那層樓妥善地提供足夠的逃生途徑，以備一旦發生緊急事故之用。

f. *Section 81E(2), Criminal Procedure Ordinance (Cap. 221)*

The appeal may be – (a) on any ground which involves a question of law;(b) on the ground that the documents and evidence before the court were sufficient to establish a **prima facie case** against the accused for the offence set out in the charge or for any other offence for which he might be convicted upon that charge.

上訴可基於以下的理由——（a）任何涉及法律問題的理由；（b）就控罪書內列明的罪行或被控人可就該控罪書而被定罪的任何其他罪行而言，在法庭席前的文件及證據足以針對被告人構成**表面證據**。

g. *Section 22(1), Complex Commercial Crimes Ordinance (Cap. 394)*

The accused may at any time before the jury is empanelled apply to the judge for his discharge on the ground that the evidence disclosed is insufficient to establish a **prima facie case** against him for the offence with which he is charged or for any other offence for which he might be convicted upon that charge.

被控人在陪審團組成之前，可隨時向法官提出釋放申請，申請理由為所披露的證據，就他被控的罪行而言或就他因該控罪而可能被裁定已犯的其他罪行而言，並不足以使該等罪行的**表面證據**成立。

h. Section 42C(1), Professional Accountants Ordinance (Cap. 50)

Where pursuant to a direction under subsection (2) an Investigation Committee informs the Council that in its opinion there is a **prima facie case** against the professional accountant, the Council may in its discretion constitute a Disciplinary Committee pursuant to section 33(3) and refer the matter to it, and the Disciplinary Committee concerned shall deal with it as if it were a complaint referred to it under section 34(1) and for that purpose the matter shall be deemed to be a complaint made to the Registrar by the Investigation Committee.

凡調查委員會依據根據第（2）款作出的指示通知理事會，指出其認為有對專業會計師不利的**表面證據**，則理事會可酌情決定依據第33（3）條成立紀律委員會，並將該事宜提交該委員會，而有關的紀律委員會須處理該事宜，猶如該事宜是根據第34（1）條向該委員會提交的投訴一樣，而為該目的，該事宜須當作為調查委員會向註冊主任作出的投訴。

使用百分比	ELDoS: 100.00%
	BLIS: 90.91%

2. 表面的案

Section 16(1), Criminal Procedure Ordinance (Cap. 221)

...the accused may at any time − ...(b) after the filing of the indictment and prior to his arraignment thereon...apply to a judge for his discharge on the grounds that the evidence disclosed in the documents handed to the court...is insufficient to establish a **prima facie case** against him for the offence with which he is charged or for any other offence for which he might be convicted upon that charge.

……（b）被控人可在公訴書送交存檔後，但須在就公訴書被公訴提控前……隨時向法官申請將他釋放，所基於的理由是……

遞交法院的文件……所披露的證據……並不足以就他所被控告
的罪行，或就他基於該控罪而可能被定罪的任何其他罪行，針
對他而確立**表面的案**。

b. Rule 4, Criminal Procedure (Applications under Section 16) Rules (Cap. 221G)

The notice of application shall be in the form prescribed in the Schedule or as near thereto as circumstances permit, and shall – (a) be signed by the applicant; (b) set out the grounds of the application particularizing in full why it is alleged no **prima facie case** is disclosed; (c) give an address at which notices relating to the application may be served on the applicant.

申請通知須採用附表所訂明的格式，或情況所容許的儘量近似
格式，並須──(a)由申請人簽署；(b)列出申請的理由，充
分詳細說明為何有**表面的案**未見披露的指稱；(c)提供可將關
於申請的通知送達申請人的地址。

使用百分比	ELDoS:	0.00%
	BLIS:	6.06%

3. 表面個案

a. Section 168IA(1), Companies Ordinance (Cap. 32)

The court may, on the application of the Official Receiver by a report stating that in his opinion a **prima facie case** exists against any person that would render him liable to a disqualification order under this Part, direct that the person shall attend before the court on a day appointed by the court for that purpose and be publicly examined as to the conduct of the business of a company or as to his conduct and dealings as a director.

法院可應破產管理署署長藉報告作出的申請(報告是述明破產
管理署署長認為有針對某人的**表面個案**存在，可使法院根據本

部對該人作出一項取消資格令的），指示該人須於法院指定的日期到法庭席前，並就公司業務的處理或就他作為董事的行為操守及事務往來接受公開訊問。

使用百分比	ELDoS:	0.00%
	BLIS:	3.03%

prima facie evidence

n. pl. prima facie evidence

/ˌpraɪmə ˈfeɪʃi ˌevɪdəns/ /ˌpraɪmə ˈfeɪsi ˌevɪdəns/

Latin prima facie=at first sight

【中譯】 香港法庭判詞 ELDoS: **1** 表面證據；香港法例 BLIS: **1** 表面
證據；其他 Others: **1** 顯證；**2** 初步證據；**3** 立案證據

Interpretations 釋義

Evidence that is presumably sufficient to establish the existence of a fact and, if not contradicted, remains good and sufficient.
被推定為可以力陳事實的證據。除非有相反證據否定，否則該證據仍可被視為妥善及充分。

Examples 例句

1. 表面證據

a. Section 22A(3), Evidence Ordinance (Cap. 8)

Notwithstanding subsection (1), a statement contained in a document produced by a computer used over any period to store, process or retrieve information for the purposes of any activities ("the relevant activities") carried on over that period shall be admitted in any criminal proceedings as **prima facie evidence** of any fact stated therein if − (a) direct oral evidence of that fact would be admissible in those proceedings....

如任何電腦是在任何一段期間內用於為在該段期間內進行的任何活動（「有關活動」）而儲存、處理或檢索資料，則儘管第（1）款已有規定，一項載於由該電腦製作的文件的陳述如符合以下各項情況，在任何刑事法律程序中須接納為該陳述內所述任何事實的**表面證據**——（a）該事實的直接口頭證據在該法律程序中會是可接納的……。

b. Section 31C(4), Legal Practitioners Ordinance (Cap. 159)

The publication in the Gazette by the Bar Council of a list of the names and addresses of those barristers who have obtained employed barrister's certificates for the period therein stated shall be prima facie evidence that each person named therein is the holder of such a certificate for the period specified in such list, and the absence from any such list of the name of any person shall be **prima facie evidence** that the person does not hold such a certificate.

凡執委會在憲報刊登載有已取得受僱大律師證書的大律師的姓名及地址的名單，而名單亦述明各證書的有效期間，則該名單即為證明每名該等大律師在其中所指明的期間持有上述證書的表面證據；而任何人如並無名列上述任何名單，此事實即為該人並非持有上述證書的**表面證據**。

c. Section 80, Trade Marks Ordinance (Cap. 559)

In any proceedings relating to a registered trade mark, including proceedings for rectification of the register, the registration of a person as owner of a trade mark shall be **prima facie evidence** of the validity of the original registration and of any subsequent assignment or other transmission of it.

在任何與註冊商標有關的法律程序（包括為更正註冊紀錄冊而進行的法律程序）中，任何人註冊為商標的擁有人，即為該商標的原有註冊及其任何日後的轉讓或其他傳轉的有效性的**表面證據**。

d. Section 20(1), Gambling Ordinance (Cap. 148)

Where in any proceedings under this Ordinance a court is satisfied that a tape recording machine or a tape recording was used in or in connexion with the commission of an offence under section 7 or 8, then a tape recording produced by that machine or the tape recording, as the case may be, shall be admissible in evidence and shall be **prima facie evidence** of any matter recorded thereon.

在根據本條例而進行的任何法律程序中，凡法庭信納有答錄機或錄音帶曾在犯有第7或8條所訂罪行時被使用或被使用於有關犯有第7或8條所訂罪行，則該錄音帶或由該機所錄音的錄音帶（視屬何情況而定），須接納為證據，並須作為其內所錄得任何事宜的**表面證據**。

e. Secretary for Justice vs. Jerry Lui Kin Hong
Case Number: FACC000003_1999

Where statements contained in documents produced by a computer, which have been adopted as part of the business records of a company, are tendered as **prima facie evidence** of the facts stated therein, is the tenderer required to comply with the provisions of section 22 or section 22A of the Evidence Ordinance. [sic]

凡載於由電腦製作之文件內的陳述被提出作為陳述內所述事實的**表面證據**，而那些文件已被公司採取為業務紀錄的一部分，則提出者是否必須遵從《證據條例》第22條或第22A條的規定？

f. Secretary for Justice vs. Jerry Lui Kin Hong
Case Number: FACC000003_1999

It lays down the conditions upon which a statement contained in a document produced by a computer must be admitted as **prima facie evidence** of any fact so stated.

它規定一些條件並表明載於由電腦製作的文件內的陳述在符合了這些條件後須被接納為該陳述內所述任何事實的**表面證據**。

g. *Secretary for Justice vs. Jerry Lui Kin Hong*
Case Number: FACC000003_1999

It will be seen that there are three conditions which have to be satisfied before a document is admissible under s.22 as **prima facie evidence** of any fact which it states. They are set out in paragraphs (a), (b) and (c) of subsection (1).

從上述所引之條文中可見，任何文件必須先符合三項條件，才能根據第22條被接納為該文件內所述任何事實的**表面證據**，這些條件已於第（1）款的（a）、（b）和c段內列明。

h. *Section 71, Companies Ordinance (Cap. 32)*

A certificate, under the common seal of the company or the seal kept by the company under section 73A, specifying any shares held by any member, shall be **prima facie evidence** of the title of the member to the shares.

任何股票，經蓋上公司法團印章或蓋上公司根據第73A條所備存的印章，並指明某成員所持有的任何股份，即為該名成員對該等股份的所有權的**表面證據**。

i. *Section 36, Evidence Ordinance (Cap. 8)*

Where any notice, order or other document is required by any enactment to be published in the Gazette, or where any document referred to in section 35(b) appears in the Gazette, a copy of the Gazette in which it is so published or appears shall be **prima facie evidence** of the facts stated in such notice, order or document.

凡任何成文法則規定任何公告、命令或其他文件須在憲報刊登，或凡有第35（b）條提述的文件載於憲報，則一份如此刊登或載有該公告、命令或文件的憲報的文本，即為該公告、命令或文件內所述事實的**表面證據**。

使用百分比	ELDoS: 100.00%
	BLIS:　　100.00%

265

pro forma *adj.*

/ˌprəʊ ˈfɔːmə/

Latin as a matter of form

【中譯】 香港法庭判詞 ELDoS: **1** 形式上；**2** 形式性；香港法例 BLIS:
—；其他 Others: **1** 按格式；**2** 形式的；**3** 表面的；**4** 由於形式
上的理由

Interpretations 釋義

As a matter of form; for the sake of form; according to formality
形式和格式方面的事情；為了追求形式的配合；根據正式手
續進行的事情

Examples 例句

1. 形式上

Lau Kong Yung and others vs. Director of Immigration
Case Number: HCAL000020_1999

The "Summary of Facts" bears a **pro forma** paragraph as follows: −...

案情簡述書內有一段**形式上**的句子如下：——⋯⋯

使用百分比	ELDoS: 50.00%
	BLIS: 0.00%

2. 形式性

Twinkle Step Investment Limited vs. Smart International Industrial Limited
Case Number: FACV000004_1999

This is an appeal by the defendant to an action relating to the sale by it of a house in Hong Lok Yuen to the plaintiff. The only contractual document between the parties is a **pro forma** one headed "Provisional Agreement for Sale and Purchase" dated 12 June 1997.

此乃被告人就一宗訴訟而提出之上訴。該訴訟涉及被告人出售一所位於康樂園之房屋予原告人，雙方唯一的合約性文件為一紙日期是1997年6月12日，名為「臨時買賣協議」的**形式性**文件。

使用百分比	ELDoS: 50.00%
	BLIS: 0.00%

pro rata *adj./adv.*

80

/ˌprəʊ ˈrɑːtə/ /ˌprəʊ ˈreɪtə/

Latin proportionately

【中譯】 香港法庭判詞 ELDoS: **1** 按比例；香港法例 BLIS: **1** 按比例；
2 按⋯⋯比例；其他 Others: **1** 按比率；**2** 按比例計；**3** 成比例
的；**4** 成比例地

Interpretations 釋義

Proportionately; according to interest or liability; by share
根據比例計算；按照權益或責任劃分；以佔有的分額分配

Examples 例句

1. 按比例

a. Section 57B(1), Companies Ordinance (Cap. 32)

Provided that no such prior approval shall be required in relation to
the allotment of shares in the company under an offer made **pro rata**
by the company to the members of the company, excluding for that
purpose any member whose address is in a place where such offer is
not permitted under the law of that place.

但公司如根據一項**按比例**向其成員作出的要約，將其股份分配
予公司的成員（就此而言，不包括該項要約未為成員地址所在
地的法律所准許的任何成員），則無須事前獲得上述的批准。

b. Samuel Tak Lee vs. Lee Tak Yan and another
Case Number: CACV000118_1999

Interest attributable to the specified sums shall include a **pro rata**
share of interest accrued on amounts (of which the specified sums

form part) placed on fixed deposits and on the savings account. In computing such **pro rata** share of interest, withdrawals made to meet the Company's expenses shall be deemed to have been made out of the Company's income.

可歸於該等指明款額的利息，包括存於定期和儲蓄帳戶裏（部分為該等指明款額）的款項，**按比例**分攤的累算利息，計算這**按比例**分攤的利息的，支付公司費用的提款，將被視為從公司的收入中提取。

c. Section 19(8), Bankruptcy Ordinance (Cap. 6)

Where the Official Receiver, after a public examination is held, is of the opinion that the application for the holding of the public examination was frivolous or vexatious, he may apply to the court for an order that the creditors who required the public examination to be held pay, on a **pro rata** basis based on value of debts, the costs incurred by the Official Receiver in holding it and the court may, if it agrees, assess the costs incurred and make an order for the pro rata payment of such costs.

在進行公開訊問後，凡破產管理署署長認為申請進行該公開訊問一事乃屬瑣屑無聊或無理取鬧的，他可向法院申請命令，飭令該名要求進行該公開訊問的債權人以債項價值為基準，按比例償付破產管理署署長因進行該公開訊問而招致的費用，法院如同意，則可評定所招致的費用並為**按比例**償付該等費用而作出命令。

d. Section 6E(5), Employees' Compensation Ordinance (Cap. 282)

In determining the amount of reimbursement payable under section 6(5), if the aggregate claimed amount exceeds the amount specified in the second column of the Sixth Schedule shown opposite section 6(5) specified in the first column of that Schedule, the Commissioner shall apportion the amount payable on a **pro rata** basis.

在裁定根據第6(5)條須付還的數額時，如申索合計總額超過
附表6第2欄中相對於該附表第1欄所指明的第6(5)條之處指明
的款額，處長須將須付的款額**按比例**分配。

e. *Section 4(a)(i), Securities and Futures (Stock Market Listing) Rules (Cap. 571V)*

...by a capitalization issue **pro rata** (apart from fractional entitlements) to existing shareholders, whether or not they are shareholders whose addresses registered in the books of the corporation are in a place outside Hong Kong and to whom the securities are not actually issued or allotted because of restrictions imposed by legislation of that place; or(ii) pursuant to a scrip dividend scheme which has been approved by the corporation in general meeting....

……藉一項資本化發行，**按比例**（零碎的權利不計算在內）向
現有股東（不論該等股東在法團簿冊內的登記地址是否在香港
以外地方，亦不論是否因該地方的法例所施加的限制，致使
該等證券實際上沒有向該等股東發行或分配）發行或分配的證
券；或（ii）依據法團在成員大會上批准的以股代息計劃發行或
分配的證券……。

f. *Section 41AB(3)(a), Employment Ordinance (Cap. 57)*

Where an employer makes an election under this section, he shall thenceforth use that 12 month period as the leave year for the purpose of calculating the annual leave entitlement of all of his employees and, where an employee has not been in employment under a continuous contract for the full period of a leave year − (a) the employer shall calculate the leave entitlement on a **pro rata** basis, based on the number of calendar days between the day the employee commenced employment and the end of the leave year, divided by 365, and any fraction of a day resulting from the calculation shall be counted as a full day's leave...

凡僱主根據本條作出決定，他須從那時起採用該12個月期間為假期年，以計算他所有僱員有權享有的年假，及如僱員並未曾根據連續性合約在假期年的整段期間受僱——（a）僱主須根據僱員開始受僱當日與假期年終結之間的西曆日日數，除以365，以**按比例**基準計算該僱員有權享有的年假，因該計算而產生的一日的部分，須算為一整日的假期……

使用百分比	ELDoS: 100.00%
	BLIS: 88.89%

2. 按……比例

a. Schedule 1-2.(2), Broadcasting (Licence Fees) Regulation (Cap. 562A)

If the remaining period of validity of a licence immediately after any anniversary of the specified day is less than 1 year, then the annual licence fee payable for the remaining period shall be calculated on a **pro rata** basis.

如某牌照在緊接指明日期的某個周年日之後尚餘的有效期不足1年，則就尚餘有效期繳付的周年牌費的數額須**按**該尚餘期佔有關年份的**比例**計算。

b. Rule 3(4), Rules For Construction of Policy, Schedule, Marine Insurance Ordinance (Cap. 329)

Where freight, other than chartered freight, is payable without special conditions and is insured "at and from" a particular place, the risk attaches **pro rata** as the goods or merchandise are shipped; provided that if there be cargo in readiness which belongs to the shipowner, or which some other person has contracted with him to ship, the risk attaches as soon as the ship is ready to receive such cargo.

凡運費（不包括租船運費）是於不附帶特別條件下須予支付，以及是「於及由」某處地方受保的，風險責任**按**貨品或商品已裝運的**比例**而起期；但如已準備妥當的貨物是屬於船東，或是

由其他人與該船東訂約同意裝運的，則在該船舶準備妥當收取
該等貨物時，風險責任即行起期。

c. Section 4(b), Securities and Futures (Stock Market Listing) Rules (Cap. 571V)

securities offered on a pre-emptive basis, **pro rata** (apart from
fractional entitlements) to existing holdings, to holders of the
relevant class of shares in the corporation, whether or not they
are shareholders whose addresses registered in the books of the
corporation are in a place outside Hong Kong and to whom the
securities are not actually offered because of restrictions imposed by
legislation of that place

以優先認股方式**按**現有持股**比例**（零碎的權利不計算在內）向
法團有關類別股份的持有人（不論該等股東在法團簿冊內的登
記地址是否在香港以外地方，亦不論是否因該地方的法例所施
加的限制，致使該等證券實際上沒有向該等股東提出要約）提
出要約所涉的證券

| 使用百分比 | ELDoS: | 0.00% |
| | BLIS: | 11.11% |

pro tanto *adj./adv.*

/ˌprəʊ ˈtæntəʊ/

Latin for so much

【中譯】 香港法庭判詞 ELDoS: **1** 在這程度上；香港法例 BLIS: 一；
其他 Others: **1** 至此；**2** 到這個程度；**3** 以此為限

Interpretations 釋義

For that much; to that extent; for as much as may be

在所敍述的幅度、層次、範圍、數額上。

Examples 例句

1. 在這程度上

Novatel Communications (Far East) Limited vs. Canadian Imperial Bank of Commerce and another

Case Number: HCA008052_1999

The cash collateral account was then debited in the like sum and ICB's loan account credited therewith, reducing **pro tanto** the amount owing by ICB to the Defendant.

然後，在該現金抵押品帳戶記入借方同一筆數而隨即記入ICB貸款帳戶貸方，**在這程度上**減少了ICB所欠被告人之數。

使用百分比	ELDoS: 100.00%
	BLIS: 0.00%

quantum *n. pl. quanta*

/ˈkwɒntəm/

Latin how much

82

【中譯】 香港法庭判詞 ELDoS: **1** 數額；**2** 賠償金額；**3** 金額；**4** 賠償
數額；**5** 賠償；**6** 損害賠償金額；**7** 損害賠償額；**8** 數量；
9 額；香港法例 BLIS: **1** 額；**2** 量；其他 Others: **1** 所索金額；
2 賠款額；**3** 定量；**4** 份量；**5** 賠償額；**6** 總量

Interpretations 釋義

A quantity (of money); the amount (of damages)
（金錢的）數額；（賠償金的）總額

Examples 例句

1. 數額

a. *Tai Chau Yung and another vs. Ng Jim*
Case Number: HCPI000753_1997

Having heard Mr Wright and after having read the Memorandum
for Settlement as well as the two written opinions by Mr Wright in
respect of liability, **quantum** and evidence in this matter, I gave my
approval to the Plaintiff's acceptance of the monies paid into Court in
full satisfaction of the Plaintiff's claim against the Defendants.

經聆聽韋先生的陳詞，又經審閱「和解備忘錄」及韋先生就本
案所涉及之法律責任、**數額**及證據所撰寫的意見書，本席批准
原告人接受被告人存交法庭之款項，以完全了結原告人向被告
人提出之申索。

b. *Ling Nam Herbalist Koon and others vs. Radio Television Hong Kong*
Case Number: HCA000263_1997

However, if it were necessary for me to do so, I certainly do not consider that the **quantum** suffered by them to be anywhere near the sums they claimed.

儘管如此，假如本席需要這樣做的話，可以肯定，經衡量後量定的**數額**，與他們所要求的數額，將會相差甚遠。

使用百分比	ELDoS: 28.00%
	BLIS: 0.00%

2. 賠償金額

a. *Tong Tim Nui and others vs. Hong Kong Housing Authority*
Case Number: CACV000281_1998

The issues relating to individual Applicants' eligibility to claim for damages and the **quantum** of damages were left to be assessed at a later date.

至於個別申請人是否合資格申索損害賠償以及**賠償金額**的問題則留待日後評定。

b. *Tong Tim Nui and others vs. Hong Kong Housing Authority*
Case Number: CACV000281_1998

Thereafter, over the course of the next few months, the Judge proceeded to determine the eligibility for and **quantum** of damages payable to all applicants on the basis which he laid down in the March 19th decision, no matter when their applications had been made.

自此，在往後的幾個月內，法官依據他在3月19日的判決所定下的基礎審定申請人的資格及厘定申請人應得的**賠償金額**而不論他們的申請何時提出。

c. *Oriental Press Group Limited vs. Apple Daily Limited*
Case Number: FACV000006_1998

The second hearing concerned damages; it is only the Judge's decision on **quantum** that has been in question, initially before the Court of Appeal and now in this Court.

第二次聆訊是關於損害賠償，法官所判定的**賠償金額**成為唯一的爭議，在其上訴被上訴法庭駁回後，上訴人現在向本法院提出上訴。

| 使用百分比 | ELDoS: 24.00% |
| | BLIS: 0.00% |

3. 金額

a. *Chan Chee Shum and another vs. The Incorporated Owners Of Gold Mine Building*
Case Number: LDBM000224Y_1998

The applicants challenged the validity and the **quantum** of the respondent's demand for renovation and repair charges, including the reserved fund and the consultation fees.

申請人質疑答辯人要求他們支付維修及裝修費用包括儲備基金及顧問費用之合法性，並質疑所須繳付之**金額**。

b. *Alucase Company Limited and another vs. Keen Lloyd (Holdings) Limited*
Case Number: HCMP003577_1998

In my view this amount (the **quantum** of which is not challenged) is recoverable.

本席認為此筆款項（對**金額**並無質疑）是可予追討的。

| 使用百分比 | ELDoS: 16.00% |
| | BLIS: 0.00% |

4. 賠償數額

Ling Nam Herbalist Koon and others vs. Radio Television Hong Kong
Case Number: HCA000263_1997

However, I shall set out my findings on credibility both for the sake of completeness and because it is relevant to the issue of **quantum** (if that needs to be decided): –

但是，本席一來為了處事徹底起見，二來亦鑒於此點會對衡量**賠償數額**那方面的爭論有重要性（若果需要決定這一點的話），因此本席會列述對可信性方面的裁斷結果：

使用百分比	ELDoS:	8.00%
	BLIS:	0.00%

5. 賠償

Ling Nam Herbalist Koon and others vs. Radio Television Hong Kong
Case Number: HCA000263_1997

Since I already found against the Plaintiffs on liability, I do not need to consider the question of **quantum**.

由於本席經已在關於責任誰負方面裁定原告等敗訴，本席實無需考慮衡量**賠償**方面的問題。

使用百分比	ELDoS:	8.00%
	BLIS:	0.00%

6. 損害賠償金額

Tong Tim Nui and others vs. Hong Kong Housing Authority
Case Number: CACV000281_1998

The Hong Kong Housing Authority opposes these appeals but has submitted to the judge's order of 27 June 1996 (against which it has not appealed) and all his subsequent decisions as to "eligibility" and "**quantum**".

香港房屋委員會反對這些上訴，但接受原審法官於1996年6月27日所作之命令，（房委會並沒有對此命令提出上訴）以及其後作出的所有關於「資格」及「**損害賠償金額**」的判決。

使用百分比	ELDoS:	4.00%
	BLIS:	0.00%

7. 損害賠償額

Tong Tim Nui and others vs. Hong Kong Housing Authority
Case Number: CACV000281_1998

As it happens, there being no-one with any legitimate claim to any relief, no-one has suffered any detriment from the judge's manner of conducting the various hearings he held on "eligibility" and "**quantum**", in the course of which he attempted to create and administer his own scheme for the determination of such claims.

事實上，由於沒有申請人的濟助申索具法理依據，所以也沒有人因原審法官在那些關於「資格」及「**損害賠償額**」的不同聆訊中所採用的方式而蒙受任何損失。（原審法官在這些聆訊中自行制定及施行一套關於這些申索的裁斷方案）。

使用百分比	ELDoS:	4.00%
	BLIS:	0.00%

8. 數量

To Kan Chi and others vs. Pui Man Yau and others
Case Number: HCMP000562_1992

The distinction between common fund and indemnity costs basis lies only on the burden of proof. It would not affect the **quantum**, see *Wharf Properties Ltd v. Eric Cumine Associates & Others* [1992] 2 HKLR 273.

「共同款項」（common fund basis）及「彌償基準」（indemnity basis）之別單取決於舉證之責任，並不影響**數量**：見*Wharf Properties Ltd v. Eric Cumine Associates & Others* 一案［1992］2 HKLR 273。

使用百分比	ELDoS:	4.00%
	BLIS:	0.00%

9. 額

a. Rule 13, Solicitors (Professional Indemnity) Rules (Cap. 159m)

Any dispute or difference concerning the existence in **quantum** of any liability for any contribution to be made or caused to be made by any solicitor in accordance with rule 4...shall be referred to a single arbitrator to be appointed in default of agreement by the President of the Society for the time being.

任何爭議或歧見是關於任何律師按照第4條將作出或安排作出的任何供款**額**的法律責任的存在……須提交單一仲裁員仲裁，而在沒有協定的情況下則由當其時的律師會會長委任單一仲裁員。

b. Tong Tim Nui and others vs. Hong Kong Housing Authority
Case Number: CACV000281_1998

Acting in person, they approached the court, by originating or ordinary summonses, after the judge had made his order of 27 June 1996 but before he had finally disposed of all the issues as to "eligibility"and "**quantum** of damages" raised in the public law proceedings instituted by the original applicants.

他們沒有律師代表，在原審法官於1996年6月27日發出命令後，但尚未就最初的申請人之公法訴訟中所提出的所有涉及「資格」及「損害賠償**額**」問題作出最終裁決前，以原訴傳票或普通傳票向法庭提出申請。

使用百分比	ELDoS:	4.00%
	BLIS:	66.67%

10. 量

Rule 13, Solicitors (Professional Indemnity) Rules (Cap. 159M)

Any dispute or difference…concerning any claim or the **quantum** of any claim to be provided with Indemnity in accordance with rules 10, 11 and 12 shall be referred to a single arbitrator to be appointed in default of agreement by the President of the Society for the time being.

任何爭議或歧見是……關於按照第10、11及12條將提供彌償的任何申索或任何申索量者，須提交單一仲裁員仲裁，而在沒有協定的情況下則由當其時的律師會會長委任單一仲裁員。

使用百分比	ELDoS:	0.00%
	BLIS:	33.33%

quantum meruit *n.*

/kwɒntəm ˈmeruːɪt/

Latin as much as one deserves

【中譯】　香港法庭判詞 ELDoS: **1** 按勞計酬；香港法例 BLIS: 一；
其他 Others: **1** 按勞計酬；**2** 按照服務計酬；**3** 相當的付給；
4 按合理價格支付；**5** 辛勞所值

Interpretations 釋義

The reasonable amount to be paid for services or work done without any prior agreement in contract law.

適用於合同法：在沒有合約的情形下，受僱人士可以根據他所提供的服務或工作而要求合理的報酬。

Examples 例句

1. 按勞計酬

a. Ko Chi Keung vs. Lee Ping Yan Andrew
Case Number: HCA018029A_1999

The claim is for, inter alia, damages for breach of contract alternatively, damages on a **quantum meruit** basis.

原告人申索的是違約的損害賠償，或是基於**按勞計酬**的損害賠償。

b. Ko Chi Keung Vs. Lee Ping Yan Andrew
Case Number: Hca018029a_1999

The plaintiff there also claims damages on a **quantum meruit** basis and the trial judge will have to deal with the extent of the work performed by him and also whether this is the same work performed by the firm of accountants in action no. 445.

原告人在這訟案中也申索以**按勞計酬**為基礎的損害賠償。主審法官將要處理的問題包括：原告人所做工作的範圍，以及這工作是否就是在第445號訟案中會計師事務所所做的工作。

使用百分比	ELDoS: 100.00%
	BLIS: 0.00%

quid pro quo *n.*

84

/ˌkwɪd prəʊ ˈkwəʊ/

Latin what for what

【中譯】 香港法庭判詞 ELDoS: **1** 交換條件；香港法例 BLIS: 一；其
他 Others: **1** 回報；**2** 誘因；**3** 報償；**4** 報復；**5** 相等的補償或
報酬；**6** 對價

Interpretations 釋義

This for that; something for something. This phrase is used to
denote the mutual consideration in a contract.

一物換一物，用於顯示合約中當事各方的相互代價。

Examples 例句

1. 交換條件

Jumbo King Limited vs. Faithful Properties Limited and others
Case Number: FACV000007_1999

The court is not privy to the negotiation of the agreement − evidence
of such negotiations is inadmissible − and has no way of knowing
whether a clause which appears to have an onerous effect was a **quid
pro quo** for some other concession. Or one of the parties may simply
have made a bad bargain.

因為法庭對各方洽商協議的情節，全然不知——洽商內容不可
接納為法庭證據——故此法庭根本無法得知某一似乎過於繁苛
的條款是否某些折衷安排的**交換條件**，又或只是協議一方做了
一宗不上算的交易。

使用百分比	
ELDoS:	100.00%
BLIS:	0.00%

quorum *n. pl. quorums*
/ˈkwɔːrəm/
Latin of whom

【中譯】 香港法庭判詞 ELDoS: **1** 法定人數；香港法例 BLIS: **1** 法定
人數；**2** 法定……人數；其他 Others: 一

Interpretations 釋義

The minimum number of members who must be present to make
the meetings, votes, transactions, etc. of a body, such as a board
of directors or the Legislative Council, valid.

一個團體（如董事會或立法會等）開會、投票、交易等必須有
的最少出席人數。人數不足，則該等活動均告無效。

Examples 例句

1. 法定人數

a. Section 74(2), Legal Practitioners Ordinance (Cap. 159)

The **quorum** for the Costs Committee shall be the Chairman and 2
members under subsection (1)(d).

事務費委員會的**法定人數**須為主席及第（1）（d）款所訂的2名
成員。

b. Francis Cheung and another vs. Insider Dealing Tribunal
Case Number: CACV000157_1999

Having the proper **quorum** at all relevant times, from the beginning
up to the very last moment is a question of principle, of public policy
and of sound and fair administration of justice.

由始至終，在有關時刻要有恰當的**法定人數**，是一項原則性問題，也是公共政策和正確合理而公平地執行司法工作的問題。

c. *Francis Cheung and another vs. Insider Dealing Tribunal*
Case Number: CACV000157_1999

A long series of cases have established a proposition which I would venture to formulate as follows: in setting a **quorum** and requiring that a minimum number of persons participate in a decision, Parliament reposes its faith in collective wisdom, does so for the benefit of the public as well as for the benefit of those who might be affected by the decision either as members of the majority or as dissenting members to act together up to the very last moment which is the making of one united, though not necessarily unanimous, decision.

一連串的案例已確立了一項命題，而我會嘗試用以下方式闡述之：在訂立**法定人數**和規定參與作出決定的至少人數時，議會兩院將信心放在集體智慧上，不論這些人是大多數人或持異見者，使他們可以同心協力至最後一刻，達致一項聯手作出的決定，雖然這未必是一致的意見。議會這樣做，除為了公眾的利益外，也為了可能受該決定影響的人之利益。

d. *Francis Cheung and another vs. Insider Dealing Tribunal*
Case Number: CACV000157_1999

While there appears to be no authority directly on the point in issue, a perusal of the jurisprudence that has examined questions related to **quorum** indicates that the courts have consistently insisted on the necessity for a decision making authority to strictly comply with **quorum** requirements at all times.

雖然看來沒有典據與討論中要點直接有關，但翻閱法理學關於檢討**法定人數**這問題時，可以看到法庭一貫堅持決策機關在任何時候，都必須嚴格遵守**法定人數**的要求。

e. Section 125H, Public Health and Municipal Services Ordinance (Cap. 132)

At a meeting of the Board, other than an appeal hearing or a meeting for the purposes of section 125B(5) − (a) the **quorum** shall be not less than half the members of the Board for the time being;(b) the Chairman or Vice-Chairman shall preside;(c) decisions are to be made by a majority of the members present and voting; and(d) the person presiding has a casting vote.

在上訴聆訊或為第125B（5）條的目的而舉行的會議以外的委員會會議上——（a）會議的**法定人數**不得少於委員會當其時的成員人數的一半；（b）主席或副主席須主持會議；（c）問題由出席並有投票的成員的多數票決定；及（d）主持會議者有權投決定票。

f. Section 2(2), Town Planning Ordinance (Cap. 131)

5 members of the Board, one of whom must be the chairman or vice-chairman, shall form a **quorum** at any meeting of the Board.

在規劃委員會的任何會議上，5名規劃委員會成員（其中一名須為主席或副主席）即構成**法定人數**。

g. Section 40C(3)(a), Building Management Ordinance (Cap. 344)

a management committee under subsection (2)(a) shall be deemed to be effected if at the meeting of owners convened under that subsection a resolution in favour of that appointment is passed by a majority vote of the owners voting either personally or by proxy at a meeting with a **quorum** of not less than 10% of the owners; and for the purposes of that meeting, any proxy appointed by an owner for the purposes of voting on that resolution shall be treated as being an owner present at the meeting for the purposes of establishing that **quorum**.

如在為第(2)(a)款的目的召開的有達到不少於業主人數10%
（「會議**法定人數**」）的業主出席的業主會議上，親自出席或委
派代表出席投票的業主以多數票通過贊成委任管理委員會的決
議，則該款所指的決議委任管理委員會一事，須當作已完成；
而就該會議而言，在確定是否達到會議**法定人數**時，獲業主委
派就該決議投票的代表，須視作出席會議的業主計算。

使用百分比	ELDoS: 100.00%
	BLIS: 99.09%

2. 法定……人數

Schedule – 6, Occupational Safety and Health Council Ordinance (Cap. 398)

The **quorum** of the Council shall be 10 and, while a member is disqualified from taking part in a decision or deliberation of the Council in respect of a matter, he shall be disregarded for the purpose of constituting a **quorum** of the Council for deciding, or deliberating on, that matter.

職安局的**法定會議人數**為10人。如有一名成員在某事項上被取消參與作出決定或商議的資格，則在計算職安局決定或商議該事項的**法定會議人數**時，不得將他計算在內。

使用百分比	ELDoS: 0.00%
	BLIS: 0.91%

ratio decidendi *n. pl. rationes decidendi*

/ˈreɪʃiːəʊ ˌdesəˈdendɪ/

Latin the reason for the decision

86

【中譯】　香港法庭判詞 ELDoS: **1** 判案理由；**2** 判決理由；香港法例

BLIS: 一；其他 Others: **1** 判決之根據；**2** 判決依據

Interpretations 釋義

The rationale for a judge's decision; the part of the judgment that explains how the court reached its decision; the legal principles on which the decision was founded.

法官作出判決的理據；判決書的一部分，解釋法庭為何作出是項判決；判決背後所根據的法理。

Examples 例句

1. 判案理由

Redland Concrete Limited vs. Hing Lee Construction Company Limited and another
Case Number: HCA008140_1998

On my analysis of the **ratio decidendi** of the Po Kwong case, the Court of Appeal held that the correct principle in deciding the setting aside of irregular judgment is the Limited Right Principle....

況且，以本席分析Po Kwong Marble案的**判案理由**所得，上訴法庭亦裁定適用於處理將不合規範判決作廢，是「有限權利」準則……。

使用百分比	ELDoS: 50.00%
	BLIS: 0.00%

2. 判決理由

Secretary for Justice vs. Jerry Lui Kin Hong
Case Number: FACC000003_1999

But so far as the decision deals with the application of the statutory hearsay exception, the true **ratio decidendi** is in my opinion to be found in a passage which the court…quotes from the unreported judgment of Pill J. in *R. v. Dobson*….

至於判決中涉及傳聞證據之法定例外規定的適用範圍方面，本席認為真正的**判決理由**可見於法庭引述自大法官 Pill J 在 *R. v. Dobson* 這宗未經報導案件中的一段文字……。

使用百分比	ELDoS: 50.00%
	BLIS: 0.00%

ratione personae *adv.*

/ˌræʃiːˈəʊniː pɜːˈsəʊniː/

Latin by reason of the person

【中譯】 香港法庭判詞 ELDoS: **1** 屬人的理由；香港法例 BLIS: 一；
其他 Others: 一

Interpretations 釋義
Because of the person concerned
由有關人士引起的

Examples 例句

1. 屬人的理由

N vs. O
Case Number: HCMP004204_1998

Article 4 concerns the scope of the Convention **ratione personae** as regards those children who are to be protected and reads − ...

第4條則按照**屬人的理由**來訂定受公約保護的兒童之範圍，內文是：──……

使用百分比	ELDoS: 100.00%
	BLIS: 0.00%

res *n. pl. res*

/reɪz/ /riːz/

Latin a thing

【中譯】 香港法庭判詞 ELDoS: **1** 爭論點；香港法例 BLIS: 一；其他
Others: **1** 物；**2** 事件；**3** 財產；**4** 標的；**5** 有體物；**6** 無體物；
7 權利的客體

Interpretations 釋義

A thing; a matter; an object; the subject matter
物件、事情、主題事項。

Examples 例句

1. 爭論點

Mui Foon and others vs. Land Development Corporation
Case Number: HCMP006219_1998

Since there was no legally binding agreement, the question whether
the Plaintiffs had good title to give to the Defendant and whether they
had answered "requisitions" satisfactorily were hypothetical only,
and it is well-established that the Court does not decide hypothetical
questions when there is no **res** between the parties.

由於欠缺有法律約束力的協議，那麼原訴人是否有妥善的業
權給予被告人的問題，和他們（原訴人）是否已完滿地答覆了
「（那些）要求」，純屬基於假設的而已，而法庭在雙方之間並
無**爭論點**存在時，不會就基於假定的問題作決定，則是確認已
久的了。

使用百分比	ELDoS: 100.00%
	BLIS: 0.00%

res gestae _n. pl. res gestae_

/ˌreɪz ˈgestaɪ/ /ˌriːz ˈdʒestiː/

Latin things done

【中譯】　香港法庭判詞 ELDoS: **1** 已成既往的事；**2** 案件事實；香港法例 BLIS: 一；其他 Others: **1** 案發經過；**2** 成就之事；**3** 真事實；**4** 有關物；**5** 犯罪構成要件事情實況；**6** 案情經過；**7** 有關事實；**8** 真實事實

Interpretations 釋義

Things done; the events that occurred.

It is a rule of evidence that hearsay evidence is generally inadmissible in a court proceeding. However, words, acts and statements of this type that are closely linked to the circumstances of the crime in question may be admissible if they form part of the res gestae by, for example, accompanying or explaining a fact in issue.

已做的事情；已發生的事件。

根據證據法則，傳聞證據一般在法律程序中是不獲接納的。然而，如果傳聞證據中的說話、行為和陳述與所述罪行的經過有密切關係（例如與有關事實同時發生或可以解釋有關事實的），則屬於「事情經過」的一部分，有可能成為可接納證據。

Examples 例句

1. 已成既往的事

Wang Din Shin vs. Nina Kung alias Nina T.H. Wang
Case Number: HCAP000008A_1999

In the end I am fully satisfied that Teresa's unshaken impression was that it was Nina who talked to her over the phone before the letter was sent and thus Nina was fully aware of the subject matter she was engaged in. Thereafter Teresa received the form with adaptations together with a letter written to her by Nina, to complete the **res gestae** sequence.

總而言之，本席裁定王德嫻所說收信前是跟龔如心通的話、而龔如心清楚是在辦什麼手續，這個印象是堅定的。之後王德嫻再收到修改後的表格，上面寫有龔如心給她的字條，接着就去辦餘下**已成既往的事**。

使用百分比	ELDoS: 50.00%
	BLIS:　0.00%

2. 案件事實

HKSAR vs. Wong Wai-Man (D1) Hau King-Yeung (D2) Lee Kar-Yeung (D3)
Case Number: CACC000315_1998

The sweeping statement about statements made outside the trial is, of course, generally true, but there are exceptions to it, as, for example, if the statements are part of the **res gestae** or made by a combination in furtherance of a common design.

對於在審訊以外所作出的陳述的涵蓋性看法，在一般情況下當然是正確的，但當中亦有例外的情況，例如，假如有關陳述是**案件事實**的一部分，或由一夥人在為了進一步達成共同計劃時而作出的。

使用百分比	ELDoS: 50.00%
	BLIS:　0.00%

res ipsa loquitur n. pl. res ipsa loquitur

90

/ˌreɪz ɪpsə ˈlɒkwɪtə/ /ˌriːz ɪpsə ˈlɒkwɪtə/

Latin the thing speaks for itself

【中譯】 香港法庭判詞 ELDoS: **1** 事實不證自明；香港法例 BLIS:
一；其他 Others: **1** 事實不證自明；**2** 事情不言自明；**3** 事物自
道緣由；**4** 事實自證

Interpretations 釋義

A rule of evidence usually invoked in tort of negligence cases.
Under this rule, the plaintiff need not induce any evidence to
establish a prima facie case against the defendant if the facts
of the accident seem so obvious that the factor which caused
the accident was under the defendant's exclusive control and
that the accident was a kind which does not usually happen
without negligence. The defendant is rebuttably presumed to
have been negligent and it is up to him to show that it is not his
responsibility.

通常在因疏忽而引起的侵權訴訟中援引的證據法規。根據本
法規，原告人毋須舉出任何證據，案件即可視作表面證據成
立，被告人亦會被推定曾有疏忽作為。因為在沒有人疏忽的
情況下，案中意外通常不會發生，而案情又明確顯示，意外
起因是被告人完全可以避免的。被告人若要證明意外並非自
己的責任，便需舉證反駁該項推定。

Examples 例句

1. 事實不證自明

    a. Wong Sze Shun Syson and another vs. Au Mei Ling Eva and others
       Case Number: HCA005646_1997

The Plaintiffs also aver that in so far as may be necessary, they will rely upon the doctrine of **res ipsa loquitur** to establish that the bursting of the said water pipe and the water leakage were caused by the negligence of the Defendants.

原告人亦堅稱只要有需要，他們會援引「**事實不證自明**」的原則來證明上述食水喉管的爆破及食水滲漏為被告人疏忽所致。

    b. The Queen vs. Kwok Yan Man
       Case Number: HCMA000665_1995

The learned magistrate in convicting the Appellant said "Obviously, the doctrine of **res ipsa loquitur** applies here. Prima facie the Defendant is careless". He did not believe the Appellant's evidence.

裁判官在裁定上訴人罪名成立時稱：「『**事實不證自明**』原則明顯在本案中適用，表面上看來被告人是疏忽魯莽的。」因此，他不相信上訴人提出的證供。

    c. Lo Yuk Chu vs. Hang Yick Properties
       Case Number: CACV000169_1996

For negligence alleging water damage to her premises and consequential loss caused by flooding as a result of a blocked sewage pipe caused, inter alia, by a failure by the defendant to inspect and maintain the sewage pipe. The appellant sought to rely when proving this allegation upon the maxim **res ipsa loquitur**.

上訴人指稱因被告人疏忽，尤其是沒有妥善檢查及保養污水渠，令污水渠淤塞，從而使她的單位的食水受到污染，並最終因水浸造成損失。上訴人在證明此指稱時尋求援引法諺「**事實不證自明**」。

使用百分比	ELDoS: 100.00%
	BLIS: 0.00%

res judicata n. pl. res judicata

91

/ˈreɪs ˌdʒuːdɪˈkeɪtə/ /ˈriːz ˌdʒuːdɪˈkɑːtə/

Latin a thing adjudicated

【中譯】 香港法庭判詞 ELDoS: **1** 已判事情；**2** 已成定案；香港法例
BLIS: 一；其他 Others: **1** 已判決的事情；**2** 既判案件；**3** 已判
決的事項；**4** 已結之案；**5** 已裁事實；**6** 已經裁判之事；**7** 定
案

Interpretations 釋義

When a matter has been fully and finally adjudicated on by
a court of competent jurisdiction, the decision is conclusive
between the parties to the action and no future action on the
same matter may be brought by them or their successors in
interest. The rule does not preclude an appeal. The rationale for
the rule is the need for finality and it is against public interest to
allow a matter finally decided to be relitigated.

當一件案件獲具有司法管轄權的法院作全面及最終判決後，
該項判決為訴訟各方之間不可推翻的。訴訟人或其權益繼承
人不可就相同案件再提出訴訟。此規令並不妨礙訴訟人提出
上訴。其理據是任何案件必要有所終結與定斷，而容許已作
最終判決的案件再提出訴訟則有違公眾利益。

Examples 例句

1. 已判事情

a. *Chan Siu Lun vs. Hui Cho Yee and another*
Case Number: CACV000171A_1999

The second question depends on the application of a doctrine of estoppel, namely **res judicata**.

第二個問題取決於不容反悔法其中之一項法則的應用，即**已判事情**這個法則。

b. *Chan Siu Lun vs. Hui Cho Yee and another*
Case Number: CACV000171A_1999

We do not see how in the circumstances of the appellant's case, the doctrine of "**res judicata**" would not prevent him from pursuing his new action which was no more than re-litigation on a cause of action which had been fully adjudicated on its merits by a court of competent jurisdiction.

從上訴人的案情看來，我等看不出「**已判事情**」這個法則，為何不能阻止他繼續進行新訴訟，該新訴訟只不過是就一項已由具司法管轄權之法庭對事非曲直作出了全面判決的訴因再次提出訴訟。

c. *Chan Siu Lun vs. Hui Cho Yee and another*
Case Number: CACV000171A_1999

The plea of **res judicata** applies, except in special cases, not only to points upon which the court was actually required by the parties to form an opinion and pronounce a judgment, but to every point which properly belonged to the subject of litigation, and which the parties, exercising reasonable diligence, might have brought forward at the time.

除了特別個案外，**已判事情**之申辯並非只適用於訴訟各方要求法庭給予意見或作出判決之論點，而是亦適用於和訴訟標的正正有關的每個論點，亦即是訴訟各方，在盡了合理之努力後，當時所可能提出的各個論點。

| 使用百分比 | ELDoS: 66.67% |
| | BLIS: 0.00% |

2. 已成定案

Vankin Investments Limited vs. Wing Lung Bank Limited
Case Number: HCA015962_1999

The plea of **res judicata** applies, except in special cases, not only to points upon which the court was actually required by the parties to form an opinion and pronounce a judgment, but to every point which properly belonged to the subject of litigation, and which the parties, exercising reasonable diligence, might have brought forward at the time.

除非案件特殊，「**已成定案**」這個答辯不但適用於那些當事人確曾要求法院下判斷或者作出判決的事項，同時也適用於做事勤奮得宜的當事人本來可以提出而又確實可以成為訴訟事項的每一事項。

| 使用百分比 | ELDoS: 33.33% |
| | BLIS: 0.00% |

sic *adv.*

/sɪk/

Latin thus

92

【中譯】 香港法庭判詞 ELDoS: **1** 原文如此；香港法例 BLIS: 一；其他 Others: 一

Interpretations 釋義

It is used to indicate that the quotation was a faithful reproduction of the original document and that any error therein is not the quoter's responsibility.

用以顯示有關引文為忠實地取自原文，因此引文中的任何錯誤並不是引述人的責任。

Examples 例句

1. 原文如此

a. *HKSAR vs. Tang Sau-Leung*
Case Number: CACC000620_1996

The log is specifically referred to in paragraph 1 of the Admitted Facts where it was admitted Tse made a 999 call to police at "7.35 p.m." (**sic**) on 21 July 1995 as shown in the "Incident Log of Royal Hong Kong Police Records".

這個日誌在「雙方承認的事實陳述書」的第1段中有特別提及到，而在第一段中大家承認：謝湛波是在1995年7月21日「下午7時35分」（**原文如此**）致電999電台報警。一如「香港皇家員警紀錄的事項日誌」所載。

b. *Liu Kin Leung vs. Tsang Mi Ling*
   Case Number: HCMP007660_1999

"The aforesaid declaration, if made [**sic**], and any transfer of interest pursuant thereto" was made subject to the approval of the Hong Kong Jockey Club and the existing mortgagee of the Property to continue the mortgage and the ownership scheme of the Jockey Club on the existing terms and conditions (Paragraph 8).

「上述宣告（如作出的話）〔**原文如此**〕及任何根據該宣告而進行的權益轉讓」，須得到香港賽馬會及該物業現時的承按人批准以現時的條款及條件繼續提供有關按揭及馬會自置居所計劃，方為有效（第8段）。

c. *Chan Ho-Kay vs. HKSAR*
   Case Number: CACC000375_1999

Quite apart from any motive Chung or anyone else had, it is open to you to find that the accused himself also had no (**sic**) motive.

除認定與鐘永青和任何其他人士有動機外，你們有權可以認定被告人本身亦沒有（**原文如此**）動機。

使用百分比	ELDoS: 100.00%
	BLIS: 0.00%

sine die adv.

93

/ˌsaɪni ˈdaɪiː/ /ˌsɪni ˈdiːeɪ/

Latin without day

【中譯】 香港法庭判詞 ELDoS: **1** 無限期；香港法例 BLIS: **1** 無限期；
其他 Others: **1** 不定期

Interpretations 釋義

Indefinitely; without appointing a date for resumption
不設限期；沒有指定恢復進行某事的日期

Examples 例句

1. 無限期

a. Rule 85, Bankruptcy Rules (Cap. 6A)

Where an examination has been adjourned **sine die** and the bankrupt
desires to have a day appointed for proceeding with his public
examination, the expense of gazetting, advertising and giving notice
to creditors of the day to be appointed for proceeding with such
examination shall, unless the Official Receiver or trustee, as the
case may be, consents to the costs being paid out of the estate, be at
the cost of the bankrupt, who shall, before any day is appointed for
proceeding with the public examination, deposit with the Official
Receiver such sum as the Official Receiver may think sufficient
to defray the expense aforesaid. The balance of the deposit after
defraying the expense aforesaid shall be returned to the bankrupt.

凡一項訊問**無限期**押後，而破產人意欲法院指定某日期以恢復
對其進行公開訊問，除非破產管理署署長或受託人（視屬何情
況而定）同意有關訟費從有關產業中撥付，否則就恢復進行該
項訊問的指定日期而在憲報刊登公告、作出宣傳及向債權人發
出通知的開支，須由破產人承擔。破產人須在法院指定任何日
期以恢復進行該項公開訊問前，向破產管理署署長繳存破產管
理署署長認為足以支付上述開支的款項。該筆繳存款項於支付
上述開支後的餘款，須交還破產人。

b. Rule 83, Bankruptcy Rules (Cap. 6A)

Where the court is of opinion that a bankrupt is failing to disclose
his affairs or where the bankrupt has failed to attend the public
examination or any adjournment thereof or where the bankrupt has
not complied with any order of the court in relation to his accounts,
conduct, dealings and property and no good cause is shown by him
for such failure, the court may forthwith commit the bankrupt for
contempt of court or may adjourn the public examination **sine die**,
and may make such further or other order as the court thinks fit.

凡法院認為破產人沒有披露其事務，或破產人沒有出席公開訊
問或任何經押後的公開訊問，或破產人沒有遵從法院就其帳
目、行為操守、交易及財產各事項而作出的任何命令，而破產
人未能就此提出好的因由，法院可立即將破產人以犯藐視法庭
罪而交付羈押，或將公開訊問**無限期**押後，並可作出法院認為
合適的進一步或其他命令。

c. Rule 84, Bankruptcy Rules (Cap. 6A)

The court may on the application either of the Official Receiver or of
the bankrupt appoint a day for proceeding with a public examination
which has been adjourned **sine die**.

法院應破產管理署署長或破產人的申請，可指定恢復進行曾被
無限期押後的公開訊問的日期。

d. *Ong Ee Chang vs. Li Tung Lok and another*
Case Number: HCA002541_1993

Apart from an order made on 14th July 1997 adjourning **sine die** another summons issued by the Defendants (this time for further and better particulars of the Further Re-amended Statement of Claim), no steps in the action were taken in this period of alleged inactivity.

而除了在1997年7月14日法庭頒令**無限期**押後另一張由被告人發出的傳票外（這一次是要求原告人就經重新再修改的申索陳述書提供更詳盡清楚的詳情），在這段被指為沒有作出行動的期間裏便沒有任何一方採取其他訴訟步驟。

e. *Rule 86, Bankruptcy Rules (Cap. 6A)*

In any case in which a public examination has been ordered under section 19(4) of the Ordinance or has been adjourned **sine die** and the court afterwards makes an order for proceeding with such public examination, notice of the date, time and place appointed for such public examination shall be sent by the Official Receiver to all persons mentioned in section 19(5) of the Ordinance, and such notice shall also be gazetted at least 7 days before the day so appointed.

凡已根據本條例第19（4）條命令作出公開訊問，或公開訊問被**無限期**押後，而法院其後作出恢復進行該公開訊問的命令，則有關進行該公開訊問的指定日期、時間及地點的通知，須由破產管理署署長送交本條例第19（5）條所提及的所有人，而該通知亦須在如此指定的日期前最少7天在憲報上刊登。

使用百分比	ELDoS: 100.00%
	BLIS: 100.00%

status quo *n.*

94

/ˌsteɪtəs ˈkwəʊ/ /ˌstætəs ˈkwəʊ/

Latin

【中譯】 香港法庭判詞 ELDoS: **1** 原狀；**2** 現狀；香港法例 BLIS: 一；
其他 Others: 一

Interpretations 釋義

The existing state of things
事物當下的狀況

Examples 例句

1. 原狀

a. N vs. O
Case Number: HCMP004204_1998

The means by which the Convention counters such mischief is by an
early restoration of the **status quo** which is achieved by ensuring the
prompt return of the child to the country of its natural environment.
If this were not done, it would allow the party who has abducted the
child to a country of refuge or wrongfully retained the child in that
country to seek the assistance of the courts there and by that means
create a jurisdiction which is more or less artificial.

至於打擊這些不當行為的方法則是早日回復**原狀**。也就是説，
法院應迅速地將有關兒童交還他們的自然環境（國家），不然
的話，就是縱容擄拐或不當扣留兒童的一方在收容他們的國家
或在他扣留兒童的國家向該地的法院求助，以及藉此造成人為
的情況來令到該地的法庭具有司法管轄權。

b. N vs. O
Case Number: HCMP004204_1998

In such circumstances, as I have said earlier, the courts are obliged expeditiously to restore the **status quo**.

本席在上文已經指出，在這種情況下，法庭須迅速處理，將一切回復**原狀**。

| 使用百分比 | ELDoS: 50.00% |
| | BLIS: 0.00% |

2. 現狀

a. Tong Tim Nui and others vs. Hong Kong Housing Authority
Case Number: CACV000281_1998

This did not allay the concerns of the residents. They petitioned the Governor to maintain the **status quo**.

然而，這份公告仍未能消除居民的憂慮，他們遂向港督提交請願書要求維持**現狀**。

b. Lau Kong Yung and others vs. Director of Immigration
Case Number: HCAL000020_1999

Mr. Dykes suggests that a more reasonable approach for the Director to adopt is to maintain the **status quo** by allowing the applicants to remain in Hong Kong pending the outcome of further discussions with the Mainland authorities and the implementation of a new scheme.

戴先生建議處長應採取一個較合理之做法，就是維持**現狀**，容許申請人繼續留在香港，直至處長和國內機關經商議後，達成協議及實施一個新的安排。

| 使用百分比 | ELDoS: 50.00% |
| | BLIS: 0.00% |

sub judice *adj.*

/səb ˈdʒuːdəsi/

Latin under judicial consideration, under a judge

95

【中譯】　香港法庭判詞 ELDoS: **1** 尚在審訊中；香港法例 BLIS: 一；
　　　　其他 Others: **1** 正在審訊；**2** 尚待判斷；**3** 在審理中；**4** 尚未判
　　　　決；**5** 在審判中

> ### Interpretations 釋義
> A case still under consideration by the court or pending for
> determination.
> 表示案件仍在審訊中，等候法庭裁決。

Examples 例句

1. 尚在審訊中

Master Zhang Chaojie alias Zhang Chao-Jie alias Cheung Chiu
Kit an infant by his mother and next friend Chau Mei Tuen,
Chau Mei Tuen vs. Director of Immigration
Case Number: HCAL000005_2000

I do not wish to go into too great a detail in this particular case, firstly
because it is **sub judice** as the matter is still being pursued.

本席不欲就該案作過分詳盡的論述，首先，因為該案**尚在審訊
中**，有關事宜仍在訴訟階段。

使用百分比	ELDoS: 100.00%
	BLIS: 0.00%

subpoena ad testificandum 96

n. pl. subpoenas ad testificandum

/səbˈpiːnə æd ˌtestɪfɪˈkændəm/

Latin subpoena = under penalty;

　　　　ad testificandum = to testify

【中譯】 香港法庭判詞 ELDoS: **1** 着令出庭作證的傳召出庭令；香港
法例 BLIS: **1** 着令出庭作證的傳召出庭令；**2** 着令出庭作證
的傳召證人出庭令；其他 Others: **1** 作證傳票；**2** 出庭作證的
傳票

Interpretations 釋義

A writ issued by a court requiring the recipient to appear and
give evidence as a witness.

由法庭發出的令狀，要求收到令狀的人出庭作證。

Examples 例句

1. 着令出庭作證的傳召出庭令

a. *Order 32 rule 10(1), The Rules of the District Court (Cap. 336H)*

A writ of **subpoena ad testificandum** or a writ of subpoena duces
tecum to compel the attendance of a witness for the purpose of
proceedings in chambers may be issued out of the Registry, if the
party who desires the attendance of the witness produces a note from
a judge or from the Registrar or any master authorizing the issue of
the writ.

如意欲證人出庭的一方交出法官、司法常務官或聆案官的短
簡，批准發出**着令出庭作證的傳召出庭令**狀或着令攜帶文件出

庭的傳召出庭令狀，則登記處可發出該等令狀，以為在內庭進行法律程序而強迫有關證人出庭。

b. *Order 38 rule 15, The Rules of the High Court (Cap. 4A)*

The names of two or more persons may be included in one writ of **subpoena ad testificandum**.

一份**着令出庭作證的傳召出庭令**狀可包括兩人或多於兩人的姓名或名稱。

c. *Order 38 rule 15, The Rules of the District Court (Cap. 336H)*

The names of 2 or more persons may be included in one writ of **subpoena ad testificandum**.

一份**着令出庭作證的傳召出庭令**狀可包括多於1人的姓名或名稱。

d. *Walton Wai-Tati Li vs. Evelyn Man-York Li*
Case Number: CACV000192_1997

A writ of **subpoena ad testificandum** or a writ of subpoena duces tecum…to compel the attendance of a witness for the purpose of proceedings in chambers may be issued out of [the Registry, various places as the case may be] if the party who desires the attendance of the witness produces a note from a judge or from the Registrar or a master, as the case may be, authorising the issue of the writ.

如意欲證人出庭的一方交出法官、司法常務官或聆案官（視屬何情況而定）的短簡，批准發出**着令出庭作證的傳召出庭令**狀或着令攜帶文件出庭的傳召出庭令狀，則登記處可發出該等令狀，以為在內庭進行法律程序而強迫有關證人出庭。

使用百分比	ELDoS: 100.00%
	BLIS: 83.33%

2. 着令出庭作證的傳召證人出庭令

Section 38A, Criminal Procedure Ordinance (Cap. 221)

No **subpoena ad testificandum** or subpoena duces tecum shall issue after the commencement of the Criminal Procedure (Miscellaneous Provisions) Ordinance 1981 (59 of 1981) in respect of any criminal proceedings for the purpose of which a witness summons may be issued.

《1981年刑事訴訟程序（雜項條文）條例》（1981年第59號）生效日期後，就任何可發出證人傳票的刑事法律程序而言，不得發出**着令出庭作證的傳召證人出庭令**或着令攜帶文件出庭的傳召證人出庭令。

使用百分比	ELDoS:	0.00%
	BLIS:	16.67%

subpoena duces tecum

n. pl. subpoenas duces tecum

/səbˈpiːnə ˈdjuːsiːz ˈtiːkəm/   /səbˈpiːnə ˈduːkeɪs ˈteɪkəm/

Latin subpoena = under penalty;

duces tecum = bring with you

【中譯】 香港法庭判詞 ELDoS: **1** 着令攜帶文件出庭的傳召出庭令；
香港法例 BLIS: **1** 令攜帶文件出庭的傳召出庭令；**2** 着令攜
帶文件出庭的傳召出庭令；**3** 着令攜帶文件出庭的傳召證人
出庭令；其他 Others: **1** 舉證傳票；**2** 攜帶證件到庭的傳票

Interpretations 釋義

A writ issued by a court requiring the recipient to give evidence in court and produce the documents specified in the writ for the court's examination.

由法庭發出的令狀，要求收到令狀的人出庭作證並出示令狀列明的文件以供法庭審閱。

Examples 例句

1. 着令攜帶文件出庭的傳召出庭令

a. Rule 19(1), Order 38, The Rules of the High Court (Cap. 4A)

The office of the Court out of which a writ of subpoena ad testificandum or a writ of **subpoena duces tecum** in aid of an inferior court or tribunal may be issued is the Registry, and no order of the Court for the issue of such a writ is necessary.

可發出着令出庭作證的傳召出庭令狀或**着令攜帶文件出庭的傳召出庭令**狀以協助某下級法庭或審裁處的法院辦事處為登記處，而發出該令狀是無須法庭作出命令的。

b. Order 24 rule 7A(6), The Rules of the District Court (Cap 336H)

No person shall be compelled by virtue of such an order to produce any documents which he could not be compelled to produce – ...(b) in the case of a summons under paragraph (2), if he had been served with a writ of **subpoena duces tecum** to produce the documents at the trial.

根據本規則作出的命令不得強迫任何人交出任何下述文件——
……（b）（如屬根據第（2）款發出的傳票的情況）該等文件是假
若該人已獲送達**着令攜帶文件出庭的傳召出庭令**狀，規定他須
在審訊時交出有關文件也不能強迫他交出的。

c. Order 24 rule 7A(6), The Rules of the High Court (Cap. 4A)

No person shall be compelled by virtue of such an order to produce any documents which he could not be compelled to produce – ...(b) in the case of a summons under paragraph (2), if he had been served with a writ of **subpoena duces tecum** to produce the documents at the trial.

不得憑藉該命令而強迫任何人交出任何下述文件——……（b）
（如屬根據第（2）款發出的傳票的情況）該文件是假若該人已
獲送達**着令攜帶文件出庭的傳召出庭令**狀須在審訊時交出有關
文件亦不能強迫該人交出的。

d. Order 32 rule 10(1), The Rules of the District Court (Cap. 336H)

A writ of subpoena ad testificandum or a writ of **subpoena duces tecum** to compel the attendance of a witness for the purpose of proceedings in chambers may be issued out of the Registry, if the party who desires the attendance of the witness produces a note from a judge or from the Registrar or any master authorizing the issue of the writ.

如意欲證人出庭的一方交出法官、司法常務官或聆案官的短
簡，批准發出着令出庭作證的傳召出庭令狀或**着令攜帶文件出
庭的傳召出庭令狀**，則登記處可發出該等令狀，以為在內庭進
行法律程序而強迫有關證人出庭。

e. *Walton Wai-Tati Li vs. Evelyn Man-York Li*
Case Number: CACV000192_1997

A writ of subpoena ad testificandum or a writ of **subpoena duces
tecum**...to compel the attendance of a witness for the purpose of
proceedings in chambers may be issued out of [the Registry, various
places as the case may be] if the party who desires the attendance of
the witness produces a note from a judge or from the Registrar or a
master, as the case may be, authorising the issue of the writ.

如意欲證人出庭的一方交出法官、司法常務官或聆案官（視屬
何情況而定）的短簡，批准發出着令出庭作證的傳召出庭令狀
或**着令攜帶文件出庭的傳召出庭令狀**，則登記處可發出該等令
狀，以為在內庭進行法律程序而強迫有關證人出庭。

使用百分比	ELDoS: 100.00%
	BLIS: 71.43%

2. 令攜帶文件出庭的傳召出庭令

Section 68(2), Landlord and Tenant (Consolidation) Ordinance (Cap. 7)

Notwithstanding subsection (1), a **subpoena duces tecum** may be
issued against the Commissioner requiring him to produce in any
proceedings an application under section 51(4), 51(4A), 56A(1),
57(1), 59(1) or 63(1), and a subpoena issued under this subsection
shall be deemed to be complied with by the production of any
document specified in the subpoena by any public officer employed
in the Rating and Valuation Department.

即伸第（1）款另有規定，**令攜帶文件出庭的傳召出庭令**，可針對署長髮出，要求署長將根據第51（4）、51（4A）、56A（1）、57（1）、59（1）或63（1）條提出的申請書，在訴訟程序中呈堂；如受僱於差餉物業估價署的任何公職人員將傳召出庭令所指明的文件呈堂，即須當作該根據本款發出的傳召出庭令已獲遵從。

| 使用百分比 | ELDoS: | 0.00% |
| | BLIS: | 14.29% |

3. 着令攜帶文件出庭的傳召證人出庭令

Section 38A, Criminal Procedure Ordinance (Cap. 221)

No subpoena ad testificandum or **subpoena duces tecum** shall issue after the commencement of the Criminal Procedure (Miscellaneous Provisions) Ordinance 1981 (59 of 1981) in respect of any criminal proceedings for the purpose of which a witness summons may be issued.

《1981年刑事訴訟程序（雜項條文）條例》（1981年第59號）生效日期後，就任何可發出證人傳票的刑事法律程序而言，不得發出着令出庭作證的傳召證人出庭令或**着令攜帶文件出庭的傳召證人出庭令**。

| 使用百分比 | ELDoS: | 0.00% |
| | BLIS: | 14.29% |

supra *adv.*

/ˈsuːprə/ /ˈsjuːpə/

Latin above

98

【中譯】 香港法庭判詞 ELDoS: **1** 出處同上；**2** 上文；**3** 如上；香港法例 BLIS: 一；其他 Others: **1** 在上；**2** 在前；**3** 上述

> ### Interpretations 釋義
> Used to refer the reader to an earlier part of the book or document.
> 用以指示讀者參閱書本或文件中較前部分。

Examples 例句

1. 出處同上

a. *Leung Sai Lun Robert vs. Leung May Ling*
Case Number: FACV000005_1998

One such purpose is that, as marriage represents a fundamental change in a person's life whereby new responsibilities are undertaken, it is appropriate to start with a clean slate. See para. 3.2, **supra**.

而其中一個宗旨是：因為婚姻代表了人生中一個根本的改變，這個改變帶來了新責任的承擔；而重新開始承擔這些責任是適當的。見第3.2段；**出處同上**。

b. *Fu Kin Chi, Willy vs. The Secretary for Justice*
Case Number: FACV000002_1997

Thus in *Police Service Board v. Morris* (**supra**) every member of the court considered not only the Police Regulation Act 1958 but also the Police Regulations 1957.

因此，於*Police Service Board v. Morris*（**出處同上**）一案，每位法官不但考慮了《1958年員警規例法令》（譯名）（*Police Regulation Act 1958*），而且也考慮了《1957年員警規例》（譯名）（*Police Regulations 1957*）。

c. *Fu Kin Chi, Willy vs. The Secretary for Justice*
Case Number: FACV000002_1997

Mr. Bleach for the appellant makes the point that the officers in *Police Service Board v. Morris* (**supra**) were asked about their conduct while on duty.

Bleach先生代表上訴人指出，於*Police Service Board v. Morris*（**出處同上**）一案中的兩名警務人員，被問及他們當值時的行為。

使用百分比	ELDoS: 57.14%
	BLIS:　0.00%

2. 上文

Ultra Eternal Limited vs. Liu Tai Cheong
Case Number: HCMP001188_1996

For reasons given **supra**, I have concluded the Defendant had failed to show a good title.

基於上文所述理由，本席的結論是，被告人未能顯示持有良好業權。

使用百分比	ELDoS: 28.57%
	BLIS:　0.00%

3. 如上

Leung Sai Lun Robert vs. Leung May Ling
Case Number: FACV000005_1998

For many years Chinese people in Hong Kong had in fact been executing Wills and in In re Tse Lai-chiu (**Supra**) it was held that the section implicitly recognised the testamentary capacity of Chinese persons in accordance with English laws.

多年來，香港的華人其實一直有簽立遺囑；而在In re Tse Lai-Chiu（**如上**）一案中，法庭裁定該條法例隱含地承認華人根據英國法律有立遺囑的能力。

| 使用百分比 | ELDoS: 14.29% |
| | BLIS: 0.00% |

uberrima fides *n.*

/uːˈberɪma ˈfaɪdiːz/

Latin utmost good faith

99

【中譯】 香港法庭判詞 ELDoS: **1** 坦率誠實；香港法例 BLIS: 一；其他 Others: **1** 坦率誠實

Interpretations 釋義

In insurance, the parties have to deal in good faith by declaring and disclosing all material facts in the insurance proposal.

指在保險合約裏面，雙方坦誠地聲明或申報所有與合約有關的實況。

Examples 例句

1. 坦率誠實

Green Park Properties Limited vs. Dorku Limited
Case Number: HCA008564_1998

To this rule there are three well-known exceptions where non-disclosure of material facts is a ground for relief: (1) where the contract requires **uberrima fides** (eg, insurance, family arrangement);

不過，這個規則容許有三個為人熟知的例外情況，立約一方可以以對方不披露具關鍵性的事實為由申索濟助：（1）合約規定要訂立**坦率誠實**合約（例如，保險合約、家事安排合約）；

使用百分比	ELDoS: 100.00%
	BLIS: 0.00%

ultra vires *adj./adv.*

100

/ˌʌltrə ˈvaɪəriːz/　/ˌʌltrə ˈvɪəriːz/

Latin　beyond the powers

【中譯】　香港法庭判詞 ELDoS: **1** 超過許可權；香港法例 BLIS: 一；
其他 Others: **1** 越權；**2** 權力之外；**3** 無權行為；**4** 超過職權；
5 越權行為

Interpretations 釋義

Referring to an act that is outside the scope of the legal powers
or authority of the person doing it.

An act by a company is ultra vires if it is not authorized by the
memorandum of the company or by the law under which it is
incorporated. So is an act if the company exercises the power
irregularly.

An act by a public authority is ultra vires if it goes beyond the
powers conferred upon the authority by law or if the authority
fails to observe any procedural requirements.

一個人作出的行為超越其法律權力或許可權所規定的範圍。

如果一間公司的作為未得公司章程或註冊成立的法例授權，
即屬越權。而公司在不符合規定的情況下行使權力，其作為
同樣被視為越權。

至於公共機構方面，如果其行為超出法律上賦予的權力或其
未能遵守任何程序上的規定，則屬越權行為。

Examples 例句

1. 超過許可權

Liem Hung and others vs. HKSAR
Case Number: FAMC000029_1999

It may well be that where it can be clearly shown that the Building Authority has acted **ultra vires**, maliciously or unreasonably, or upon a mistaken factual basis, the validity of the order can and should be raised in the magistrates' court.

當清楚顯示建築事務監督的行事**超過許可權**、惡意或不合理、或基於錯誤事實時，那麼，該命令的有效性就可以或應該在裁判法庭提出。

使用百分比	ELDoS: 100.00%
	BLIS: 0.00%

virtute officii *adv.*

/vɜːˈtjuːtiː əˈfɪʃiːaɪ/

Latin by virtue of the office

【中譯】 香港法庭判詞 ELDoS: **1** 憑藉其身分；香港法例 BLIS: 一；
其他 Others: 一

Interpretations 釋義

By virtue of the powers or authority vested in a person as the
holder of the particular position or office.

一個人憑着其特定身分或職位而獲賦予的權力或許可權。

Examples 例句

1. 憑藉其身分

Ultra Eternal Limited vs. Liu Tai Cheong
Case Number: HCMP001188_1996

"Executors, no doubt can sell **virtute officii**, but that must be with a
view to performing their officium." (See : In re Molyneux & White
15 L. R. Ir. 383 at 386.)

「毫無疑問，遺囑執行人可**憑藉其身分**作出售賣行為，但必須
是以履行彼等之職責為目標。」（見：In re Molyneux & White
15 L. R. Ir. 383 at 386。）

使用百分比	ELDoS: 100.00%
	BLIS: 0.00%

vis-à-vis *adv./prep.*
French

【中譯】 香港法庭判詞 ELDoS: **1** 關於……；香港法例 BLIS: 一；其他 Others: **1** 和……相對；**2** 同……相比；**3** 對……而言

Interpretations 釋義

In relation to; concerning; as compared with

與某事物相關；有關某事物；與某事物相比較

Examples 例句

1. 關於……

a. *Tse Wai Chun Paul vs. Albert Cheng and another*
Case Number: CACV000170_1998

I have decided that there is no evidence of malice against the 2nd Defendant; that means that if jury finds defence of fair comment proved by Defendants, then jury must find that 2nd Defendant is not liable to Plaintiff **vis-a-vis** any defamatory comments (as distinct from defamatory facts, for which 2nd Defendant has to prove justification).

本席裁決，並無證據針對第二被告人，顯示他懷有惡意；意思是假若陪審團裁斷被告人就公允評論抗辯舉證成功，陪審團必定要裁斷，**關於**任何誹謗性評論，第二被告人毋須對原告人負法律責任（這與誹謗性事實不同，因為第二被告人須證明有正當理由）。

使用百分比	ELDoS: 100.00%
	BLIS: 0.00%

viva voce *adj./adv.*

103

/ˌvaɪvə ˈvəʊtʃi/ /ˌviːvə ˈvəʊsi/

Latin with living voice

  also: voire dire

【中譯】　香港法庭判詞 ELDoS: **1** 口頭；香港法例 BLIS: **1** 口頭；**2** 口
    頭……方式；**3** 口頭方式；其他 Others: 一

> ### Interpretations 釋義
> This phrase means "orally" (as opposed to "in writing") when it
> comes to the giving of evidence. With regard to voting, it means
> "by voice" as opposed to "by ballot".
> 在作證時，作出「口頭」證供（相對於「書面」證供）。若在
> 投票的情況下，則指以「口頭」表決，與透過「選票」形式
> 表決相反。

Examples 例句

1. 口頭

  a. Appendix A Form 35 – Letter of request for examination of
  witness out of jurisdiction – The Rules of the High Court
  (Cap. 4A)

And I further request that you will permit the agents of both the
plaintiff and defendant or such of them as shall be present to examine
(upon interrogatories and **viva voce** upon the subject-matter thereof
or arising out of the answers thereto) such witnesses as may, after
due notice in writing, be produced on their behalf, and the other party
to cross-examine the said witnesses (upon cross-interrogatories and
viva voce) and the party producing the witness for examination to re-
examine him **viva voce**.

本人又要求閣下准許原告人及被告人兩者的代理人或他們當中在場者（就質詢書及就質詢書的標的事宜或就對質詢書的答覆所產生的標的事宜而**口頭**）訊問妥經書面通知後為他們而交出的證人，並請求閣下准許另一方（就交相質詢書而**口頭**）盤問該等證人，以及准許交出證人以接受訊問的一方對其所交出的證人作**口頭**覆問。

b. *Novatel Communications (Far East) Limited vs. Canadian Imperial Bank of Commerce and another*
Case Number: HCA008052_1999

Moreover, in the context of an Order 14 application, the willingness of a former employee to provide a signed witness statement indicates that he may potentially be available as a witness to give **viva voce** evidence should the matter proceed to trial.

再者，鑒於一項用第14號命令申請之背景，一名前僱員願意提供由其所簽署的證人陳述書，這表示他或有潛在可能出任證人；倘若整件事發展至審訊階段，他可以**口頭**作證。

使用百分比	ELDoS: 100.00%
	BLIS: 84.62%

2. 口頭……方式

Section 100(5), Bankruptcy Ordinance (Cap. 6)

Subject to general rules, the court may in any matter take the whole or any part of the evidence **viva voce** or by interrogatories or upon affidavit or, out of Hong Kong, by commission.

除一般規則另有規定外，法院可就任何事情而以**口頭**、質詢或誓章**方式**或在香港以外地方以委託方式錄取全部或部分證供。

使用百分比	ELDoS: 0.00%
	BLIS: 7.69%

3. 口頭方式

Section 5, Evidence Ordinance (Cap. 8)

In all proceedings before the court, the parties and the husbands and wives of the parties thereto, and the persons in whose behalf any proceedings may be brought, or instituted, or opposed, or defended, and the husbands and wives of such persons shall, except as hereinafter excepted, be competent and compellable to give evidence, either **viva voce** or by deposition, according to the practice of the court, on behalf of either or any of the parties to the proceedings.

在法庭席前進行的所有法律程序中，法律程序的各方及其丈夫及妻子，以及由他人代表提出、提起或反對任何法律程序或由他人代表對任何法律程序進行抗辯的人及其丈夫及妻子，除如下文屬另行規定者外，均有資格並可予強迫按照法院常規以**口頭方式**或以書面供詞為法律程序的其中一方或任何一方提供證據。

| 使用百分比 | ELDoS: | 0.00% |
| | BLIS: | 7.69% |

voir dire *n./v.*

104

/ˌvwɑːˈdɪə/   /ˌvɔːˈdɪə/

Latin to speak the truth

【中譯】 香港法庭判詞 ELDoS: **1** 翻供聆訊；**2** 案中案聆訊；**3** 案中案程序；**4** 審查供狀的特別程序；香港法例 BLIS: 一；其他 Others: **1** 審查

Interpretations 釋義

Preliminary examination by a judge of a witness as to his competency or of a juror as to his qualification and suitability. Such an examination may also be conducted by a judge in the absence of the jury to determine the voluntariness (and hence the admissibility) of the confession made to a law enforcement officer by an accused.

法官對有關證人的作證資格，或對有關陪審員是否合乎資格及適任此職而作出的初步審查。該審查聆訊可在沒有陪審團在場的情況下，由法官主持，以斷定被控人向執法人員供認時是否自願（及其證供可接納與否）。

Examples 例句

1. 翻供聆訊

a. *Fan Koon Hung vs. HKSAR*
   Case Number: FAMC000031_1999

…those questions read as follows: "(1) whether after a **voir dire** a trial judge who refuses to admit into evidence written post records of certain verbal admissions should allow oral evidence of those same admissions to be given by the same witness whose 'writings' he has refused to admit, without stating his reasons for so doing …"

該三個問題內容如下：「(1)經過**翻供聆訊**後，主審法官既然不接納證人書寫的『補錄口頭招認供詞』，那麼他決定接納同一證人口述證據的『口頭招認』為證據是否正確？何況他亦沒有陳述他作此決定的理由……」

b. Fan Koon Hung vs. HKSAR
Case Number: FAMC000031_1999

…those questions read as follows: "…(3) whether a trial judge giving a ruling on a **voir dire** which has included allegations of serious police misconduct at the time of arrest should specifically state that he has considered his general discretion to exclude (as well as matters of voluntariness) before deciding to admit the verbals whilst excluding the written records of them."

……該三個問題內容如下：「……(3)在**翻供聆訊**中，既然有人提出嚴重指控，投訴警方人員在執行拘捕時的不當行為，那麼，法官作出裁定時，是否應該特別說明他在決定接納該等口頭說話而拒絕接納該等書面記錄前，已考慮過其拒絕接納的一般酌情權(以及有關自願性的事項)。」

c. Fan Koon Hung vs. HKSAR
Case Number: FAMC000031_1999

I am satisfied from the evidence which I have heard in the **voir dire** proceedings that, if they were said, the defendant said them voluntarily. The prosecution may, therefore, lead evidence of their being said before the jury.

於聆聽過**翻供聆訊**中的證據後，本席確信若被告人有說過這些話，他是在自願的情況下說的。因此控方可在陪審團席前，引導證據證明被告曾說過這些話。

使用百分比	ELDoS: 45.45%
	BLIS: 0.00%

2. 案中案聆訊

a. HKSAR vs. Yu Chi On
Case Number: HCMA000140Y_1999

Mr. Lee submitted that what was allegedly said by the Appellant amounted to an admission and the Special Magistrate should have held a **voir dire**.

大律師李先生陳詞說，上訴人被指所說的話，構成了招認的供詞，特委裁判官應展開**案中案聆訊**才對。

b. HKSAR vs. Yu Chi On
Case Number: HCMA000140Y_1999

In my view, the question of voluntariness does not arise. There is no need for the Special Magistrate to hold a **voir dire**.

本席認為此案並不存在自願性的問題，特委裁判官不需展開**案中案聆訊**。

| 使用百分比 | ELDoS: 27.27% |
| | BLIS: 0.00% |

3. 案中案程序

HKSAR vs. Tang Sau-Leung
Case Number: CACC000620_1996

A **voir dire** was held to determine the admissibility of the oral answers the Applicant had allegedly given to police.

審訊過程中曾進行**案中案程序**，藉以裁決（控方指稱）申請人對警務人員作出的口頭答覆可否接納為證據。

| 使用百分比 | ELDoS: 18.18% |
| | BLIS: 0.00% |

4. 審查供狀的特別程序

Wong Wai Man vs. HKSAR
Case Number: FAMC000028_1999

A judge in a voir dire is required to look at the narrative of each confessional statement in order to judge whether or not there are similarities or inconsistencies between statements by different defendants which indicate that they were not made in the manner the prosecution say, see *R v. Li Kar Wah* [1970] HKLR 572, a case to which defence counsel referred the judge at the conclusion of the **voir dire**.

在進行審查供狀的特別程序時，法官必須留意每一份供認供詞的內容，從而判斷不同被告人所作的供詞有沒有相似或不一致之處，標示該等供詞並不是如控方所言般作出；參閱*R v. Li Kar Wah*（［1970］HKLR 572）一案，此案例由辯方代表律師在結束**審查供狀的特別程序**時向法官提述。

使用百分比	ELDoS:	9.09%
	BLIS:	0.00%

volenti non fit injuria _n._

/vəʊˈlentɪ ˈnɒn fɪt ɪnˈjʊərɪə/

Latin to a willing person there is no injury

105

【中譯】 香港法庭判詞 ELDoS: **1** 自願者不受損；香港法例 BLIS:
　　　 —；其他 Others: **1** 自願招致傷害；**2** 自願招致傷害者不得提
　　　 起訴訟；**3** 對自願者不構成侵害；**4** 自願招致損害者不得主張
　　　 所受的損害

> ## Interpretations 釋義
>
> A tort defence in an injury claim that the plaintiff cannot sue
> because he has full knowledge of the danger and has voluntarily
> assumed the risk of being injured.
>
> 在人身傷害訴訟中的侵權法辯護理據。如果原告人事前已充
> 分瞭解事情的危險性，並且自願承擔受到損害的風險，他便
> 不能就受到的損傷向被告人提出訴訟。

Examples 例句

1. 自願者不受損

a. _Tso Yung vs. Cheng Yeung Hing and Secretary for Justice_
Case Number: HCPI001509_2000

According to Clerk & Lindsell on Torts (18th Ed., 2000), the tort
of false imprisonment is established on proof of : (1) the fact of
imprisonment; and (2) absence of lawful authority to justify that
imprisonment (para.13–19). The maxim **volenti non fit injuria**
applies to actions for false imprisonment (para.13–24).

根據Clerk & Lindsell on Torts（2000年，第18版），要確立侵
權法下的非法禁錮，必須證明以下事項：（1）禁錮的事實；

（2）禁錮是在沒有合法許可權的情況下發生（第13–19段）。**自願者不受損**（volenti non fit injuria）這法諺在非法禁錮的行為上適用（第13–24段）。

b. Tso Yung vs. Cheng Yeung Hing and Secretary for Justice
Case Number: HCPI001509_2000

The meaning of volenti: **Volenti non fit injuria** is a voluntary agreement by the claimant to absolve the defendant from the legal consequence of an unreasonable risk of harm created by the defendant, where the claimant has full knowledge of both the nature and extent of he risk. When it applies it is a complete defence; the claimant recovers nothing. On this basis there are at least three requirements for the defence to apply:(1) Agreement by the claimant to waive a claim against the defendant;(2) This agreement must be voluntary, not due to compulsion by the defendant or external circumstances;(3) The claimant should have full knowledge of the nature of the risk.

volenti（自願）的意思：Volenti non fit injuria（**自願者不受損**）指申索人自願同意免卻被告人因製造不合理的傷害的風險所招致的法律後果，且對該風險的性質及程度完全瞭解。符合這條件便是一個完整的抗辯理由；申索人是得不到任何賠償的。基於此，是項抗辯理由需要起碼符合以下三個條件方能成立：（1）申索人同意放棄向被告人索償；（2）申索人必須自願同意，而並非因遭被告人強迫或其他外在因素影響而同意；（3）申索人應對所涉風險的性質完全瞭解。

c. Tso Yung vs. Cheng Yeung Hing and Secretary for Justice
Case Number: HCPI001509_2000

Now that contributory negligence is not a complete defence, but only a ground for reducing the damages, the defence of **volenti non fit injuria** has been closely considered and in consequence, it has been severely limited. Knowledge of the risk of injury is not enough. Nor is willingness to take the risk of injury. Nothing will suffice short of an agreement to waive any claim for negligence. The plaintiff must agree, expressly or impliedly to waive any claim for any injury that may befall him due to the lack of reasonable care by the defendant.

既然共分疏忽不是完整的抗辯理由，而只是減少賠償額的理據，便仔細考慮了**自願者不受損**的抗辯理由。考慮的結果是這抗辯理由是有種種限制的。光是知道有受損的風險，又或光是願意冒受損的風險都是不夠的。唯有願意放棄就疏忽而提出索償才足夠。原告人必須同意（明示也好、暗示也好）放棄就被告人因沒有作出合理的謹慎措施致令他受損而提出索償的權利。

使用百分比	ELDoS: 100.00%
	BLIS: 0.00%